T0193860

FROM WOLFENBÜTTEL TO CURRY'S REST

FROM WOLFENBÜTTEL TO CURRY'S REST

A Personal and Professional Memoir

JOHN CARSON

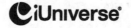

FROM WOLFENBÜTTEL TO CURRY'S REST
A PERSONAL AND PROFESSIONAL MEMOIR

The author acknowledges use of material from the following publishers: *Instead of a Book: Letters to a Friend* by Diana Athill, London: Granta Books, 2011; *My Promised Land* by Ari Shavit, New York: Spiegel and Grau/Penguin Random House, 2013; *The Idea of Israel* by Ilan Pappe, London: Verso Press, 2014; Eric R. Kandel, *In Search of Memory: The Emergence of a New Science of Mind*, New York: Norton, 2006; "Food for Thought: Crustaceans and Molluscs" by Renate Carson, originally published in the Royal Ontario Museum's *Rotunda* magazine, Spring 1979, permission granted by the Royal Ontario Museum for reprint of article, and by Zile Zichmanis for reprint of the drawings; *Israel's Holocaust and the Politics of Nationhood* by Idith Zertal, originally published in Hebrew as "Ha'Umah ve Ha'Mavet, Historia, Zikaron, Politika," Dvir Publishing House, 2002 and ©2002 Idith Zertal. English translation ©Idith Zertal 2005. Published by Cambridge University Press, 2011. Reprinted with the permission of Cambridge University Press; W.G. Sebald, translated by Michael Hulse, from THE RINGS OF SATURN, copyright ©1995 by Vito von Eichborn GmbH & Co Verlag KG, Translation ©1998 by The Harvill Press. Reprinted by permission of New Directions Publishing Corp.

iUniverse books may be ordered through booksellers or by contacting:

iUniverse
1663 Liberty Drive
Bloomington, IN 47403
www.iuniverse.com
1-800-Authors (1-800-288-4677)

ISBN: 978-1-5320-6982-6 (sc)
ISBN: 978-1-5320-6983-3 (e)

Print information available on the last page.

iUniverse rev. date: 03/20/2019

Contents

For Rene and Jacki
and

Ann and Nicholas

Acknowledgments

I am greatly indebted to Rene for two documents. First, a long letter written to me on our 50th wedding anniversary about our relationship, highlighting how she saw the important events, happy and sad, throughout the fifty years. The second document is her detailed diary, written during our year in Indonesia and the year travelling home. The diary was especially important in helping me to begin to understand what was happening to us during those difficult years.

Our daughter, Ann, apart from being responsible for prodding me to write my memoir, undertook the hard job of transcribing Rene's pencil-written diary.

Last but not least, my supportive editor, Beth McAuley, deserves special thanks. Beth was indispensable to me because my previous writing experience, though extensive, consisted solely of technical reports—I had no preparation for writing a memoir. Beth led me on the path to writing prose.

PROLOGUE

When I was born in Wolfenbüttel, Germany, my father, Hermann Cohn, was the headmaster of the Jewish high school, in addition, he and my mother, Anna, were operating a humanitarian enterprise: they brought boys from Krakow, Poland, where my father was born to attend the high school. My mother, Anna, put them up in our large house and looked after them. So, both of my parents were working all day. A nanny looked after me and my sister, Ruth, who was three years older than me, played with me, even when she started school.

Photo of Hermann Cohn / Credit: Taken by John M. Carson ca. 1931.

Only after our family returned to Berlin, when I was five years old, and where I started school, did I get to know my parents properly; and both of them spent much time with me. Especially my father's pedagogical instincts began to have their effects on me. He continued for the rest of his life, about a dozen years, to ensure that I would have a good education: after elementary school he got me into the Fichte Gymnasium, for as long as they accepted Jews. Thereafter, he sent me to a technical school in the German speaking part of Czechoslovakia, until Hitler occupied the Sudeten Land.

Above all and over time I began to understand how my father's self-development from an orthodox, insular Jewish family and community background moved towards an enlightened, questioning, liberal, educated young man in Berlin. And I began to understand and grasp his *Weltanschauung*, that is, his world view.

After my parents' death and in the turmoil of my life on leaving Germany, the essence of my father's outlook on the world and the individual in it gradually became a stabilizing and central guide in my life.

INTRODUCTION

We, as human beings, are landed with memory systems that have fallibilities, frailties, and imperfections – but also great flexibility and creativity …

Memory is dialogic and arises not only from direct experience but from the intercourse of many minds.

—Oliver Sacks, "Speak, Memory"
The New York Review of Books, February 21, 2013

Writing about one's own life presents problems similar to those that historians face: what do we remember; what don't we remember; how selective or faulty is our memory; even if what we do remember is accurate, how honest are we going to be? Historians, for the most part, have a hypothesis to prove: they develop theories and select from what is known to fit their theories.

Famous memoir writers are writers first and know what makes a good story despite the facts or the truth. So, you are warned. I am neither famous nor a writer nor a historian; although I have a degree in Political Science – which is a branch of historical studies. I had an interesting life and my family wants to know about it. I have no reputation to protect and therefore can be honest to the best of my "memory."

But I had some help: Rene wrote a long letter to me on our 50th wedding anniversary in 1995, which is about some of the more important events in our lives. Then, when clearing through Rene's private papers, I found her diaries, kept intermittently, and it seems she only wrote in her diaries when she was confused or unhappy during two years – one year in Indonesia and the following year travelling back to Toronto. (Rene's text is in *italics*.) Finally, I found Google immensely helpful.

CHAPTER 1

Childhood

I was born in 1921, three years after the end of the First World War and twelve years before Hitler's rise to power, in northwest Germany in Wolfenbüttel. Actually, my birth was in a hospital in Braunschweig, a bigger town ten miles away. Wolfenbüttel is about 125 miles west of Berlin and 100 miles south of Hamburg.

They called me Hans Walfried. "Walfried" is a very Germanic name like Wilfried or Wotan and was chosen in memory of a well-liked family friend.

Wolfenbüttel, a beautiful town established in the sixteenth century, is famous because of the philosopher and writer Gotthold Ephraim Lessing (1729–1781), who lived there in his later years and was the librarian of the Herzog-August Bibliotek, founded in 1572 – one of the first lending libraries in Europe. In fact, the town is often referred to as Lessingstadt. Fortunately, the town was spared the heavy bombardment of most German cities because it was of no strategic significance.

With few authentic documents and only the memory of a very young child, it was difficult to come up with a reliable account of the circumstances of our family when I was born.

I do not know when my parents arrived in Wolfenbüttel. I do know that my sister, Ruth, was born in the Braunschweig hospital. I do not know where my brother Max, nine years older, was born.

And I do know that our family left Wolfenbüttel for Berlin in 1926 where my father became the director of a Jewish school.

Whenever my parents came to Wolfenbüttel my father taught, and for a time was the director, at the Samson Schule. This Jewish school was established by Philipp Samson in 1786 in the centre of the town. In 1896, a new, large building was erected at the edge of the town.

At some time, when I became conscious of what was going on in our large house, a number of Polish boys enrolled at the Samson Schule and lived on the top floor of our house. I believe that later some additional Polish boys were taught in a private school by my father. The boys' quarters were run as a *pensione*, or a boarding house, and our mother managed it.

The Family

My father was an intelligent and learned man. He had the greatest influence over me as I grew up. His only brother died in the First World War.

My father was born in Krakau, Poland, into a very orthodox Jewish family. His father, my grandfather, was a famous cantor because of his exceptionally fine voice. He was no longer alive when I was born, but his wife, my father's mother and my grandmother, a tiny woman called Otta, lived with us; more about her later.

My father's education, especially after he left Poland and moved to Berlin, turned him into a scholar. He earned a Ph.D. in philosophy and a Ph.D. in philology. He taught Latin, Greek, Hebrew, and Arabic, as well as theology. His studies and his work turned him slowly but decisively into a liberal Jew.

My mother, Anna, nee Engel (Angel), was from Cologne. She was much younger than my father (by thirteen years). Her religious background was less strictly Jewish, though one of her ancestors was a Chief Rabbi of Cologne. My mother was an only child and I never knew her parents.

━ ✿ ━

One interesting fact of the origins of my parents is that they came from the two main divisions of the Jewish people. My father was an Ashkenazi (from Eastern Europe) and my mother was a Sephardi (originally from Spain).

My father was a quiet and gentle person who left all family affairs to his wife. She dealt with all financial matters: she gave her husband money for his books, clothes, etc., but she managed all the rest. She decided where to go for our summer holidays and made all the arrangements.

Of course, my father was concerned and took a great interest in his children's education. I know that I was a great disappointment to him after I started school because of my lacklustre educational progress. But he was too good a pedagogue to show anger or to scold me about my lack of progress at school. Rather, he tried to find out why I did not do better. Fortunately, my older sister, Ruth, made up for it. She was a top student and, having inherited our father's gift for languages, did well in Latin and modern languages.

My mother was an accomplished *hausfrau* – she was a great cook, she could sew, and she could generally run all aspects of a large household. In addition, she had managerial skills (probably learned at a special school) which were put to good use in Wolfenbüttel.

My brother, Max, was nine years older than me and, because of this great age difference, we had few common interests. Imagine, when I was three years old he was practically a teenager – I was just a baby to him. In my memory of life in Wolfenbüttel, Max is not really there. Later in life, in Berlin, when I was over ten, this changed a bit, but not much. I was never as close to him as I was to my sister who was just three years older.

Ruth was a wonderful sister. I probably idealize her because she played with me and looked after me when I was very young, at a time when my mother was busy running a large household. I did have a *kindermädchen*, a nanny who washed, clothed, fed, and put me to bed, and who generally looked after all the chores of bringing up a young child. My sister's "looking after me" meant something more. Yet, away from me, her life left no memories. For example, I do not remember her going to school or having girlfriends.

The kindermädchen was a strict disciplinarian, probably under instruction from my mother. She may have had other, additional household duties. Her punishment for me included shutting me in a large dirty linen basket for a while – maybe until I promised to be a good boy. I have a few other memories of her washing, dressing, and feeding me, and when I was a bit bigger, she seemed to enjoy playing with me to give me an erection. I did not tell my mother or anyone else about it. How should I have known, at perhaps two-plus years of age, that this was sexual abuse? It did not hurt.

Otta, my grandmother, may have lived with us in Wolfenbüttel, but I do not remember her there. Possibly, she still lived in Poland with her husband until he died, at which time she joined us in Berlin. She was a quiet, kind old lady dressed all in black as all older women were in those days. She taught me to write the German script, which is full of letters with straight strokes, and she used to follow my writing efforts carefully, saying *"rauf und runter"* (up and down) to make sure I made no mistakes. I well remember both my grandmother and how she and I liked eating candy together.

That was our very small family. I respected my father and admired him. Had life been kinder and he had lived longer, we would have had a rewarding adult relationship. My mother was very competent, and I could always rely on her to give me whatever I needed or desired. Ruth gave me love; we would have been lifelong friends. Max, my brother, the only family member apart from me to survive the Second World War, left little mark in my memory, except that he went off to Buenos Aires with all of the family's liquid assets and changed them into strips of pure gold. After we left Berlin in 1938, we never saw each other again.

There was no aunt, no uncle, no nephew, no niece, no cousin twice removed (whatever that is). I grew up lacking all experience of an extended family life, and did not know what this meant until I married Rene. She came from a very large family that was spread out over Europe, North America, and Israel.

Our House and Surroundings and a Wonderful Life

The Samson Schule faced the main road leading out of town. In fact, it was the last building at the corner of a country lane. Our house was immediately behind a wall that enclosed the school playground. The country lane ran along a forest.

Our house was very large. Not just in the memory of a small boy. It must have been spacious enough for a family of five plus the *pensione* that housed about a dozen high school boys as well as the servants' quarters. The main entrance door opened onto a large hall with a sweeping staircase that led to a balcony on the second floor overlooking the entrance hall. This enormous space left a strong impact on me. In later life I had dreams, repeated over and over again, about frightening scenes in our large hall and staircase. It took me years as an adult to banish the dreams by finally associating the setting of the dreams with our large hall and the sweeping staircase.

There was also a third floor, I believe, where the schoolboys' dormitory and bathrooms were located. However, my indoor life was confined to the nursery and the passageway, where the nasty laundry basket was kept, that led to the bathroom. The life I remember best was spent outside the house.

I could not guess the acreage of the grounds belonging to the house. There was an orchard, there were stables for cows and horses, and there were ducks and chickens. Beyond the stables were the fields for vegetables that were of no interest to me. The orchard gardener was my special friend. In season, he always left a ladder propped against any tree that had ripe fruit for me to pick: apples, plums, peaches, cherries, and other nameless but tasty fruit. I was free to roam around the farm and animal shed. The great excitement on one of those days was watching a calf being born.

My constant companion was a dog, an Alsatian called Filax. He was a big, strong dog and rough to play with, but he never hurt me even when he tore my shirts and shorts. At some stage Filax was suspected by neighbours of killing chickens and other small animals. Eventually, Filax was gone and I was a very sad boy – but for a short time only because there were always new things to explore, especially in the forest on the other side of the country lane. This was a natural forest without paths, benches, tables, or other amenities. In fact, in some places you could hardly get through the bushes, weeds, or trees.

I was warned not to walk alone into the forest or I might get lost. More important: gypsies camped in the forest and gypsies were known to kidnap children and take them away with them. Well, this sounded exciting. Possibly, I was looking for children to play with – there were none at home. I did meet children of my own age to play with occasionally. For example, when I was old enough to join the mountain hikes with the family, we used to go with other families to the nearby Harz Mountains to climb its highest peak known as the Brocken (1,140 m). This was also where I discovered my fear of heights. The path leading to the top of the Brocken was steep in parts but not difficult for me. But near the top, the narrow path ran along a precipice with a sheer drop into a void. I was scared to move. Only the strong arms of some young man we were hiking with rescued me from immobility. But let's return to my forest.

The gypsies had lots of children and I played with them without coming to any harm. One trip into the forest led to another. Short excursions went unnoticed. But once I got to know the children I, of course, stayed longer, until one day I was gone so long that I was missed at home and a search party was organized. My parents found me playing happily with the gypsies. I was told again not to go into the forest by myself, but I continued. I believe that my parents, seeing that I was not getting into any serious trouble, let me continue my long walks into the woods.

Gypsies roamed about in groups all over Europe at the time and were allowed to camp on public land, but they were prohibited to settle. Then one day "My Gypsies," the gypsy children I had befriended, had gone. They had moved on. Yet I continued to explore the forest by myself and never stopped as long as I lived in Wolfenbüttel. What kept me going into the forest after my playmates had left? I think I went back because there was so much to see; I must have liked what I saw and wanted more. I would explore the different trees, shrubs, ferns, and mosses. I remember trying to climb a tree without a ladder.

This was the beginning of my interest in forests. Wherever I went during my life, I discovered forests: evergreen forests, tropical forests, and rain forests. As I grew older, the names of the trees did not matter too much: what interested me was the great variety and beauty of trees to be admired. This changed some thirty years later when I was a planning officer in West Ham, in the east end of London of all places and became involved with the new Tree Preservation Regulations under the Town Planning Act. This time, knowing the names of trees did matter. The preservation orders not only asked for the location and the number of trees to be preserved but also asked for the type, age, and life expectancy of every tree in order to justify its preservation. At that time, I both admired the beauty of the trees and I got to know their names pretty well. As a boy in Wolfenbüttel, though, I did not have to worry about these details.

But then, my life in Wolfenbüttel came to an end and my family moved on just like "My Gypsies" had. It was 1926 and I was five years old.

Berlin

Going to Berlin meant the start of a new life for me: starting school, living in an apartment, and having to get used to a big city. People were everywhere and everything was different from Wolfenbüttel.

The apartment in the west end of the city near the fashionable Kurfürstendamm was certainly large enough. There were eight rooms, two bathrooms, a front and rear hall, and two balconies – a large one on the street side and a smaller one overlooking the landscaped courtyard. We had a maid named Mia who had her own small room. She was a young, buxom country girl who cleaned the apartment, helped with the cooking, and washed the laundry in the basement of the building. The drying was done in the courtyard, or in the spooky attic when it was raining.

When I was old enough for a bicycle, there was the problem of where to store it. Outside was not advisable. To carry it up the main staircase was not permitted; this left the winding, spiral back staircase which gave access to the kitchen. This was all right, but where to keep it? My brother came up with an idea: he fixed a pulley on the back hall ceiling so I could then haul the bicycle up to our landing.

I do not remember being unhappy about all the changes in my new life. It was all new and therefore exciting. Just one small example: I enjoyed going with my mother to the Kaufhaus des Westens (Department Store of the West) in Berlin. This huge, multi-storey department store was nicknamed KaDeWe (pronounced Kah-Day-Vay) and sold everything imaginable, including food. On the food floor there were large glass-sided water tanks full of live fish.

Once, an eel escaped the fishmonger's net and slithered along the tiled floor. I tried to pick up the eel but it was too slippery.

The year of our move to Berlin was 1927: six years before Hitler came to power. You will note my memory's fixation on Hitler and what he stood for in my Berlin life. By the time he became the Chancellor of Germany I was a student (not for long) at the Fichte Gymnasium, a boys' grammar school. Out in the streets around the school, noisy gangs of the extreme right and left parties marched, often leading to fights.

At school the Jewish boys discussed "the situation" in the streets and the rising tension between us and the boys who belonged to the Hitler Youth. We also talked about what we heard at home when our parents discussed political events in Germany with their dinner guests. We, the school boys, seemed to be more worried about the situation than our parents were.

One day at school, during recess in the yard, a big Hitler Youth boy attacked a little Jewish boy, a friend of mine. I rushed over to try and stop the fight. The big guy hit me in the face with a hard object. This made me really mad and I wrestled him to the ground, sitting on top of him with blood from my face trickling all over him. The hard object turned out to be an illegal weapon – a knuckle-duster – which was a brass gadget worn with four fingers through four holes as a grip in the palm of the hand. By the time a crowd had formed to watch the fight, the duty-teacher was alerted and came to separate us.

I was reminded of this time in Berlin when reading Erik Larson's *In the Garden of Beasts*, a remarkable and well-researched book about William Dodd's (U.S. ambassador) failure to persuade the State Department of the seriousness of Hitler's aims. Ambassador Dodd's views were influenced by Konstantin von Neurath, Germany's minister for foreign affairs, who believed that others in the government could control Hitler. Dodd said: "Hitler will fall into line with these wiser men and ease up on a tense situation." That was also the initial view of Germany's middle and upper classes. It is important to remember that Hitler had admirers elsewhere, in England and the United States. He was praised for being a strong leader who "got things done," unlike the officials of the Weimar Republic.

The Jewish middle class was just the same at first – they were unconcerned about their future in Germany. They were Germans first, they had fought for Germany in the last war and they were among the leaders in science and the arts, and in commerce and industry. And like the rest of the educated Germans and Austrians the Jews felt safe – until it was too late, and Hitler was unstoppable. This attitude was well expressed, perhaps in its extreme form, by Sigmund Freud: "My language is German. My culture, my achievements are German. I consider myself intellectually to be a German, until I noticed the growth of anti-Semitic prejudices in Germany and German Austria. Since then, I prefer to call myself a Jew."

We, the school boys, however, having a "front seat" so to speak, seemed to have had a better sense about what was to come. Had our elders been less blasé they could have left Germany in time before it was too late – as some of them did – like Rene's uncle Fritz Neuburg. He left with a substantial part of his fortune. Freud left Vienna rather late in 1938 when he and his family escaped to England with the help of Ernest Jones, president of the International Psychoanalytic Association.

These thoughts may show my hesitant hindsight as well as the grown-ups' failed foresight. But I think it is an issue well worth further re-examination (by someone else), considering the inconceivable number of people killed. The criticism of the allies for not bombing the railway lines leading to the concentration camps during the critical years of 1943 to 1945 is a different issue. After all, Hitler's *Mein Kampf* explicitly described his aims well before he took power.

This may be a suitable point at which to consider my belief – my Judaism. I never denied my Jewish ancestry. I mentioned my father's orthodox background and how he became a liberal Jew. There was also a rabbi somewhere in my mother's ancestry. When I was growing up in Berlin I went to the synagogue on Saturdays and during the holidays. I learned to read Hebrew and had my bar mitzvah, at which I not only recited the Torah blessing but I also read the weekly portion from the Torah. But none of these Jewish practices had any meaning for me. I now rationalize that I followed tradition out of respect for my father.

I do remember on my bar mitzvah day being upset that the ceremony interfered with a rehearsal at school. I was clearly more interested in activities with my school friends than in my religious duties. It is hard now for me to pin down my passage or my drift to agnosticism – a kind of continuation of my father's religious passage. But I clearly recall my, perhaps immature, reasoning at the time: if the Jews were God's "chosen people" how could I believe in Him when He had abandoned us or failed to protect us, not only now but throughout history.

I had to grow up, read more, and above all get some education before I could sort out my disturbed and young mind. I found that chance after the war at the London School of Economics (LSE).

Though the 1930s were uncertain times that affected all of us, young and old, our Berlin days were not all bad. We had lots of good times, too. For the summer holidays we usually went to the mountains in Austria, mainly because my father was under his doctor's orders to spend as much time at higher altitudes for the benefit of his heart. Our favourite places were in the region of Tyrol in northern Austria where we usually stayed on large farms in the foothills, not in hotels in the towns. The food was good and we could start hiking from the front door of any farmhouse we might be staying in. We did visit towns like Innsbruck where I had another fright one afternoon as I crossed the Inn River on a rickety footbridge. The gaps between the boards were so wide I feared that I might fall through them and drown: it seems that I had an instinct for my safety.

On one of the farms in Tyrol, the family produced honey. One day, the son responsible for looking after the operation took me along on his motorbike to help him collect the honey. At each station, with up to a dozen hives, the routine consisted of spinning the honey combs to separate the honey from the wax, putting the honey through a sieve to catch bits of wax and other impurities, and finally – the best part of the job – tasting the honey. Small amounts of honey were poured into a paper cup for tasting. It was like a wine tasting, except you didn't spit out the honey. I concentrated on "quality control," often tasting the honey from the same hive several times to make sure that the honey conformed to my standard.

At home, throughout the year, we used to go on day trips either sightseeing to places like the Schloss in Potsdam southwest of Berlin or to lakes on the outskirts of the city, where Max and Ruth liked to row. Visits to the Berlin Zoo were frequent as it was within walking distance of our home. Curiously, in addition to the zoo's large number of animals, there were exhibits of humans, too. These were families from different African tribes or from Asia. The zoo built replicas of their villages and brought groups of "natives" to show how they lived in their home countries: what they ate, how they dressed, how they danced, and so on. This, I believe, was an early manifestation of Nazi propaganda used to draw attention to the inferiority of the coloured races.

Another enjoyable activity we shared was acrobatics. Max, Ruth, and I loved sports and gymnastics and we developed an acrobatic performance. Max was strong and tall like my father (about 6 feet) and he was the prop of the team. By prop I mean that he lay on the ground and Ruth and I balanced in different positions on top of him. He was also the prop for our grand finale in which Ruth stood on Max's shoulders and I on hers. We were so popular that we gave performances at parties and festivities.

Mentioning that both my father and brother were tall reminds me of my parents' attempts to "make me grow." I was always called *der Kleine* (the little one), not because I was the youngest in the family but because I was the shortest. The family doctor suggested I should "run a lot." I already belonged to a sports club, so I started to concentrate on running medium distances and cross-country. I got good at it and made the team to compete against other clubs. But I did not grow any taller, though my chest expanded and I am certain that my good health is mainly due to my many years of running regularly during my younger years.

Looking back on the peaceful times in Berlin, I have but one regret: my parents suggested I take music lessons to learn to play the piano or violin. I showed little interest; I was probably too busy with my friends. I wished my parents had been more persistent or had asked again a bit later.

My father occasionally gave private lessons to foreign university students in need of help in their philosophy or history studies. One Indian student seemed to need a lot of help; he was around for a long time. He liked my father's library and used it all the time, almost becoming a part of the family. It was unusual for a student in those days, but he had a car – a leather-upholstered Mercedes, no less. I believe now that he may have been a Maharaja's son who had come to Berlin to study Western culture. In return he told us about exotic India. To seal the friendship, he took us in his car to the more inaccessible places on weekends – giving me my first ride in a private car.

When there was less time on the weekends for long trips, the family went for walks in one of the nearby parks. My father might talk about his early teaching experiences and my mother about growing up in the Rhineland.

Then there was Uschi, my first girlfriend at thirteen. By common consent, beautiful and mysterious Uschi was the most desirable girl at school and, unbelievably, she was mine – for a time – in an innocent way. It made me deliriously happy and boosted my ego. This happened at a Jewish school in Berlin because, after my first two years at the Fichte Gymnasium, Jews were no longer allowed to attend the public school system.

My parents became increasingly concerned about our education. Max seemed all right by this time. He would have liked to become a dentist, but this was no longer possible for a Jew; he became a dental mechanic making crowns and bridges for the patients of dentists. Ruth was looking forward to becoming a teacher. I had no idea what I wanted to do when I grew up.

I was sent to an occupational institute for tests to determine what I might be good at. Apart from the expected tests in math and language skills, there were different manual tests like bending wires, building odd constructions, sketching, and copying given scenes. The verdict was that I would likely do well in engineering.

My parents first attempted to send me to Palestine, as it then was known, to the Technion – Israel Institute in Technology – in Haifa, later to become as prestigious as the Massachusetts Institute of Technology (MIT). I was accepted, but the monetary restrictions on the transfer of funds on a regular basis from Germany to Palestine made it impossible for me to go there. The next attempt worked: a private technical school in Bodenbach in the German-speaking Sudetenland of Czechoslovakia. I was admitted for a three-year course in electrical and mechanical engineering.

When I went to Bodenbach I was fourteen. I was living away from home for the first time in a house with other lodgers. There was no bathroom; one had to go to the public bathhouse for a shower or, at a higher price, to use a bathtub. The house was none too clean. When I got some itchy, red marks on my body I showed them to Frau Goldberg, the landlady. Her instant response was "I don't have any bedbugs." I had never heard of bedbugs or any other biting creatures that lived in one's bed. It was then that I realized that I had been living a very sheltered life at home.

Curiously enough, Rene, my future wife lived a mere thirty miles from Bodenbach in Leitmeritz. We might have met then but had to wait a few years for fate to bring us together in Northampton, England. After the war, Rene and her older sister, Dorli, found refuge there and worked for a doctor's household as the cook and maid.

In 1936, after my first year at the technical school, my father and my mother died within a few months of each other. My father's cause of death at sixty was angina pectoris. It seems that spending vacations "in the mountains" was an inadequate cure for his heart condition. My mother took an overdose of sleeping tablets and our family doctor was unable to save her.

I accepted my mother's decision to end her life at forty-eight without speculating why she had done so. I assumed she was unable to face life without her husband, especially during such uncertain times in Berlin. She probably thought that her children were old enough to look after themselves. This was certainly true about my brother, and my sister had a steady boyfriend whom she married shortly afterwards. And I, after all, was living by myself.

My mother, Anna, chose a better way to end her life than the death she would have faced like my sister, Ruth, did in Auschwitz in 1942. I like to think that my mother sensed, as I did, that the situation in Germany was more dangerous than her adult friends imagined. Anna was a loving mother who gave me all I needed or desired and she would not have abandoned me indifferently.

I felt no bitterness or anger, then or since, about my mother leaving me on my own. Though, I had grown used of living by myself, the realization of actually being on my own sunk in more slowly. While my mother's suicide was not traumatic at the time, it may have affected my psyche – but this would be for others to say. The long-term effect on me, I believe, was to make me independent – I became an adult at an early age and made decisions readily if not always wisely.

I continued my studies and, when I could, visited my sister in Berlin. During one of these visits I got into serious trouble. I had previously taken photos in Berlin of interest to the media outside Germany. For example, I took a photo of a sign in a public park reading Hunde und Juden VERBOTEN (Dogs and Jews strictly prohibited). On this visit an even better opportunity presented itself. The Luftwaffe staged a mock air attack on Berlin to test the city's defences and air-raid precautions. When the sirens went off everyone had to go into a shelter. I lingered on the balcony of our apartment when the first waves of planes appeared in the sky and – surprise – all the planes had British or French insignia on their wings. I got my Kodak box camera and took pictures, using up the whole film.

The air-raid wardens in the street spotted me and shouted for me to go to the shelter. After the exercise was over, I received a call at the apartment from the police telling me to report to the police station with my camera. I had enough sense to seek advice before going to the police. As my father had been a respected member of the Jewish community, I called the community organization. A lawyer directed me to remove the film from the camera, destroy the film, and take pictures on a new film of the empty sky.

At the police station my camera was confiscated and I was locked in a cell to await the arrival of the Gestapo (Secret Police or Geheime Staats Polizei). The Gestapo arrived in style in an open Mercedes and took me to their headquarters near the Potsdamer Platz where I was interrogated at length. By the time the lawyer from the Jewish community organization arrived, I had been locked up in the dreaded Gestapo prison, but the lawyer was allowed to see me briefly. His strategy was to plead my youth and inexperience in photographing fast-flying aircraft. He knew that the film would show the blank sky. Of course, there was no way I could have missed the planes because they flew in tight formation and covered the whole sky.

The Gestapo kept me in their prison overnight because they had more questions about me and my friends at the school in Bodenbach. I spent a sleepless night in my cell listening to the bells of St. Lucas Church chiming every quarter hour. In the morning, after further questions, they let me go and I hastily returned to Bodenbach.

Escape

Soon after the beginning of my final year at school, on the first of October 1938, the German army marched into the Sudetenland "to protect" their countrymen living there. I left ahead of them for Prague where, as a German citizen, I was not welcome. What really mattered was that I could not speak Czech. In any case I soon ran out of money. Having had a steady monthly cheque for so long, I had gotten used to spending it.

The only solution for my predicament was to return to Berlin, but the borders were closed. Even worse, the road, rail, and air transportation systems were not operating. I learned to sleep on park benches, stuffing newspapers into my jacket to keep warm. Sometimes I slept on the floor at friends' apartments. They were in the same position as me, wanting to get back to Germany. Through these friends I also began to earn money. They introduced me to the risky black market in British 5-pound notes. English money was the only trusted currency in Prague at the time and it was in great demand. After a frightened start, because I had never seen a British 5-pound note before – it was just a large white piece of paper with black printing on one side only – I began to earn money.

Rumour had it that one could walk into Germany at Hrádek, the three-country border town between Germany, Czechoslovakia, and Poland. My two friends and I decided to make a try for the Czech border, and the three of us set off by train to Hrádek. The normal trip of a few hours took all night because military transport had priority. On arrival we were surprised to hear loud gunfire. Poland was trying to take advantage of the German-Czech dispute to gain some land as well and was attacking the town. This mini-war was never reported in any history of that time. We decided to retreat and made our long trip back to Prague.

Eventually, flights between Prague and Berlin resumed and I experienced my first trip by airplane. When I arrived at the Templehof airport in Berlin, my passport was confiscated and I was told to report to my local police station. This I did the next day and was informed that I had to leave Germany within a month and that I had to report to the police before leaving. Yet they kept my passport, which I would need in order to leave the country. So, one way or another, my future arrest was predictable.

I paid a return visit to my helpful lawyer friend who had gotten me out of the hands of the Gestapo over the camera incident. He organized my escape. Agreement had been reached at that time between the British and German governments and the British Jewish community organization for the Kindertransporte of children (without their parents) under the age of 15 from Germany and Austria to England. No passports were needed; the children were listed by age. Although I was seventeen, I was entered as fifteen. Further, the lawyer instructed me not to report to the police before my departure; he would inform the police after I had left.

⸙

While waiting for the Kindertransporte, "Kristallnacht" (the Night of Broken Glass) took place in Berlin and across Germany. It was November 10, 1938. This was the first organized, countrywide operation of violence against the Jews in Germany; synagogues were set on fire, Jewish shops were destroyed, and in the following days some 30,000 Jewish men were indiscriminately arrested. Once again, the Jewish organization looked after me. I was moved around almost daily from safe house to safe house all over Berlin, and especially its suburbs, until the day of my departure on the first train that left on December 1, 1938. Each child was allowed to bring a small suitcase and 10 Reichsmark – the equivalent of about $50 Canadian today.

CHAPTER 2

Arriving In England

The train with some 200 children went via Hoek van Holland, Netherlands, and arrived by ferry at Harwich, England, on December 2, 1938. It was a cold and snowy day. The English being spoken by the dock workers did not sound like the language I had learned at school. We were taken by bus to one of the popular Butlins Summer Camps on a beach at Lowestoft in Suffolk. The huts were nice with comfortable beds but no heating. The outside temperature was well below freezing. At night time we were given these funny rubber things – hot water bottles – to pretend that the bed was warm. Actually, on some nights the water started to freeze inside the bottles.

Other transports arrived to fill the camp, but the organizing committee in London soon realized that warmer quarters had to be found for the children. Soon I was in a small group of boys on a train to Charing Cross railway station in London where we got a meal at the station hotel before being put on another train to Broadstairs, which was near Ramsgate on the southeast coast in Kent.

It was night when we arrived at Ramsgate station. As the oldest child in the group, I was put in the first taxi with other kids. We stopped in the driveway of a large, imposing building. The driver must have said "all right, hop out" and pointed to a large door at the top of a stone staircase. I opened the tall, squeaky door and we entered a huge, silent stone hall with steps curving to another large door – we were alone, waiting.

The little boys around me were scared; a tall woman cloaked in black descended the steps to meet the children. She looked at me – the oldest of the group and not quite a child. She was the mother superior of the convent for novices. The convent had offered to take in young children and look after them until families could be found for them.

We, some four dozen boys, were put in a dormitory. On the floor above was a similar dormitory with the novices, who were about my age; they crowded the upper landing in their nighties gaping at us, the little foreign boys. We had arrived shortly before Christmas and the novices and the teaching nuns gave us a wonderful time with all the traditional food. But moves were afoot to remove me from the scene – to get me away from the novices. In the New Year I was sent by myself back to Suffolk, to Barham House outside Ipswich.

Barham House consisted of a number of eighteenth-century Poor Law buildings that once housed the impoverished and which were now used as a holding centre for refugees looking for work. Having been the oldest of the "children," I was now considered the youngest of the adults. Everyone participated in the running of what was in effect an "employment exchange." Everyone helped in running the place: cooking, cleaning, maintaining the place or dealing with the administrative work of finding jobs for everyone. I was put in the post office. The leader of the operation was a Dr. Ettlinger, a learned German refugee.

Requests arrived from all over the country from companies looking for cheap labour. Job offers were pinned on a board and anyone was free to respond after registering. My first application was in response to a posting for a "butler trainee" – the "trainee" was to be the driver for an aristocrat and would be taught other duties required to serve him. The real butler came to look me over and I was found wanting – no surprise.

My second application was successful and I went off to work as a fitter in the village of Weedon, near Northampton. The workshop was owned by Captain Gardner, a retired naval captain, and we produced battery cages for hens. These battery cages were a new invention at the time and were used for housing hens and controlling their egg production. Captain G. may have been a good sailor but he knew little about metal work. There were few tooling machines, so most of the work was done with hand tools. His battery cage design consisted of a double-sided, three-level structure that was suspended on wires; there was one cage for each hen. Belts between each level caught the droppings. The eggs rolled out in front of each cage. Except for the foreman, the workers were unskilled. Captain G. invited ideas from his workers, and he paid five pounds for each good idea he accepted that led to better production. A few of my suggestions earned me a better income.

The battery cages were shipped unassembled, by rail, for assembly on farms. The best part of the job was to go with the foreman in the sidecar of his motorcycle to the farms to install the battery cages, mainly in Devon and Cornwall. We stayed on the farms during this time and had better food than we might have had in the local hotels. The young hen-minders, boys and girls, taught me a new game: throwing raw eggs some twenty or more yards and catching them in your hand. I crushed most of them.

While I worked in Weedon, I lived in Northampton and commuted daily by bus. I shared a bedroom at Mrs. Hazeldine's with Leo, another refugee from Vienna. Leo had a wonderful voice – good enough for the Vienna Opera. His favourite aria was "Un bel di vedremo" from *Madama Butterfly* by Puccini.

Mrs. H's house was a typical English row house with one water tap at the kitchen sink, an outhouse, and no heating other than the open-hearth cooking fire. There was a gas heater in our bedroom and when I suggested using it on winter mornings, Mrs. H. had a fit: "Heating in the bedroom?!" Her husband was a coal miner. He washed off his coal dust every evening in a metal tub that was in front of the fire. Leo and I used the tub every night, too, and we went once a week to the public bathhouse.

My daily commuting left me little time in the evenings during the week. The work in Weedon was easy and not unpleasant, but the pay was small. Leo was one of a group of twenty refugees who worked in Northampton at Rice & Co., an iron foundry, as a grinder (handling power-driven grindstones) finishing cast-iron products; it was extremely hard and dusty work. Their pay was small, like mine, but I wanted to earn a bit more and had an idea.

I paid a visit to Rice & Co. and asked whether they could use a fitter with some engineering training (which I had). They hired me at a better pay than they gave their grinders. I became the assistant to an old fitter who needed help because of his age. The job consisted of repairing casting boxes used with fine sand to make the cast-iron products. In addition, we repaired whatever else was broken in the factory.

The furnaces at the foundry operated continuously for six days but not on Sundays when they were inspected and, if necessary, repaired; that was also our job. Next to the foundry was a greyhound race track with Sunday races, which we watched from the roof of the foundry.

My work was not hard but it was monotonous, as much factory work usually is. But the atmosphere in the foundry was suffocating from the fine, black sand used in the casting process. We breathed in the dust and it went right through our clothes. At the end of the day our bodies were covered in black sand. This sand had to be scrubbed off daily. Looking back, I am surprised that we put up with such working conditions, considering our sheltered upbringing. I guess when you are young and have no choice, you get used to hardship.

Working in Northampton, I now had more time in the evenings to meet people and make friends. Leo, of course, knew other refugees and some English people. The first English person I remember meeting was Sadie Simon, the daughter of a prominent family who took an interest in refugees. She invited a few of us to her house on Sunday afternoons, fed us and entertained us. We, Sadie and I, liked each other but the main benefit for me in meeting her was that my English improved – a little. She had a way of gently correcting my faulty and mispronounced words. That we liked each other was a bonus.

After I had left Germany I had no wish to speak German, yet my English was poor. Most of my friends either continued speaking German or spoke what we called "Emigranto": German, Viennese, or Czech mixed with a few easy English words. They made little effort to learn English. So, Sadie's assistance was very welcome.

A few of us talked vaguely about forming a discussion group to talk about world events, music, or anything other than work. I remember going with Leo to a few of the group meetings where we met the Neuburg sisters, Dorli and Rene, who, as I mentioned, came from the Sudetenland and were working as the maid and cook for a doctor and his wife. I do not remember subsequent meetings very well, except for a few parties. They were very frugal affairs because we had little money for drinks and goodies – not like Sadie's parties.

At one of these parties, I took notice of the Neuburg sisters, especially Rene. It was the occasion, which I have often talked about, when Rene and I stepped onto the balcony to talk alone and eat cherries – Rene was spitting the stones on people in the street and hitting them; that registered as a qualification for a wife. After that event I took a detour to work, riding my bicycle past the doctor's house and waving to Dorli, who was often outside polishing the doctor's brass plate.

Here is how Rene remembered our first encounter; it is taken from a long letter she wrote to me in 1995 on our 50th wedding anniversary:

After I had seen you for the first time, I never forgot your face. My sister and I thought that you resembled our cousin Frank. He had been shot dead walking illegally across the border from Czechoslovakia into Poland.

Frank had problems with all the Leitmeritz cousins. He came from Bodenbach and had been educated at Oxford, wore English tweed, he was interested in art and literature, and he was smarter than all the Leitmeritz cousins. My cousin Lisette was his sister.

Because of the apparent resemblance, Dorli and I called you Frank when we talked about you before we knew your proper name. Because of your smile we called you at other times the Cheshire cat, as Arthur Reckham wrote of the broad grin under the illustration in my copy of Lewis Carrol's Alice in Wonderland ...

You spoke to my sister for the first time when you saw her polishing the brass plate outside the doctor's house where we stayed.

In summer 1940, we all had to leave Northampton on account of the war. We organized a farewell party for the members of the discussion group.

CHAPTER 3

Into The Army

All foreigners had to leave Northampton, as well as other areas of "war production" because of the government's fear of spies and the possibility of sabotage. This happened after the fall of Norway to the Germans; "Quislings" (enemy collaborators) and German spies had been active behind the lines.

Most of my friends decided to move to the nearest large town: Leicester. I chose to go to Birmingham, a much larger city with, I assumed, better job opportunities. I quickly landed a job at Cadbury's preparing cardboard boxes for the shipment of chocolates. Cadbury's rule about eating chocolate was simple: you could eat as much as you liked but you were not allowed to take any with you out of the factory. A very shrewd policy because, after gorging yourself for a couple of days with all the different kinds of chocolates, including eating it in its liquid state with a spoon, you did not want to even look at the stuff anymore.

The opportunity to eat chocolate for free was short lived. Fresh rumours – this time about German paratroopers descending on England in preparation for an invasion – led to orders that all German and Austrian men over sixteen years of age were to report for internment.

We were taken by train from Birmingham to the nearest internment camp at Hyton, north of Liverpool. The response to this unexpected experience depended largely on the age of the refugees.

The youngsters like me thought it was just a lark. For example, as we walked with armed guards from the station to the tent encampment, one Liverpudlian in the crowd watching the procession shouted, "Where did you jump?" (meaning by parachute) and one young internee shouted back, "From the bus!" For some of the older refugees, the internment was distressing. Having escaped Nazi Germany, they now seemed to face persecution again, especially as our compound was next to a barbed-wire camp of German prisoners of war. This created tension between old and young internees. The elderly criticized our frivolous behaviour, and the young internees failed to explain their sympathy with Britain's action.

At this time, in a seemingly complementary decision, the government allowed, for the first time, refugees to join the British Army. A few, like me, joined at once. I was glad that I did not hesitate because many were shipped to Canada and Australia. Dorli's future husband, Salo, was sent to Canada where he worked for the rest of the war on a farm near Trois-Rivières, Quebec. Walter Foster, who I was to meet later in the Army, was sent to Australia, but he returned to England after only one year.

All this confusion is normal in wartime. Conflicting and piecemeal decisions are made by different government departments in response to isolated events. Later in the war, Japanese living abroad suffered a worse fate than some of us did.

At first aliens could only join the Pioneer Corps – the unit of labourers. Our status as refugees in the Army was defined in a meticulous correct British fashion as "friendly enemy aliens," and we remained enemy aliens throughout the war – though friendly – until discharged from the Army, when we became naturalized British subjects.

I spent five dull and tedious years in the Army, learning the full vocabulary of English swear words: the most colourful ones from the female soldiers of the ATS (Army Territorial Service). I also picked up some choice "merde plus" phrases from the French Foreign Legionnaires who joined our company after the evacuation of Norway.

I did not fire a Lee Enfield rifle or Sten gun in earnest, though I was trained to fire and clean both of them. I never went overseas until after the war in Europe had ended. I did suffer from the poorly trained Army dentists. One of them pulled a healthy tooth before he agreed with me that it was another tooth that needed attention.

Entering the Army long after the start of the war created a handicap in getting out after the end of the war. The demobilization policy was first in, first out. This meant that the friendly alien soldiers left the forces well after most of the service men had returned to civilian life, finished their education, and got jobs. We latecomers were at the end of the queue. Finding jobs was not a problem, but advancing to senior positions was almost impossible because they were all occupied by young people who were not due for retirement.

After the basic training, I was posted to an open-air rail depot handling barbed-wire coils and building materials by hand. The depot was in a western suburb of Chester, and we were housed in requisitioned mansions.

The French Legionnaires proved very useful to us. These strong men not only shifted the heaviest boxes but also taught us how to lift heavy loads without suffering a hernia. In addition, they managed to find rationed or rare food on nearby farms or in town.

On one morning's parade the command was "anyone who can drive a crane, three steps forward." A number of us stepped forward and three were selected. How they made the selection I do not know, but I was one of them, and none of us three had ever sat in the cabin of a crane. We were told to take the new mobile crane to the railway siding and start unloading the newly arrived train.

The crane was a wartime utility machine without a manual and none of the levers and buttons had tags identifying what they were for. We had little difficulty starting the diesel engine. Then we puzzled over the function of every lever and button. We gingerly pulled and pushed each one to find out. Then, we attached temporary labels to avoid accidents. In a couple of days we were proficient crane operators.

What started as a dare to escape monotonous and hard physical work turned into a lesson: "you learn by doing." Many years later, our son Nicholas discovered the same truth on his own. He barely finished high school, pushing himself to the finish line only because of his mother's insistence. Afterwards, he started odd jobs like painting and helping carpenters and other construction workers. He soon hired himself out to do work on his own account. Eventually, he became, without formal training, a custom builder relying solely on recommendations.

Having settled down as a pioneer at Chester my thoughts must have turned to Rene and her friends in Leicester; but where were they in Leicester? On my next leave I just went there. How I located them I cannot remember. In her letter to me in 1995, Rene wrote that she could not remember either:

> *How you traced Herta, Dorli, and me in Leicester, I don't know to this day. You appeared in the summer of 1943 dressed in uniform. You had leave and decided to visit the three Northampton girls. By that time I had started to work in an office as an offset printing operator and was due for a vacation. I was not earning badly and could afford a trip to the Lake District. As you had your next trip planned for early October, we decided to go hiking in the Lake District together. The weather was pretty chilly with a lot of rain, but*

*we sat at night together on a bench at the shore of
Derwentwater, gazing at the stars ...*
You visited again during the following summer ...

⟶

After Chester, my next posting was to Bicester, not far from Oxford, where a large Ordnance Depot was under construction. Here work became more interesting when I was assigned to a group building Nissen huts, which were made from sheets of corrugated iron bent into half cylinders. Four of us from Chester, having learned how to put up these huts, formed a team. We soon found that we could erect a Nissen hut faster than it took regular British soldier pioneers. We persuaded the officer in charge of the Nissen huts project that the four of us should be allowed to finish work for the day whenever we had finished putting up one hut. The officer readily agreed because it had never been done before.

The following day we finished early, perhaps at 3:00 pm, and went by train (soldiers could travel for free) to Oxford for the rest of the day. We got to know Oxford pretty well in the following weeks.

While at Bicester the Army decided that "friendly enemy aliens" would be permitted to transfer to other branches of the Army. Walter Fast, who had returned from internment in Australia some months ago, and I were sent for a trade test to Woolwich Arsenal. Having passed the test we were posted to No. 4 REME (Royal Electrical Mechanical Engineers) workshop at Donnington Ordnance Depot in Shropshire. And that is where I was stuck until the end of the war in Europe, when I was sent to Egypt.

At Donnington, my work consisted of servicing and repairing guns: Beaufort anti-aircraft guns, 17-pounder anti-tank guns, and 25-pounder field guns. It was a semi-skilled job, but it was repetitive and boring work. Quite frankly, we were cheap labour compared to unionized mechanics doing the same work. Turns out that some of the anti-tank guns we serviced were sent to Russia from Donnington.

I hope they were used in the decisive Battle of Stalingrad, so I can feel that I had some direct involvement in the victory.

In December 1943, an Army Order suggested that German- and Austrian-born soldiers change their names to avoid "difficulties" in case they were taken as prisoners of war. This was not a direct order, but merely advice. Walter chose Foster. My only concern was to keep my "C" because the weekly pay on Fridays was in alphabetical order. If you wanted to catch a train to go away for the weekend it was better to get paid early. An ATS girl's first suggestion was "Churchill." Eventually, she came up with the name "Carson."

At some point, when victory for the Allies seemed assured, Walter and I started talking about what we would do after the war. Our education, especially mine, was incomplete. Above all, we had not written the matriculation exam (the Matric), which was required in order to enter university. After enquiries, we decided to register with a correspondence school in London. But to study in the barracks would be difficult. We searched in the adjoining village and rented a room: the "parlor" in a house owned by an old lady. The parlor was the front room and was used only for weddings and funerals. She gave us the keys to the house and we could come and go anytime, evenings and weekends. She even brought us coffee sometimes.

Walter was the driving force in this initiative, especially when it came to the actual study part. He was more mature than me. Without his push I might never have completed the course and I have been grateful to him ever since. We needed to pass in five subjects, three of which were compulsory – English, math, and one foreign language – plus a choice of two from a long list of subjects. We naturally chose German for the foreign language, and I picked geography and mechanical drawing as my two choices. We sat the examination at the Imperial Institute in London. There are things you do, decisions you make which at the time you do not notice too much, but which in retrospect are crucial to your life – tipping points. Taking the Matric was one of them.

After the Matric, Walter and I had free weekends again. Walter's time off from the Army was mostly spent in Ilford with the Mann family who had befriended him when he was staying at a hostel after his arrival in England in 1939. Myrtle, one of the Mann's daughters, by this time a lieutenant in the ATS, had been posted near Donnington. As Walter wrote in his memoir, "that was great, but given the Army's caste system, very difficult. She was by then a lieutenant and I was a private soldier. For her to be seen with me was a disciplinary offence. We found little cafes and quiet country lanes to go cycling."

For me, visits to Leicester became more frequent. Whenever I could get away from the Army, I was with the refugee crowd in Leicester, and with Rene, who wrote:

> *The following winter we met mostly in Leicester. I had found lodgings for you near Ashleigh Road … You visited for the youth march and for the dance when I wore the national costume. On that occasion you took "French" leave. Not so much to see me as to prove that in the British Army you could get away with anything … By that time I had proposed to you several times. You said nothing.*

On my visits to Leicester I imperceptibly noticed the presence of a few older Germans from London among the refugees. They talked a lot about returning home to Germany, Austria, and Czechoslovakia to help with reconstruction. It soon became clear to me that this clandestine group was a communist cell recruiting and indoctrinating refugees to their cause.

Like most refugees, I took an interest in politics. I had read Orwell's *Homage to Catalonia*, the earliest critique of Russian communism. The secret and conspiratorial manner of the communists did not appeal to me. The Molotov–Ribbentrop Pact of August 1939 sealed my opposition to communism.

Nevertheless, the recruitment for communist, post-war leadership in Leicester was, at least partly, successful. Two refugees became bosses in the DDR (Deutsche Democratische Republik). Werner Pincus became a member of the inner circle of the Communist Party, and Hans Herzberg became the DDR's correspondent in Bonn and, I believe, he was a spy.

I did not have to worry about Rene. Although she was not well versed in politics, she was independently minded enough not to accept prescribed doctrine; but nonetheless she had come under suspicion by the communists as a "capitalist lackey" on account of her war production work, the only refugee in Leicester to do so, and she was a friend of a British soldier, another no-no. Not that this mattered. The communists held no sway over us; it was all intimidation.

Rene had given up her office job and was trained as a centre-lathe operator, making among other things release buttons for parachutes. She was too short to reach the levers of the machine, so they had to build a platform for her. She acquired an impressive vocabulary of obscene swear words. When I asked Rene if she knew the meaning of some of the words she said, "No, but they all use them at work." Her co-workers elected her shop steward to represent them at management meetings – I believe because she could read and write and was not afraid to speak up on their behalf.

When the last pre-war Czech president, Eduard Benes, visited Leicester on his tour of England to rally the Czech community, he presented Rene with a signed copy of his book *Democracy Today and Tomorrow* in recognition of her war production work.

Throughout my years in the REME I regularly volunteered to be posted overseas for active duty. I never succeeded. Yet, predictably, after getting married to Rene on a weekend in Leicester, I was posted to Egypt. By then, I was no longer interested in leaving England and, in any case, the war in Europe was over.

I landed just outside Cairo, near the Heliopolis Airport, at the Abassia Depot, the British Army's largest overseas depot, where many of its soldiers were due to be "demobbed." We, the new recruits, had arrived to replace them. The officer interviewing me in order to decide where to place me noticed from my record that I had changed my name. He almost shouted "Why did you not call yourself Smith instead of Carson which is an Irish name?" – a bad start to the interview. However, he noticed that I could read and write and had some education, so he assigned me to the position of registrar of incoming mail, which meant I was in charge of an immense filing system.

The pile of letters arriving daily had to be sorted and the appropriate letter attached to the appropriate file or files and sent to the responsible officer for action. There were thousands of files, well organized and categorized. The system had obviously been set up by an experienced administrator. Many of the incoming letters gave references or file numbers, which was helpful, but some did not and some referred to more than one subject without a reference. Apart from learning the filing system, I also had to understand the office organization in order to send files to the correct office.

I learned how to manage the volume of files quickly and the orderlies did not have to wait long with their trolleys to start their rounds distributing them. I was also occasionally on night duty answering phone calls and taking messages from all over the Middle East. Once I had settled in, it became like a peacetime office job with regular hours, which left me free time to explore Cairo, although with care. British soldiers were not a popular presence in Egypt. It was unsafe to walk by oneself, especially down back alleys.

I went, of course, to the pyramids and the Great Sphinx at Giza, and crawled through the narrow tunnel of the largest pyramid to reach the burial hall in its centre. The room was dark and musty with a stone sarcophagus in the middle, plus there were all kinds of presents and utensils the awaking Pharaoh might need – should he arise. Many visitors climbed up the walls of the pyramid, which had become possible ever since the smooth alabaster cladding of ancient times had been taken away long ago and used for other constructions, leaving it a bit more scalable. The stone blocks were about three-foot square and to climb up was dangerous – it was definitely not for me. On the day I was there, I was walking away from the pyramid when I heard a sudden commotion and saw people pointing at the pyramid and shouting "*Shufti, shufti!*" (Look, look!). I turned around to see a Yankee soldier tumbling down head-over-heels like a dummy, arriving dead at the bottom. I don't know when exactly, but climbing up the pyramid was stopped some time ago.

Leaving through the main gate of the Abbasia Depot one day to go to town, I saw a crowd of people lining the main road leading from the airport into Cairo. Eventually, an open Mercedes passed by, whose passengers were King Ibn Saud and King Farouk. They were rather like Hitler and Goering, only Farouk was much fatter than Goering.

For my leave I went to Palestine by train via Al Arish to Gaza and then hitchhiked to Tel Aviv. I first stayed with Father Fritz, Rene's uncle, and his wife, Leni, in their spacious apartment; really two apartments turned into one unit. The place was like a small museum, filled with his glass collection and other *objets d'art*. The three of us then went to Netanya, a seaside resort to the north of Tel Aviv where we joined Janne, Honza's sister, and her baby son, Dodi. Many years later, Dodi remembered being carried on the shoulders of a soldier from "Australia or some place."

Before returning to England and finally getting out of the Army, I benefitted from an enlightening Army policy: service men intending to return to school were invited to spend some time getting reacquainted with study habits like reading, listening to learned talks, and writing essays. Some of the soldiers based in Egypt agreed to go, and we found ourselves housed in a magnificent building on top of Mount Carmel in Haifa. I never learned what the building's original use was, but the ground floor had been converted into a library, and reading and lecturing rooms, and the upper floors had become bedrooms and bathrooms. I stayed there for a month in the spring of 1946.

The program offered voluntary lectures with optional discussions on a wide range of subjects. I chose history and spent most of my time reading. There were no tests or examinations. The teachers were ready to discuss whatever was on our minds and they understood that the most important part of our time there would be to get used once again to serious reading.

For relaxation we went for swims in Haifa Bay. Unfortunately, this was a time of conflict between the British Mandate forces, the Palestinians, and two Jewish armed groups: the Haganah, the future Israeli Army, and Irgun, a militant group actively engaging the British forces. This meant that we, the British soldiers, had to go to the beach with our guns ready to defend ourselves from the Jews.

One evening, our school received a warning about a pending attack aimed at the armory in the building. This warning was taken seriously. All of us were deployed in and around the building with rifles and Sten guns. I was stationed at one of the two entrances and found myself in a disagreeable position: I did not want to shoot a Jewish attacker, however misguided, nor did I want to be shot at. The elaborate design of the entrance's porch provided the solution. I could hide in a deep alcove. Luckily, it was a false alarm, nobody turned up all night. But the alarm was not frivolous. A short time later, on July 22, 1946, the King David Hotel in Jerusalem, headquarters of the British Mandate administration in Palestine, was blown up by the Irgun.

A final note on my month in Haifa. While I was there, I struck up a friendship with another soldier-student. We had common interests and spent much time together exploring the city: seeing the sights like the Technion, where I might have been a student, and talking to the people in the way journalists prepare for their dispatches home. But being in British Army uniform did not help, we were not trusted. To the Palestinians, we were the representatives of the 1917 Balfour Declaration promising the Jews a homeland in Palestine. And to the Jews, we were there to uphold the Mandate dating back to the League of Nations in the 1920s, supposedly assuring an even-handed treatment of both sides.

What we learned can be summarized as follows: the future of all the people in this rather small area of land looked hopeless. Unless all three or four parties – the United Nations, the Palestinians, the British, and the Jews – showed a respect for each other and an uncommon willingness to find a mutually acceptable accommodation, there would be no solution.

Strange to say, the Jews who are said to be very intelligent failed from the beginning to see the obvious. Put candidly, the Israelis, from the establishment of their country onwards, refused to acknowledge that they were located in a region where they were surrounded by enemies. Some accommodation should and could have been established for all of them to live in peace instead of continuing to follow the historic colonial policies of claiming complete control over other people's lands. Israel could have led development in the Middle East as a leader and a partner.

Today, when unexpectedly, the future global oil supply is changing radically, it is not fanciful to expect that the United States will dump its "vital Middle East interests" and, when it does so, we will watch a catastrophe in the making.

After the very pleasant farewell from the British Army in Haifa, I returned to England for my demobilization. I sailed on an overcrowded troopship from Alexandria to Toulon, France, and then travelled by train to Calais, Dover, and Aldershot, where I received civilian clothes and instructions about converting my "friendly enemy alien" status into "a British subject."

CHAPTER 4

Into The World

Starting Work and a Family

Arriving in London in 1946 after many wasted years marked the beginning of my real life. With the uncertainties awaiting me, it should have been an anxious time for me. But being reunited with Rene and having to find somewhere to live kept me happy and busy. Housing was in very short supply in England and especially in London.

There was no urgency for both of us to find jobs just yet. Rene had already started her biology studies at Chelsea Polytechnic and I expected to go to the London School of Economics (LSE). I had visited the school after writing my Matric in Cambridge, where the school had been evacuated to during the war.

We settled in one good-sized room, perhaps 15 feet by 15 feet, in South Kensington, minutes from Kensington Gardens. Most of the imposing four- or five-storey terrace houses in the area were partitioned into one- or two-room units with shared bathrooms on the half landings. Our room had a wash basin in one corner, which became the kitchen – covered by a custom-built table most of the time – and an electric hotplate on a trolley in another corner, also covered when not in use. With a fold-out bed, we had a living room, kitchen-dining room, and bedroom all in one.

Both of us were out most days at school, so life did not feel too confined. The FET (Further Education and Training) grants – similar to the American G.I. Bill – were available to ex-service men and women wishing to return to their previous studies. I decided not to return to engineering or start learning any other "practical" subject. I chose what was called "government" at LSE, or political science, a branch of history.

Not long after Rene and I had settled down in South Kensington and I had started at college, Rene suffered a traumatic experience. Her school friend at Chelsea Poly, Vasant, who was a student from India, took his life one night in a dramatic and very public way at the Peter Pan bronze statue in Kensington Garden, a fifteen-minute walk from our flat. The London papers were full of the incident, not because of Vasant but because of Peter Pan's popularity. I had met Vasant but cannot say that I knew him well. He was reserved, lonely, and came from a well-to-do family. I think Vasant hoped Rene might change partners. Rene and I never spoke about him – before or after. There was little I could do to help her other than be extra considerate – only time could heal her hurt. This was my second encounter with a suicide caused by lost love – a powerful motivation.

When I went back to LSE, I had applied for a grant, but to obtain a grant required taking an exam. LSE had its own exam consisting of an essay and an interview. The essay was about *The Managerial Revolution* by James Burnham, published in 1941 and much talked about. I had read the book before, so I had no problem writing about it or discussing it. The interview seemed a pro forma affair considering that the professors knew that I had passed the written exam. Still, the younger professor took his job seriously and asked some difficult and almost unanswerable questions. The older professor, who I later learned was Edward Shils, a distinguished American sociologist, merely had a pleasant chat with me.

LSE was an important milestone in my life. Just having been at LSE impressed people and, no doubt, was a help when applying for a job. Yet I did not benefit as much as I might have done had I been better prepared for a college education. Never having finished my secondary education in Berlin, my general knowledge of literature, science, and history was sketchy. The month at Mount Carmel library had been helpful, but it could not fill the many gaps in my education.

I did not have to go to LSE to find out that I was ill prepared for a university education. Rene, one year younger than me, had a comprehensive knowledge of literature, science, and history. She was always my encyclopedia or, as I would say now, my personal Google. Though not a good student, I enjoyed my time at the school. Nearly all the students were ex-service, the rest were either straight from public school (meaning private school in England) or from the ex-colonies who were studying to become the future leaders of their countries after independence.

The lectures were interesting, and some were outright entertaining. One example was a lecture course given by Harold Laski, a member of the Labour Party executive and head of the political science department, who mixed information, analysis, and jokes to hold our attention. Because of some of his outlooks, the school had a reputation of being "left wing," when in fact most professors and lecturers were conservative. The economics faculty under Lionel Robbins was wholly conservative.

We also had much freedom regarding the lectures we could attend, and were invited to attend any of interest to us outside our discipline. A good example was a lecture given by the renowned philosopher Karl Popper on logic. While only a handful of students actually attended his course, the school had to assign him the largest theatre for his lectures because of his popularity – and even then many had to stand.

On the social side, there were a number of clubs and societies sponsored by students of different faculties or interests that were active. Casual cliques of friends were always ready to chat and drink coffee in the cafeteria any time of the day. Future long-term friends included Walter, who was studying international relations; Peter Block, the returned paratrooper from Italy; Martin Ennals, later to be the first secretary of Amnesty International; and Bernard Levin, one of the youngsters from public school, who was an exceptionally gifted young man soon to become a household name in Britain as a controversial journalist and broadcaster. One of his interests and subjects he wrote about was opera. Bernard insisted that I go with him to Covent Garden and listen to the complete Wagner Ring cycle just a couple of weeks before our final examinations.

Other LSE students included ex-lieutenant Myrtle Hirsh (nee Mann), Walter's friend, who put in an appearance at the cafeteria, but not very often; she was more mature and a serious student. In his memoir, "The History of Young Walter," he wrote: "She [Myrtle] was the first to point me in the direction of LSE as a place for study after the war." Therefore, by association, she pointed me in that direction, too.

Then there was Rachel Ginsburg, another friend of Walter; and Walter wrote about her: "We met at LSE during the Lent term of 1948. She was really interested in John Carson, and I in her friend Tamara." I recall Walter telling me one day, "When you walked into the cafeteria, Rachel said, 'He looks rather interesting,' and I said, 'Rene would not like to hear you say that,' and Rachel's response was, 'Who is Rene?'" When Rachel and Walter did get married in January 1949, Rene and I moved with them into Mrs. Miller's house in Wembley Park. Mrs. Miller, her sons Reg and Stew, and the four of us shared one bathroom. Rachel and Rene shared the downstairs kitchen. This was the beginning of our close and long-lasting friendship.

Howard Salis, a Welshman and wartime merchant seaman, also became a close friend of mine. We went together for a short vacation to Sweden. From among this group, we became close friends with Walter and Rachel, Joe and Myrtle, and Howard and Joan. Like Rene and me, they were well-matched couples.

Among the private events at the clubs I mentioned, the most memorable occasion for me was a debate, organized by the political science club, between Arnold Toynbee, the proponent of a "rise and decline" predictive view of history, and Karl Popper, author of *The Poverty of Historicism*, who argued against it. Harold Laski was the moderator, and the debate was held in a drawing room with comfortable chairs and was attended by just twenty students. The brilliance of both speakers and Popper's ability to counter Toynbee's every argument made it an unforgettable experience and established my continued interest in history and how it is written.

I do not know why I took a special interest in the U.S. Constitution; it was possibly because of Denis Brogan's books on American law and politics. Brogan, educated at Oxford and Harvard, was a professor at Cambridge and, in his younger days, was a lecturer at LSE. In any case, this early interest, strengthened by the thirteen years we lived in Boston and Washington, has given me much amusement in following the U.S. Supreme Court's antics in interpreting the meaning of the writings by the framers of the Constitution on political decisions of the twentieth and twenty-first centuries.

Summer vacations from LSE offered opportunities for varied diversions. During the first vacation in 1947, we joined the "youth train" to the World Youth Festival in Prague so Rene could introduce me to her parents who had lived in Czechoslovakia throughout the war. Her father had spent several months in Theresienstadt concentration camp towards the end of the war.

Grete and Erich (called Poxl) Neuburg were a mismatched couple who lived a devoted, long, and difficult life together. Rene's mother was a Catholic whose father, a wealthy, philanthropic businessman, gave her a private education that included time in Switzerland. This was probably one reason why Grete engaged a private Swiss governess for Rene and her sister when they were teenagers. Grete spoke German, Czech, French, and English, was well read, and had developed an interest in philosophy, which had made her – privately – a non-believer. Grete and I established an early and close relationship. Sometime after our first meeting, I gave her Bertrand Russell's *A History of Western Philosophy*. She kept it on her bedside table and read a chapter each night before going to sleep, or so she told me.

Poxl, Rene's father, was born in Budapest into a Jewish family. Religion was a matter of convenience to him. In order to join and become an officer in the Austro-Hungarian Army, he converted to Christianity – this did not protect him from the Nuremberg Laws, though being married to a Christian did delay his arrest. After the war he reverted to Judaism.

Poxl was talented in writing, speaking, sketching, and handicrafts. He regularly wrote feuilletons – short literary essays – in the *Prager Tageblatt*, some of which were accompanied by delightful sketches. Much of his writing was based on their frequent travels. Poxl also loved to give talks on literary subjects and public events to private groups. Later, when they lived in Santiago, Chile, he started making silver jewelry and copper ashtrays; they sold well as "local handicraft." For a real income, Poxl worked in his brother's leather factory; Fritz Neuburg was his brother's keeper.

The following summer I landed a job, organized by the British Foreign Office, giving lectures to German prisoners of war still held in England. The subject of the lectures was "The Marshall Plan," named after the U.S. Secretary of State, George Marshall. This imaginative plan remains one of two very successful initiatives of President Eisenhower's administration; the other one was the construction of the interstate highway system, although that was not known at the time. The Marshall Plan, officially called the

European Recovery Plan, provided considerable funds for a four-year period to help Western European economies, including West Germany's.

The purpose of the Plan seemed altruistic, but the real purpose, which was appreciated by most, was to recreate trading partners for the U.S., and in this respect the Marshall Plan was an enormous success. I dare say that Eisenhower and Marshall, both military men, had never heard of Maynard Keynes.

I visited several prisoner of war camps and explained the Marshall Plan to my audiences, encouraging questions and responding to their scepticism. The German prisoners were not prepared to accept the notion that America, the recent enemy, would help reconstruct Germany. It was a tough assignment; I deserved my fee.

Near the end of my time at LSE, we had another, more pleasant diversion when we made a snap decision to go on a holiday. It would be the last chance for a long time to relax: Rene was pregnant and I would have to find a job. That we had little money did not bother us. We did not worry about the uncertainties ahead – we would find a way. This behaviour became typical throughout our life: not to make decisions based on monetary considerations alone. Repeatedly, a move to another job or another country was not determined by immediate income prospects. For example, our move from London to Toronto with three young children initially meant a drop in salary.

All of our major life changes arose from my career opportunities and once from my decision to resign from a project. With one exception, these decisions always met with Rene's approval. I will come to the exception in chapter 5 where I discuss selected projects.

To return to our deserved and wonderful if not reckless holiday in the summer of 1949. We decided to hitchhike our way through France and into Italy. It was the halcyon days of hitchhiking for youngsters when almost every car or truck with spare seats would pick you up. Starting at Calais, we quickly went through France to Provence, taking our time making our way from Sisteron to the French Riviera, visiting the Côte d'Azur, Nice, Monaco, and Menton before heading into Italy. On to Genoa, Milan, and Como, before travelling along the west coast of Lake Como and along Lago Maggiore and into the Alpine region of Aosta and Col du Petit St. Bernard, where we took a bus along a frighteningly steep road to Séez on the River Isere, and then back to Calais.

During our travels, to make it even easier to get a lift, Rene would stand on the road with her thumb out while I hid behind a tree. We landed quite a few interesting rides with interesting people, like the nun in a Deux Cheveau, and the truck driver who took us a long way and even stopped for lunch. Rene and I offered to pay for his meal, which is when we learned that Frenchmen do not just have a hamburger for lunch but take a full three-course meal with a bottle of wine – we could have paid for a bus ride.

Wherever we decided to stay, our routine was for Rene to sit and rest while I went scouting for a cheap room. My choices were not always acceptable: the sheets may have been slept in, so we'd have to creep out the back way. At Como, I picked a nice clean *camera matrimoniale*, a room with the biggest bed I have ever slept in, big enough for a family of five. But when I brought Rene, the landlord refused us entry. I thought it was because he suspected Rene was a prostitute, but the reason was money. I had paid for a one-person room. I gladly paid for two, or two and a half persons, just to test the enormous bed. Rene appreciated my efforts, for the most part.

> *I was fussy – you had courage.*
> *By the time it was summer 1949, I was pregnant;*
> *it was time to go on a honeymoon – the beginning of*
> *many travels to come in future years. We had very*
> *little money but you wanted to go to France and Italy.*

Hitchhiking was safe and easy. I was your "shingle" hung out at the road side; you had to find shelter for the night.

Sometimes you found a place and you took in our bags. Then you came to get me from the spot where I was waiting. I would enter and turn back the bed covers to see if the sheets had been slept in before. I refused to sleep on soiled sheets. When that was the case, out came the bags and you had to find another place we could afford.

How much had I changed by the time we travelled in Sulavesi [Indonesia, many years later]! We slept on a filthy quilt thrown on top of a door with a big hole in it and the privy doubled up as a rabbit cage.

The most memorable stay was on the west side of Lake Como. We asked to be dropped at a small, deserted beach for a swim. After hours of bliss on the sand we noticed an odd house just up the hill, very narrow and four storeys high, and the only house for miles around. We asked whether we could stay for the night. The woman agreed, although she normally had no guests.

The house was built against a vertical rock and had just one room on each of the four floors; we had the top floor overlooking Lake Como and the area around both sides of the lake. The kitchen occupied the ground floor. A large open fire with pots hanging on chains was used for cooking. The good woman watched Rene trying to cook in this primitive way and came to her rescue, and she cooked for us for the rest of our three day-stay. She even asked Rene to let her know whether she had a boy or a girl. So ended our carefree prologue to "Starting Work and a Family."

Looking for work with a degree in political science and not much else to offer was not easy. Fortunately, in England at the time if you had a college degree you were permitted to teach elementary school without teacher training. I was sent as a supply teacher to a school in the poorer part of Willesden in northwest London and put in charge of a class of girls, almost forty of them, in their final year, and had to teach them all of the required subjects. The girls could quit school on reaching the school-leaving age, and they did so right on the dot. Some of them had to leave even sooner because they were pregnant.

The headmaster told me that this was the rowdiest class, and only later did I find out that the regular female teacher was away because she had had a breakdown from trying to control the girls. Entering the classroom for the first time I gave them a stern pep talk and stopped any unnecessary chatter instantly. During the first morning the headmaster came in and whispered to me, "What did you do? It has never been so quiet in this classroom." Thinking that I had established control on that first day, I made the fatal mistake of believing the girls were really all right and I relaxed my vigilance. I never regained control. I did not have a breakdown, but I did come home exhausted every day.

About one month before Rene delivered our first child, Ann, who brought me luck, I got my first job in urban planning. The British Town and Country Planning Act of 1947 created the basic system for guiding urban and rural development by local government units. Towards the end of 1949, Middlesex County Council, of Greater London's western half, began recruiting its planning staff. I was one of a large crowd of applicants to be interviewed at Great George Street next to Parliament Square.

The interviews were scheduled over most of one day. Westminster Cathedral was just around the corner from the new Middlesex planning office. Waiting applicants went into the Cathedral, some to pray for an appointment. I also went in, never having visited it before. I did not pray, yet I was one of the chosen, and started my professional life with a sufficient income to look after Rene and Ann.

Over the next nine years Rene delivered two more babies, Nicholas (born 1953) and Jacki (born 1956), and I concentrated on learning the tricks of British planning as well as qualifying as a town planner at University College. I was fortunate in that my first boss at Middlesex, Moira Shields, was one of the four chief area planning officers and was an experienced architect, a good teacher, and a pleasant person. I participated at first in the land-use survey of the county, walking the streets with a base map on which I recorded the use of every parcel of land and building. I then graduated to writing reports on development applications concerning changes of land use and the construction of new buildings. This applied to major developments only; minor new developments were dealt with by the local authorities.

Britain's planning administration did without North America's inept "zoning" process and was more concerned with urban design and livability. There were, of course, land-use plans which served as guides. The process is stricter than that in Canada or the U.S. and produced results. The prime example of this is the London Green Belt which was being implemented under the Town and Country Planning Act of 1947. Without it, the explosive growth that took place over the next fifty years would have created super-suburbia. Unfortunately, more recent policies in England are pointing in the wrong direction. The Green Belt is being nibbled at and building-height controls that were put into place to preserve views of historic buildings like St. Paul's Cathedral are being abandoned. Washington, D.C., may be the only city left that observes a strict law prohibiting the construction of any structure higher than the Capitol Building. Back in the 1950s, there was an appeal process against refusals of development applications in England, and appeals were dealt with by highly experienced professional planners from the Ministry of Town and Country Planning, unlike the infamous Ontario Municipal Board which continues to operate like a lottery, usually in favour of the developer, but then, in its defence, the Board gets very little guidance from city plans or policies.

But getting back to my job in Middlesex, I well remember Ms. Shields once calling me into her office to discuss one of my draft reports on a large development proposal. She asked me whether I had visited the site. When I said I hadn't but I knew the area well, she gave me back my report saying, "Then I cannot read your report." Lesson learned: it is the context that matters, in this case, the surrounding environment of the project.

When I applied to University College, London University for admission to its two-year evening course in Town Planning, I was asked to see Professor William Holford, the head of the department. Holford told me that although I had the relevant experience, he could not admit me because the Royal Town Planning Institute only recognized architects, engineers, and surveyors as basic professions for admission to the Institute. Luckily, a year or two later, a Royal Commission on the Qualification of Planners declared that a degree in one of the social sciences was a suitable basic education for town planners – thereby recognizing that town planning dealt with people as well as bricks and concrete and allowing me into the program.

When I felt I had learned all there was to learn at the county level, I got a job at West Ham, a county borough, which was unusual for the London area. Most "local" authorities were and are boroughs, while county boroughs were local units with all the additional county powers. West Ham in London's east end included much of the London Docks which, with the surrounding areas, were almost completely destroyed during the war. The northern part of West Ham includes Stratford and the site of the 2012 Olympic Games. It was in Stratford where I introduced the new tree preservation orders, which I described earlier in the section about my childhood. Because I had to know not only the names of the trees but also their age and life in order to justify their preservation, I got to know a lot about the trees in the area.

⁓

While working in West Ham I advanced to chief planner. Meantime, we had moved to our first house in Reigate, Surrey, just after our second child, Nicholas, was born. We chose Reigate because Rene's cousin Micki, who was a doctor, lived in the adjoining town of Redhill, where three years later Micki delivered Jacki, our last child. Reigate is a pleasant place, a historic market town going back to the thirteenth century when the Reigate Priory (monastery) was established. Reigate sits at the foot of the North Downs ridge, and as the saying goes, "It's a good place to bring up children." We enjoyed living there, but the journey to work was long for me. On evenings when I had to attend committee meetings, I would get home pretty late.

Most of our houses in England, Canada, the U.S., and Indonesia were in some way special and even unique. The first house in Reigate, Surrey, was the narrowest detached house I had ever seen. It was 14 feet wide (measured on the outside) and stood on a 16-foot lot. The house originally had three bedrooms but the rear bedroom had been converted into a needlessly large bathroom. In one corner of the kitchen was the original toilet directly opening into the kitchen, by now illegal. The cellar was for coal storage that was delivered through a chute at street level. Coal fuelled the furnace that supplied both hot water and heat for the house.

The house needed redecorating and repairs, but it served us well, at least until Jacki arrived, and then we had a problem: where to put her. The bathroom being too large was the solution, but it had only one window. So I built a wall through the centre of the room with the window serving both the nursery and the bathroom – which was strictly illegal to do.

In retrospect, our move to Reigate was a success. Rene had the support of some older members of her family living in Redhill, and I was introduced to the new experience of mixing with an extended family of aunts, cousins, and nephews, all of whom spoiled the children. Not that we minded.

In Micki's large and beautiful Redhill house and garden, just half an hour's walk from our poky house, also lived Micki's sister Liese with her Australian husband Bob, and Marta, Micki and Liese's mother (Rene's aunt). Aunt Marta, as the children called her, had grown up as a member of the prosperous class in Bohemia and Vienna and she never lost the outlook and manner of an affluent person. Marta spent the war years in Florida earning some pocket money by making junk jewelry, but she had lived with her sister who fortunately had managed to escape Europe, like her brother Fritz, with her husband's fortune. This allowed Marta to prolong her comfortable lifestyle until joining her daughters in post-war England.

Marta still visited her sister in Florida every winter, sailing there in a cargo boat with just a few passenger cabins and choosing the boat based on whether she liked the captain. Her boat travels one year led to an unusual and scary experience for me. On the morning when Marta was about to depart from the London Docks, I got a call from Micki in my West Ham office. She was highly agitated because she discovered that she had given her mother the wrong mix of pills. Would I go to a pharmacy, get the correct medication, then go to a certain dock, get on board a certain ship, exchange the pills, and above all be sure to take the wrong pills from Marta with me?

I found the ship in a lock ready to sail, managed to hold the departure, climbed on board by a swinging rope ladder (it seemed at least 50 feet long) and was led to Marta's cabin. She was delighted that I had come to say goodbye and started to show me around her nice cabin and have a good chat. I had been told that I had two minutes before the ship would be on its way to Florida. Giving Marta the new medication was easy, but she had great difficulty finding the pills Micki had given her. After a frantic search, I found them in her handbag and was off to scale back down the scary rope ladder – mission accomplished without being shipped prematurely to America.

In 1957, Rene's parents came from Santiago to visit and stayed with our relatives in Redhill. They came every day to be with Rene and the "new" grandchildren. We took them for long walks along the North Downs and proudly showed them Reigate's Priory Park and the old town centre. Ann had started grade school by then and Rene had put Nicholas in a "progressive" kindergarten. This did not last long because Nicholas did not like the care he was getting, and Rene was reprimanded by the director of the kindergarten for the defective upbringing of her son. No problem as far as I could see: Ann actually was the best nanny for Nicholas. The two of them naturally grew up together and became good friends for life. Lesson: it is helpful when the first child is a girl, they make the best nannies and it gives them a chance to practise for their own motherhood later on.

When Jacki was born that year, she settled quite comfortably into her nursery-cum-bathroom.

My work in war-damaged West Ham inevitably made me aware of England's drastic changes in public policies. Coming out of a ruinous war as a bankrupt nation, having lost hundreds of thousands of its young men, losing its once lucrative colonies, and kept in debt to America due to the Lend-Lease Act of 1941, the Attlee Labour Government quickly set out in a new direction.

From today's perspective, it may be impossible for people to understand the disregard by the government of the costs involved in the "social engineering" embarked upon when there was "no money in the kitty." Today – in 2014 – England is a very rich country compared to then – in 1945 – yet the government continues to talk about austerity, which means reduced spending on social services.

The British Labour Government lost no time. Within a few years – between 1964 and 1950 – the National Health Service Act, National Insurance Act, New Towns Act, and the Town and Country Planning Act had all passed Parliament, and new towns were under construction beyond the Green Belt.

The legislation on health and social insurance, on urban planning and new towns were all based on official reports prepared in the latter stages of the war, largely on the initiative of Labour ministers in the coalition government: the Beveridge Report on social security, the Barlow Report on new towns, and the Abercrombie Greater London Plan.

The Planning and New Towns Acts plus the Greater London Plan and the definition of the Green Belt were, of course, of primary interest to me. My urban planning thesis at University College, "The Movement of Families from Willesden to New Towns," examined the joint movement of factories and of workers with their families during the 1950–53 period, mainly to Hemel Hempstead in Hertfordshire, and evaluated the government's success in attempting to improve the housing conditions of those remaining behind.

Together, the Green Belt, the new town developments, and the movement of factories with their workers and families was meant as a combined operation to alleviate the living conditions of families trapped in overcrowded areas. This initiative provided three additional benefits: (1) the prevention of urban sprawl, (2) better use of bypassed, undeveloped sites, and (3) an increase in residential densities with the construction of mid-rise buildings in established residential areas.

Nye Bevan, the health minister at the time, was also responsible for the government's housing policy and programs. Bevan was one of Attlee's shrewd appointments. A fiery Welshman, he was not only a good speaker and debater but also an excellent administrator and negotiator. His main legacy was the National Health Service Act, which tested his abilities in getting the British Medical Association (BMA) to accept serving under the act. In the final showdown, when he had to make a concession, it is reported that in order to broker the deal with the BMA, Bevan said he had "stuffed their mouths with gold." Today, the health service – which used to be universally admired and was abused by foreigners who came for a visit to get free treatment – is underfunded and split between the well-off who use their private doctors and the rest who get inadequate service. Why this change?

That is a big question which I will not attempt to answer here. Instead, I would like to talk briefly about the people's enthusiastic acceptance of the Labour government's sweeping changes after the Second World War. Who the godfather of the social programs actually was is difficult to say. The two likeliest suspects are Karl Marx and Maynard Keynes, the political ideologue and the economic theorist. I am convinced that neither of them was responsible. I believe it was Karl Mannheim, the sociologist and original thinker, who was the main influence for what happened under the Attlee Government.

Mannheim was born in Budapest; he taught and wrote in Germany before coming to England in 1938. He became very influential though generally not widely known. His best known books are *Ideology and Utopia* (1936) and above all *Man and Society in an Age of Reconstruction* (1940) and, of course, he taught, among other places, at LSE.

A recent documentary film, *The Spirit of '45* (2013) by Ken Loach, revisits the year that Britain ushered in the National Health Service, public ownership, and the concept of public – not private – good. He traced the spirit of '45 and spoke to some who remembered "the dawn of the new life." "We had won the war together; together we could win the peace. If we could collectively plan to wage military campaigns, could we not plan to build houses, create a health service, and make goods needed for reconstruction? The spirit of the age was to be our brother's and sister's keeper." Loach said, "He was motivated to make the documentary because the achievements of the Atlee generation were at risk of being reduced to a footnote to Thatcherism."

The documentary was not generally released in Canada, but I managed to see it in Toronto. It completely brought me back to those years of life and work in London. It was exciting to work in London at that time and to be part of one of the spheres of change – town planning.

The immediate post-war period in Britain and the Labour government's enactment of its sweeping program of social reform under the Attlee government is forgotten history – but not for those who lived there at the time. Today, it seems inconceivable that the Labour government achieved all that it did during its six years in power (1945–51).

One fine morning at the West Ham planning office, a senior planner and friend of mine burst into the office calling out across the drafting room, "John, I've got a job for you," and showed me a notice in his surveyors journal from the Metropolitan Toronto Planning office. They were looking for a planner interested in research. My friend knew that I had some interviews for positions in larger cities in England, and he was eager to step into my shoes. I applied for the Toronto job, giving Professor Holford as a reference, and was accepted for the position. We would be leaving for Canada in the coming months.

Into the Wider World

Landing in freezing-cold weather at Malton Airport in Toronto on January 3, 1959, at 1:00 a.m., was the beginning of forty years of wandering around the world chasing our luck and having an exciting life: first in Canada and the U.S., followed by short and long assignments in the Caribbean Islands, Africa, and Asia.

John and Helen Bower met us at the airport in the coldest temperature we had ever experienced before. John was a senior member of the Metropolitan Toronto Planning Board staff and later became the commissioner of planning. John and Helen drove us in the deep snow to our pre-arranged, temporary accommodation in downtown Toronto. We soon bought a barely finished house in Don Mills – a planned suburban community à la the new towns of England at the time.

Over the course of our first year in Toronto, the family settled well into life in Don Mills. The children were at school all day, which allowed Rene to attend a teachers training program, qualify for teaching, and start a position at a Catholic school. We had friends and enjoyed the parks, museums, and other entertainments Toronto had to offer. By chance, Rene met her best school friend, another Renate, and her husband, Robby, a rare Auschwitz survivor, at the Czech club. We felt at home.

I arrived at Metro at the time when the preparation of the Metro Plan was in its later stages. My focus, among other matters, was on estimating future industrial land needs. My one contribution of some influence was a report I wrote entitled "Towards a Waterfront Plan," which recommended the preparation of a plan covering the entire forty miles of Metro's waterfront – the Metro area went well beyond the amalgamated Toronto of today.

The waterfront plan report turned out to be the beginning of a long and very limited process, which lost its focus when Metropolitan Planning ended. Yet, in a sense, it is still ongoing in a piecemeal fashion today, but only in the eastern section of the original City of Toronto.

Metropolitan Toronto's planning was an enlightened but short-lived experiment in trying to plan and control the development of a growing urban area consisting of numerous local authorities – rather like the London County Council (LCC). Alas, both the LCC and the Metropolitan Toronto Council were to disappear for political reasons involving the value of area-wide urban planning. But that was in the future, long after we had left Toronto.

In the early 1960s, all the signs for dealing with Toronto's population growth were there to see: two subway lines were in use and being extended; several highways of a planned overall system had been completed; extensions and enlargements to water supply and waste disposal systems to serve the far-flung communities were under construction. There was a general optimism that the City of Toronto, the suburban municipalities, and some of the growing rural villages would be able to deal with the present and expected future growth with Metro's assistance.

But the honeymoon did not last. Opposition inevitably surfaced against different planned aspects. Aside from the political issues leading to the demise of Metro Toronto, which I will address below, it is relatively easy to pinpoint the chief cause of the discontent: the automobile and the relentless growth of traffic. More could have been done to explain the issues of public and private transportation, the alternatives, and the costs, and especially the actual aim of the Metro highway plan. Of course, Fred Gardiner's almost dictatorial leadership did not help to quiet criticism. But Gardiner did bring in the vast loan funds from his Wall Street contacts to pay for the major public works.

The focus of the opposition, as so often elsewhere, was how to tame the private automobile or how to accommodate it. And it was here that the unequal Toronto battle took shape: Jane Jacobs, the People's Saint from Greenwich Village, New York, against Sam Cass, Metro Roads Commissioner, who failed to explain the overall highway plan with a cross-town highway along the disused railroad line.

There is no arguing with the neighbourhood protection idealism of Jane Jacobs – it is important and people deserve it, and much can be done and has been done elsewhere in support of it. But it cannot be an absolute imperative, unless money is no object, as has been shown in Boston's old Inner Harbor area where an incomplete, elevated Interstate 93 was taken down and put underground all the way to the bridge across the Charles River. Or alternatively, with tongue in cheek, you find a way to wean modern society away from the car.

Haussmann built the Paris highway system well before the advent of the motor car and the extensive Metro (subway) network, which continues to serve Paris well and connects the downtown core to its two airports. London did not build the Abercrombie highway plan but restricted car access to its central area and kept adding to its Underground network. British Railways developed an extensive commuter rail service into London from beyond the Green Belt. London's airports are served by both underground and surface rail.

Toronto started building highways but stopped before they became a functioning system. Toronto started building subway lines but stopped when the need for them increased. Toronto even has a rail-right-of-way from Union Station to Lester Pearson airport but has yet to build the railway line. Toronto does have its GO-Train for commuters, built by the Province of Ontario.

Older and bigger cities than Toronto with longer histories, greater problems, and equally alert citizens have managed better. Why? To try and answer that question would be interesting, but I am not up to it. The present political situation in Toronto, or in Canada for that matter, does not point towards a happy solution.

The end of Metropolitan Toronto and the amalgamation of the suburban communities with the City of Toronto into one administrative unit – Toronto – have had several untold consequences, one being the neglect of urban design in downtown Toronto. The high-rise condominium towers have begun to mimic Hong Kong where residents have the privilege of looking into each other's bedrooms. I expect that before long Toronto will also copy Shenzhen's "handshake buildings," so-called because you can reach out from the window to grasp the hand of someone in the next building. Shenzhen is the city across the river from Hong Kong, which I visited when it was a small village in the 1980s. It now houses more than 10 million people and produces much of what people in Western countries buy daily.

The present control of Toronto's downtown development by "guidelines" is, for the most part, a negation of planning. The guidelines are vague and subject to wide interpretation, but above all of no assistance to the Ontario Municipal Board (OMB) which invariably follows the developer's definition. To stop the OMB from interfering is for the city to have a proper "urban design" official plan for Toronto's downtown. The OMB cannot overrule an adopted Official Plan.

Toronto's love of the streetcar being "on the street" as opposed to on its own right-of-way (now called LRT) causes much of the traffic delay we experience, mainly because of passengers needing transfers at major intersections; which brings me to my startling discovery: Berlin has an honour system that keeps streetcars and busses moving and subway stations less congested. You can buy your ticket from little machines, available everywhere, and can purchase a one-day, two-day, or three-day ticket, or a week-long ticket for a variety of zones (distance) and hop on a street car through several of its open doors and off you go. No line ups, no hassle, and you can go unchecked down into the subway. It's an honour system because an inspector may ask you to show your ticket on the train or street car at any time. Imagine the savings on staff and costly machines in return for faster service. But in London, New York, and Toronto people tell me that "it would never work here, most people would never buy a ticket." A praiseworthy reflection on Berliners, but a sad comment on the rest of us.

I mentioned that the disappearance of the London County Council and the Metropolitan Toronto government were politically motivated not because the systems did not function. In London, the LCC had always been controlled by the Labour Party and when she came to power in 1979, Prime Minister Margaret Thatcher felt her only way to break the impasse was to abolish the LCC. In Toronto, then Premier Mike Harris proposed the amalgamation of six municipalities into one Greater Toronto Area and, despite the resistance from Torontonians and then mayor Barbara Hall, the breakup of Metropolitan Toronto took place in 1998.

There were, however, major differences in the post "area-wide" political authorities. In London, the demise of the LCC produced two results: (1) enlarged local authorities (usually combining two boroughs into one) continued to function as before, each borough dealing with local issues to the satisfaction of their people, and (2) for area-wide functions a new office was created – the mayor of London – a somewhat unique office: one elected mayor without borough councillors, but with an elected twenty-five member assembly (each representing a number of newly enlarged boroughs) but with restricted authority – mainly granting approval of the mayor's budget. But the mayor administered with a large professional staff, housed in a handsome new building.

In contrast, the premier of Ontario created problems without solutions: (1) amalgamating the inner six local authorities and the original City of Toronto into one City of Toronto set the original City of Toronto at loggerheads with the sprawling suburbs, and (2) the other growing suburbs beyond these limits were left on their own – these included the second ring of communities like Mississauga to the west and Markham to the northeast, as well as smaller growing rural communities beyond the intended Green Belt.

The comparison between London and Toronto is really false in another way: at the back of London is the national government with its interest in the capital and with its financial resources; whereas in Toronto the back-up is the Province of Ontario without meaningful resources. There is the Government of Canada as the last financial support, but with its country-wide obligations very unreliable. When the Government of Canada does make financial contributions, as in the case of Toronto's waterfront lands, cumbersome and bureaucratic offices are created that not only eat up much of the funds but take years to come to decisions and even more years to implement them. But all these problems occurred long after our family had left the city.

After a few years in Toronto, I once again felt at loose ends; the work had become less exciting, I had learned about planning at the metropolitan level but there were no opportunities to "move up" because, with the exception of Hans Blumenfeld, all members of the staff were young. Blumenfeld's presence made it worthwhile to be around. He had been recruited as deputy commissioner after an outside review of the staffing recommended the addition of a professional with a longer and more varied experience – which certainly was a fit description of Hans. He did not really function as a deputy but was available to the young chief, Murray Johnes, as a consultant. Murray would discuss current problems and major issues of regional planning with Hans who invariably would go into his office and write a paper about it.

Hans Blumenfeld was THE authority on regional planning. He was a native of Hamburg, and he was educated and had practised as an architect and urban planner in Germany. He had worked in Russia on the Moscow subway. In the late 1930s, he went to Philadelphia to work for the city, and he published many papers, which were published as a collection in *The Modern Metropolis: Its Origin, Growth, Characteristics and Planning*. Because of his left political views, he faced some difficult times during the McCarthy era and had to leave the U.S. It turned out that Toronto needed him.

As a writer, and I mean the actual writing process, Hans was astonishing to me: he wrote on lined paper in his tiny, neat script with practically no corrections or alterations. His secretary had an easy time, and the finished product was a pleasure to read: it was well organized, and he gave a clear and logical presentation of his views. It was a sign of having thought through an issue and wishing to help the reader understand his reasoning.

It was a pleasure and educational to have known Hans Blumenfeld. After Metro he was a professor at the University of Toronto and a consultant for the city. Another exceptional planner at Metro was Eli Comay, who was the commissioner before John Bower. He came to Canada from Detroit during the McCarthy era because of the left-leaning views of his French wife, Helen. Eli did not get on too well with Hans, but he wrote most of the Metro Plan. He later taught at York University and, as a consultant, he frequently asked for my assistance, even after I had moved to the U.S. He died in 2010 at the age of 90.

My look for interesting work led to a successful interview at the American Institute of Certified Planners (AICP) annual conference in Detroit. Facing all five partners of a growing planning firm from Cambridge, Massachusetts, I managed to persuade them that I knew a lot about planning, either that or they were so desperate for staff to hire almost anyone. The Planning Services Group (TPSG) was named in imitation of The Architects' Collaborative (TAC). The Walter Gropius architect firm, also in Cambridge, had their office at the back of Harvard Square.

This new job meant a lot of changes: from public service to private consulting, from the stricter planning regimes of London and Toronto to a more relaxed development supervision of Boston, and, of course, all the changes that are associated with moving into a new country. We moved into the best house we ever lived in up until that time. The large house was in Watertown, just west of Cambridge, and was a typical New England clapboard house built around the beginning of the twentieth century for the then editor of the *Boston*

Globe newspaper. It had a large entrance hall with a fireplace and a winding staircase with a double-high window. There was a library and four bedrooms. One of the bedrooms on the third floor used to be the maids room and it had its own staircase. Ann claimed it for its privacy.

For over a month, before we could move into the house, we lived in tents at a summer camp about halfway between the Cambridge office and Springfield town hall where I used another office to look after a couple of jobs. Private consulting came to me all at once, and I managed without the internet or a cell phone. Plus, the family could enjoy a summer holiday at the same time.

TPSG was a young firm, both in its existence and personnel (except for the senior partner), and had grown rapidly in recent years. All the partners and most of the staff were Harvard or MIT graduates. Their clients were New England cities and towns. The Federal Urban Renewal Program provided much of the work: preparing plans, applying for HUD (Department of Housing and Urban Development) funds, and supervising projects.

A different project, also funded by HUD, called the Boston Project, included an overall appraisal of the Boston region's infrastructure and the region's future needs. It was one of several similar projects that were underway in major U.S. cities to help the federal government decide on its fund allocations to the largest cities. All sector studies were in various stages of preparation, except the port and airport studies, which became my assignment. In effect, there was a decline and growth situation. The port was on its way out for various reasons, and the growth of air transportation called for a major airport and other airport access investments.

Urban renewal funding applications required, among other details, an economic base study for the city or town in which urban renewal was contemplated. These economic base studies were assigned to me. A further request for assistance, which was unusual for America, asked for help in setting up a regional planning body for almost a dozen communities on both sides of the Connecticut

River, close to Springfield in western Massachusetts. The region was to be called the Lower Pioneer Valley Regional Planning Area. With the assistance of a recent graduate from Mount Holyoke College, I embarked on this project too. That project alone provides material for an interesting report on Massachusetts politics and corruption. I will just mention one early incident.

I made a quick round interviewing mayors and other elected leaders in member communities to find out why they decided to join the regional planning effort and what they hoped to gain – in other words, I wanted to find out what their main problems were. Unquestionably, their main concern was garbage collection and disposal. So, instead of first preparing a traditional population growth (or decline) report, I looked into the garbage problem. Part of my reason for going about it this way was to rally support from some leaders who were not really sold on "regional planning."

My young graduate assistant went out to gather information from each city and town to learn about the collection and disposal methods, whether there were responsible collectors, how frequently collection occurred, what the costs were, and so on. Within a couple of days she returned to tell me of "interference and obstruction" in her information gathering: some rough guys told her to stop whatever she was doing and started to push her away. I took over; I was prepared to get into a fight. Almost all of the communities used private, competing contractors who were loath for anyone to find out about their contracts and how they obtained them. In the end, municipal officials provided me with the necessary information.

Our report with recommendations for more favourable arrangements managed to skirt around "dishonest practices" of the communities and concentrated on the technical details of a proper sanitary landfill.

Rene had no problem getting a job at the local school. Much of the Boston area is Irish and Catholic; Rene came with the proper qualifications: an Irish name and a Catholic background. Although Rene's teaching was, I think, a bit of an embarrassment for Ann – when Rene was in her class, kids would whisper "that's Ann's mother."

Watertown has an interesting history. During and after the Armenian genocide (1915–23), Armenians were recruited by Good Year Tires and they came to live in the town, and many of their descendants were still living there. I believe Nicholas's favourite teacher was a young Armenian woman.

All of us in the family settled down quickly – not just at work and school but in the Cambridge-Watertown-Boston community overall. Through TPSG contacts, we made many friends. Justin Gray, one of the partners, and I became special friends; he was the partner who was in charge of most of the jobs I did. Through him I met professors like Kevin Lynch of MIT, who also lived in Watertown; Ken Arrow, Nobel economist from Harvard (later at Stanford); and many others. I had my own contacts at Harvard and arranged for their students to take summer jobs with us.

Within six months we felt as if we had lived there for years, and we might have stayed for a very long time. But it was not to be – it came to an end after about four years. The Boston project mentioned above had been completed and, after its review, HUD acted on its recommendations calling for proposals to implement a wide range of projects. Unsurprisingly, TPSG, having laid the foundation, got the nod for a large job. But then a professional ethics issue arose. The Massachusetts government set up in its legislature a monitoring committee to supervise the project. This committee invited the partners for a discussion and revealed that its operation would have to be financed out of the monthly contract fees – also known as "baksheesh," or a bribe.

The five partners were split on this issue 3 to 2 against accepting this condition. Bitterness affected the whole firm with, I think, the majority of the staff in agreement with the baksheesh decision. The two partners who were ready to pay the bribe were soon hired by the legislative committee to be their professional advisors. Gloom descended on the firm and this was the beginning of its break up.

Around that time, I ran into a Harvard professor friend and his question was "What are you going to do, John?" TPSG's problem by this time was common knowledge around town. My brief reply was "I don't know." He suggested that I come to his office and go through his files of enquiries for planning staff. Although most letters asked for recent graduates, there were a few for experienced planners. I spent a morning going through his files. One interesting letter was from a Malcolm Rivkin at Robert Nathan Associates in Washington. At lunch, the good professor asked me what I had found. In return I asked, "Who is Robert Nathan?" He was appalled – everybody knew Robert Nathan!

Malcolm Rivkin had established a planning section at Robert Nathan Associates (RRNA), a large firm of economic consultants, reasoning that economists and urban planners often work on projects where both disciplines are needed. The next time that Malcolm came to Boston to visit his family, he and I met; shortly after, I became an associate of RRNA.

Before I leave my account of life in Massachusetts, I would like to relate one more story about its politics. Soon after Ted Kennedy was elected senator in 1962, the mayor of Springfield, another Irishman, invited him to Springfield so he could hear directly "what he could do for his city" (John F. Kennedy's election slogan was "Ask not what your country can do for you, but what you can do for your country"; Ted Kennedy was elected senator after John Kennedy became president). The mayor, councillors, department heads, and a city consultant (me) were introduced to Ted Kennedy and the meeting began. Questions and demands flew at Kennedy and he invariably started his answer with the questioner's first name – how could he remember thirty or more names after one introduction, I wondered in my ignorance. "Simple," explained one of Kennedy's staff members afterwards. "I give him a sheet of the table with all the names on it."

⌒*ℳ*⌒

Our move to Washington was marked by a surprising event. We readily found a buyer for our attractive house in Watertown. I went ahead to Washington to start at RRNA and, on weekends, I looked around for a suitable house. It became apparent that house prices in Washington were higher than they were in Boston. When I went back to Watertown to visit, the purchaser of our house asked me how the house hunting was going. I told him that house prices were higher in Washington and that I was still searching. He asked about the price difference and to my astonishment he asked, "How much more do you need?" I told him, and would you believe it? He offered to pay the extra. I was embarrassed but relieved.

To explain this uncommon generosity: the gentleman – and he obviously was a gentleman – was the son of a wealthy Boston manufacturer, but he took no interest in the family's business affairs. His vocation was education and he had established a school for young children, which was near our house. He needed more space, but above all our house was closest to a public playing field, and he wanted to convert the large basement into a changing room and shower.

This financial help increased our choices for a new house in Washington and Rene came down to look at a couple of places I had selected. We settled on a four-bedroom house with a screened-in porch and good-sized garden on the D.C. side of Western Avenue in Washington's Chevy Chase area. It was a nice house, but it was nothing special. There was also a good basement and a garage – both of which became the preserve of Nicholas: he moved into the basement which had its own entrance from the garden and the garage was to become the workshop for his car – an Austin-Healey

Sprite – that he stripped down completely and, to my surprise, reassembled so that it was in running condition.

Little did we know, as we settled into Washington, how long we would stay and how important it would prove to be for our future. Rene would, at last, return to her biology studies. She got her master's at American University, specializing in Bryozoa (aquatic invertebrate animals), and she worked at the Smithsonian Institute. Ann would begin her studies at Antioch College in Yellow Springs, Ohio, and continue at Aix-en-Provence, France; Jacki first went to Tufts near Boston and continued at Columbia in New York City; and Nicholas, who was not interested in higher education, started work at the bottom most level of the building trades in Washington and became an accomplished and much sought after builder; and he never left Washington.

As I continued my work at Robert Nathan Associates, it became clear that Malcolm's idea of joint economic/urban planning projects was sensible but failed in practice. Robert Nathan never quite understood what planners did and potential clients seemed uninterested in getting involved with economists. In any event, the six members of our "planner group" worked mainly on RRNA projects. I essentially was a regular Nathan associate. (The exception was a fluke, as I will describe in chapter 5, "Selected Projects," when I was sent to Nigeria.)

But our experiences paid off. We made contact with organizations which later came to our own firm, and certainly I learned an enormous amount and used some of what I had learned at the London School of Economics. The greatest gift for me during these years at Nathan Associates was Robert Nathan himself – learning from him, actually working directly with him on some projects, and becoming friends with him.

Nevertheless, Malcolm Rivkin, his wife Goldie, and I decided to set up our own shop (Rivkin/Carson) and we left RRNA on friendly terms. The three of us made a good team, professionally. Malcolm was a Harvard graduate who had a master's in city planning from MIT and the first PhD in planning from MIT, plus he had wide experience in the U.S. and abroad. Goldie was a graduate of Radcliffe College and received her master's in city planning from Harvard, and she had practical experience working for private clients and public agencies.

We made a good start from an office in the Georgetown district of Washington. We had up to three professional assistants and the use of specialists as required. We also worked closely with a firm of architects from Baltimore on developments in New England and Florida. I also managed to fit in two personal assignments in Toronto at the request of my former colleague, Eli Comay. Things were going well and we did some interesting work for several years. Our best project, which was for the National Water Commission, is described in the next chapter. Apart from leading to other work, I used what I had learned over the years about urban development.

The study for the National Water Commission (described more fully in chapter 5) generated a wealth of data for our analysis of the relationship between metropolitan population growth and water resources development. I thought this information should be used in the discussion and legislation about a national urban growth policy. I therefore wrote a paper entitled "A National Urban Growth Policy" for presentation to the next annual conference of the American Planning Institute (API) in San Francisco. It so happened that I wanted to go because our very good London friends, Rachel and Walter, were going to visit San Francisco at the same time.

I believed that the discussions of a national urban policy were escapist for three reasons: (1) "cultural lag," the habit of identifying problems after they had ceased to be such; (2) the "Garden of Eden complex," which is the yearning for some ideal, and it takes many forms; and (3) "the cure-all approach," best illustrated by the

Urban Growth and New Community Development Act, which was an attempt to heap purpose upon purpose and overburden each policy and program to the point where policies became aimless and programs unworkable. I suggested: "An effective urban growth policy must recognize that (1) intervention is more effective if it channels rather than generates momentum, (2) opportunities for drastic intervention are limited, (3) the problems must be faced where they are – in and within the sphere of metropolitan areas, and (4) the public must participate actively in the urban development process."

I recommended five elements of a National Urban Growth Policy: (1) planning general distribution of urban land, (2) controlling urban development, (3) public ownership of urbanizing land, (4) a public urban development organization (like the New York State Urban Development Corporation), and (5) changes in the real estate tax. All these suggestions and recommendations really incorporated the lessons I had learned in my twenty-one years of urban planning and dabbling in economic analysis.

The reception of my paper was interesting. The Urban Land Institute published the paper in full in its *Urban Land* magazine, and the National Urban Coalition published extracts in its *City* magazine. I had an invitation from a Phoenix businessmen's group to discuss the paper with them, and they put me up in the Frank Lloyd Wright–inspired hotel the Arizona Biltmore. The professional head of HUD in Washington sent me a nice letter. But the professional planners at the conference were uninterested, as shown by the spare attendance, even though I quoted Hans Blumenfeld's words that were spoken at an API conference three years earlier: "The expressions for a 'national policy' are varied and vague, they tend to be rich in emotional appeal, but poor in clear definition and quantification of objectives."

During this time in Washington, I reached middle age. On a sudden impulse, I bought an Alfa Romeo sports car in order to get to the office and back home faster, at least that was my excuse for spending the money. The ladies at the office wagged their heads and had their own explanation: "He has entered the dangerous age." Whatever the reason, Rene liked to ride in it too.

Joys and Toys

Many years passed. We had spent exciting years in Washington. The children were teenagers. They were fun and took care of themselves. You were successful in your profession. You deserved a reward and you bought a red Alfa Romeo. We took off, just the two of us on a Sunday afternoon. We drove to the Blue Ridge. It was early fall. With the roof down, it felt like flying. The air was crisp but warm still. We hiked in the woods, and then returned ...

When a general downturn in the economy hit in 1971, there was not enough work for the three principals, and I left the firm. For the rest of our time in Washington, just short of two years, I worked as an independent consultant, which included an unusual assignment at the World Bank.

I was invited by the World Bank to help with one of their sector studies on housing. The Bank had published a number of evaluation reports in their different investment areas: agriculture, transportation, water, energy, etc. These were all "in-house" exercises. The housing sector report presented difficulties, and after nine failed drafts (which were not endorsed by the Bank's board), it was decided to ask an outsider to join the staff to add a different perspective. It was uncustomary, but I accepted and had my own office at the Bank.

Near the end of a meeting one morning of the supervising group, the chairman said to me, "John, you have been listening to us all morning and have not said a word. We don't pay you to just listen to us." To which I replied: "I have been surprised that you are no different from the commercial bank down the street." And Helen Hughes (director of the Economic Analysis Department at the Bank), the first to respond, said, "Of course not, John, what did you expect?" This brief exchange exposed the problem of producing a persuasive housing sector report, or it exposed the glaring conflict between the Bank making money and its supposed aim of providing housing for the poor.

After a fact-finding trip to Nairobi, Delhi, Ahmadabad, Chennai (Madras), and Hong Kong, one of my contributions to the tenth draft was a spurious calculation of the relationship between a country's financial support to public housing, the average cost of family accommodation, and the number of families living in inadequate housing (or in the street).

I do not know what my negligible contribution to the final report was. It was accepted by the Bank. But as I was never shown any of the failed draft reports, I cannot say what had changed.

Helen Hughes was an Australian who had been born in Czechoslovakia, which she left just before the Second World War. She went to London and studied at the LSE – what a small world. After her responsible position at the World Bank, she set up the Australian National University's Development Studies Centre.

With my by-now-customary luck, Robert Nathan called me saying they were in a fix and could I help. Then, and even now, one fairly common problem on international projects financed by public agencies is delays. Nominated staff cannot hang around for months until the job comes through. Frequently, regular staff members are sent elsewhere to follow up on projects. In the particular case that Robert was calling me about, there was an additional problem.

The case involved Marietta Tree, who was an irrepressible socialite, Democratic activist, confidante, and one-time U.S. representative on the UN Commission on Human Rights. At one time, she had suggested to Robert that RRNA and Llewelyn Davies

Associates (LDA), an international firm of architects with which she was associated, should collaborate on international and other high-profile projects. Robert had agreed reluctantly, hoping nothing would come of it. Well, a project in Trinidad did materialize after a long wait, but RRNA's man was by then working in Africa.

Robert said if I was able and willing I would have to do the work under the RRNA label. No problem there. The job was for the Trinidad and Tobago government, making recommendations for the use of the former U.S. naval base at Chaguaramas, located on an otherwise unused peninsula to the west of the capital, Port of Spain. The government had for years pleaded with the U.S. to return the land to Trinidad. When the U.S. finally released the land, Trinidad had no idea what to do with it.

I knew about Llewelyn Davies because the head office – Llewelyn Davies Weeks – was in London. My role in the Chaguaramas project turned out to be a minor one because almost any use of the land was economically feasible, which somewhat annoyed the LDA team since they were looking for constraints in selecting the best use for the land. Since I wasn't very busy, they gave me some of their work to keep me occupied.

During my months in Trinidad I also spent short periods in Sydney, Nova Scotia. Eli Comay, now a consultant, had asked me to assist him in a study of the depressed coal mining town. This was in the middle of winter and I commuted between hot Port of Spain and very cold Sydney – a new and surprising experience. I found that coming from the semi-tropics can keep you warm for about a week in sub-zero temperatures. I remember walking just in my shirt sleeves through the snow to fetch coffee for my colleagues, who were horrified to see me run out in the freezing cold without a jacket.

At the end of the Trinidad project, the LDA architect in charge, who was also the LDA New York office manager, asked me for my

CV in the event of future projects I could work on. Unbeknown to me, LDA was interested in working in Toronto. The company did some work in Kingston, Ontario, out of their Houston office, which specialized in hospital architecture. The Province of Ontario had told LDA that the company would have to set up an office in Canada if it wished to compete for contracts in Toronto or elsewhere. My Metro Toronto experience, listed in my CV, led to an offer to open an office for LDA in Toronto. Rene's wish was fulfilled at last: she could return to Toronto. Once we had moved back and settled in, Rene, with her Smithsonian experience, was able to immediately find a job at the ROM (Royal Ontario Museum).

I at first returned by myself to Toronto to find an office, hire staff, and find us a place to live, in that order. I was contacted, by a Mrs. S., a friend of Marietta Tree. She (Mrs. S.) had been selected, without my knowledge, to bring in contracts and look after me; or, shall we say, to keep an eye on me. However, she did not possess the finesse of Marietta. She had already appointed a company lawyer. Fortunately, she chose a very eminent man who acted entirely in my interest. He incorporated the new firm as LDC (Llewelyn Davies Carson). Along the way he gave me some advice: he said that, when he was a young man, his uncle had impressed upon him the importance of always looking after himself first in life.

Mrs. S. showed me an unsuitable office which, I found out, was partly owned by her husband. She received a monthly stipend and took me regularly to the best restaurants in town for lunch, paid for by the office. She never brought in a job. After a while, I let her go. Luckily, recruiting the other staff I needed was easy. Old friends were helpful and good people were always on the lookout. Eli Comay recommended one of his past secretaries to me.

For the house search I used an agent to make a selection for Rene and Jacki to look at. They came up from Washington and we did a tour with the agent. As we passed an old house in Cabbagetown, which was rather big for the area and that had a FOR SALE sign on the lawn, Jacki piped up, "What about this one?" I told her I had looked at it but the agent thought it was overpriced and also that it would need a lot of work as did most houses in Cabbagetown. I was in no mood to fix up a house all over again, quite apart from the fact that I would not have the time. The agent put in, "We can go and have a look at it," and that did it. Remember, Jacki was studying historic preservation at Columbia. She later stripped all the layers of paint from the bannister and helped restore the house to its former glory.

About half the houses in Cabbagetown (so called because the Irish families who settled there, refugees from the Irish famine, grew cabbages in their front gardens) at the time had been renovated while the rest remained in very poor condition. Our house was rather unique. It was the second oldest in the area and faced a park. It was said to have been built for a doctor – and it was also said to have been haunted. Many years later, when we were ready to retire and move to Dominica, the house was highly prized and priced.

At some point, LDC started getting jobs. This was for three reasons: I still knew planning professionals, I associated with other firms, and, in at least two instances, I picked up assignments outside Canada through prior contacts. But first let me explain about Richard, also known as Lord Llewelyn Davies, a fascinating and complex life peer whose wife, Annie, was a life peeress in her own right and the Labour government's chief whip in the House of Lords. Richard was not involved in my joining his firm. I had first met him in Cleveland. He took me for lunch and said, "In your CV, I see that you went from working in large organizations to smaller ones and ended up as a one-man consultant, why did you decide to join our firm?" I answered honestly, if not tactfully, that my main reason was to get back to Toronto.

Richard and his partner in London, John Weeks, became prominent in hospital architecture. I believe they were the first architects to study the needs of doctors, nurses, and patients for the efficient administration of health care. John Weeks remained principally a hospital architect. Richard embarked on urban planning both as a practitioner and teacher. His reputation got a big boost as the designer of the latest (Mark II) new town, Milton Keynes, in Bedfordshire, forty miles northwest of London. Before my association with his firm, Richard had founded Llewellyn Davies International (LDI), a worldwide group of architects, engineers, and urban planners that would send its staff to projects anywhere in the world; that is to say, they would send professionals with particular skills and experience to work on projects anywhere they were needed. London's LDW, New York's LDA with a branch in Houston, together with an engineering firm in Australia were the first partners in LDI.

It was a grand concept that failed for several reasons. The main one, I believe, was because of Richard's personality and concern for absolute control. The concept was not really new but was practised more informally, as it is today in various arrangements. Leading firms collaborate on new and innovative projects everywhere.

We at LDC operated in the spirit of Richard's policy. Arthur Muscovitch from our office went to Australia to help on a new town project and my visit to Cleveland was not to meet Richard but to participate in whatever it was LDC was doing there.

As we became established in Toronto, we came to be well known through some notable projects, one of which was a new town plan for Townsend near Hamilton that was intended to serve the residential needs of a new steel manufacturing plant by Stelco. We acted as project managers for the plan preparation. Townsend was never built, however, because Stelco did not proceed with its steel plant proposal. Regrettably, Stelco never paid the Province of Ontario for its troubles.

It was during this time that sorrow struck our family. Our daughter Jacki was killed in an accident. I found out first and went to find Rene.

Sorrow

You called me out of a meeting at the Museum. We sat on the stairs and you told me the sad news. There was no way of consolation. The hurt was too deep. In the night I could not sleep; and I know you were lying next to me, wakeful.

We planned a simple funeral. We invited our most intimate friends only. You asked Sam to play the violin. You spoke briefly about Jacki as we saw her and I read her little story called "Me" which she had written in grade school. Nicholas lowered the box and Ann interred it. The pain is with us always. I draw strength and consolation from the photo album you made. It is artistic and covers her childhood and adolescence. The number of times I looked at it? I've lost count.

Jacki died on Broadway on her way home on her bicycle from Columbia University. I was asked to speak at the memorial service given by the Graduate School of Architecture and Planning's class of 1982. I said:

> We all have our special memories of Jacki but the real Jacki we all readily recognize. Jacki had a definite view of life and was guided by strong principles. She cared for the truth and disliked hypocrisy. Jacki was a no-nonsense girl who was not taken in by pretensions. She liked a simple life and was on the side of the underdog. Her outlook made life sometimes difficult for her because she was not always prepared to compromise her principles. Jacki's intelligence and experiences shaped her views. She had a quick and critical mind. But unlike most critics she was modest about herself. She could not advertise her knowledge, gifts and talents. Aside from being a bright girl she was very good with her hands in arts and crafts, and we will treasure

> the things she made for us. Although she liked a simple life, she was curious and enquiring about society. Jacki loved cities because they could satisfy that curiosity, and she knew many in Europe and North America. London perhaps was her favourite, particularly the museums. New York may have been a close second. Above all else, Jacki was a gentle soul and a warm generous human being. To have lost her is unbearably painful, but Jacki leaves many wonderful memories of a lovable daughter, sister and friend.

Among the letters we received from family and friends, the one from Ann Jabine was particularly apt because it complemented my expressions of Jacki's character. Ann, or Angie as she calls herself now, was Jacki's high school friend and they kept in touch wherever they lived. Angie wrote:

> I remember her loyalty and interest in my well-being, even in the midst of her own life's ups and downs. Also very concrete to me is her independence and adventurousness, which I admired ever since we became friends. Jacki was much more level-headed than I was.
>
> She loved getting around cities and tracking down their treasures. When I'd visit her she would always come down to the subway or train station and lead the way. When I visited her in Somerville one summer we must have walked all over Boston and Cambridge, looked at her favourite architecture and art museums. I couldn't have had a more companionable guide.
>
> I've got most of the letters she ever wrote me, and I went through them last night – all about her life at

Tufts, Michigan, in England, D.C., at Columbia. She wrote to me in good and bad moods, but always with wit. What comes through all over again when I read her letters is Jacki's constant evaluation of her life. She was always concerned about the best course to follow, and very honest about examining her motivations. What also comes through is her individualism and integrity – she never did or liked anything just because someone else did. She had her own values, and she was consistent.

When I was deciding whether or not to join the Peace Corps she wrote saying not that it was poorly paid and dangerous (as other friends did) but with some valid criticism of their role politically, at the same time admitting her knowledge was incomplete. This was typical of her character as I recall it.

I hope my memories of Jacki will make grief more bearable and not less. She did so many kind things for me that I don't want to be the only one to remember them.

Another project we began to plan at LDC was a town centre for Mississauga, again paid for by the province. Richard came to the presentation of the plan to show the flag and because North Americans fawn over aristocrats and royalty.

For contrast, I was asked to take on one of the oddest jobs I have ever done, and I only accepted it because an old friend from London, Wojciech Wronski, asked me. (Wronski went on to become the Ontario deputy minister for municipal affairs.) The job was in response to public concerns that wanted the province to pass bylaws under the planning acts in order to regulate the operation of adult entertainment establishments – also known as strip joints. I went to

Los Angeles and other cities that have experience with such bylaws. I talked to their officials, obtained copies of their different bylaws, and learned the legal language used in the bylaws for describing and identifying the female anatomy. My report reviewed the cities' experiences and recommended that this field of public policy and regulation was not a proper one for urban planning; rather, any apparent problems should be dealt with by social workers and the police.

Another interesting project at LDC sent me to Nassau, the capital of the Bahamas. The Government of the Bahamas was in discussions with the World Bank about urban renewal for the original downtown area called Grants Town (generally referred to as Over the Hill), and the World Bank was going to finance the project. The process of urban renewal that would replace poor housing with new buildings had been discredited because the people living in these renewed areas could not afford the new housing once it was built. The government agreed to a renewal approach that would improve living conditions without dislocating the people already living in Grants Town.

The Government of the Bahamas was unfamiliar with firms that could do the work, so it asked the World Bank for advice. Following its usual practice, the Bank recommended only a few firms; in this case, just three: one each from England, the U.S., and Canada (us). We were selected and I put together a team for the project. Since we did not have a suitable project director, I asked Doug King from LDA in New York to take the job. We had gotten to know each other during the Chaguaramas project. The other person I asked to join our team was my Toronto friend Martin ter Woort, an economist. This led to the three of us collaborating on other projects and started a long friendship between us that has lasted until now.

The detailed recommendations for public works and especially for government loans to homeowners for improving their houses were accepted by the government and renewal started even before the World Bank had reviewed our report. To crown it all, the government signed a personal contract with Doug King putting him in charge of the renewal process.

One other project came to us at LDC through some previous work in Washington (with the National Water Commission, described in chapter 5) that is worth mentioning. A phone call from the regional office of the U.S. Army Corps of Engineers in Omaha, Nebraska, asked me whether I was the person who had been in charge of a study for the National Water Commission in the early 1970s. If so, I might be able to help them. The Corps were ready to build a dam in a canyon south of Denver to create a reservoir to increase the water supply (and/or electricity supply) for the Denver area. Construction was held up because the U.S. Environmental Protection Agency (EPA) was dissatisfied with the environmental impact study which had not assessed the dam's role in facilitating further growth of the Denver area, whose citizens were strongly opposed to increased population.

The Corps had told EPA that they had not been able to find any study on the relationship between increased water or electric power supply and urban growth. EPA's response was, more or less, that it was the Corps' problem and, due to the strong objections against further growth, the Corps was obliged to address the issue. In the pre-Google days, it had taken the Corps quite a bit of time to find our book, *Community Growth and Water Resources Policy* (the published findings of our work with the National Water Commission, described in chapter 5), and, when it did, I was asked if I would come to Omaha for a discussion.

On arrival I was introduced to a group of senior officers (mostly colonels, even though they were not wearing uniforms) and they explained their problem, showed me documents from EPA, and asked if LDC could help. I replied that I thought we could. I would take all the documents back to Toronto and send them a proposal. "Oh no, we have no time for that. You can stay in this conference room, a secretary is available full time and we'll meet again here at 4:00 p.m. to review your proposal."

I had never, before or since, produced a proposal under such pressure. We met at the appointed time. The colonels hardly read the proposal and, without discussion, the chairman accepted it, save for one problem: the fee for preparing the report was slightly above the amount the regional office was permitted to approve. To send it to Washington would mean a very long delay – there was no time for that – could I stay within the permitted ceiling? Exhibiting professional ethics, I said I would have to delete some less important aspect of the proposed study. They gave me time to do that and then asked me to start work on it as soon as possible – like tomorrow.

Karen Bricker from our office and I did the work, which included taking a scary bubble helicopter ride into the canyon to look at the proposed dam sight. Sometime later I learned that the colonels were satisfied with our report and had sent a letter to Mr. Llewelyn Davies in New York, which said, "Your man in Toronto did a fine job, giving us exactly what we needed." I suppose, then, that the EPA let them have the dam.

Things were going along uneventfully at LDC in Toronto when out of the blue I received a call from an American consulting firm I had never heard of before. They asked me whether I would be prepared to become the project manager for a World Bank–financed project in Indonesia. It was a fateful decision for me, and it is the last one I described in the next chapter, "Selected Projects."

CHAPTER 5

Selected Projects

> There's something to be said for staying in one place
> over a long period of time. I just don't know what
> that is.
> —Alan Cheuse, *A Trance After Breakfast* (2009)

My experiences in urban planning and economic research were wonderfully varied. A third of my working life was spent in public planning offices in London and Toronto. The more exciting projects took place over a longer span of time and found me working as a consultant in Canada, the United States, Africa, Asia, and the Caribbean Islands. The nature of the work ranged from detailed, site-specific plans to regional or country-wide planning and policy issues.

Over time I worked increasingly in so-called developing countries, trying in various ways to improve the living conditions for the majority of the population. My role often changed from being part of a team in small and large projects to being in charge of projects or, at the opposite end, doing freelance work on my own. This illustrates my restlessness "to get on" – to make up for the lost years in the army – as well as my grasping at opportunities and accepting tempting offers that found me working in the competitive, private consulting market with its economic ups and downs.

I may be accused of being a "Jack of all trades and master of none," to which I would reply with another proverb: "An expert in a narrow field does not see the wood for the trees," which appeals to me because of my love of forests. My restlessness may also prove that I have no *Sitzfleisch* (the ability to sit still for a long time). Regardless, whatever the cause, it made for an educational, satisfying, and rewarding life, and with a bonus: I worked with many experienced and knowledgeable colleagues who taught me a lot and with whom I became friends for life.

Before I begin describing the selected projects (which I discuss in the order of most importance to me), I'd like to say a word about two odd experiences: visiting Cuba on behalf of Cyrus Eaton, and a brief encounter with American poverty.

Cyrus Eaton was a Canadian-born investment banker, philanthropist, and proponent of world peace – he financed the first of the Pugwash Conferences in his hometown of Pugwash, Nova Scotia. He had a hunch in the 1970s that the U.S. government was going to relent towards Cuba and establish friendlier relations. Having made investments in Russia and other communist countries, Eaton pursued an offer for building a luxury hotel on the north coast of Cuba, and he asked LDA in New York to give him a preliminary appraisal of the site. Because of the prohibition against Americans visiting Cuba, an architect from the New York office went to Cuba via Toronto, where I joined him.

We met Eaton's right-hand woman, who handled investments in communist countries, at the Havana Hilton. She explained the results of Eaton's discussions with the government. The next morning the architect and I met a small group of government officials who flew us in a one-engine Russian plane to Camaguay in central Cuba, and then drove us by car to a pristine location that was on the north coast and out of sight from any development. We had a good look around, took photos, walked along the beach, sampled the sand and generally satisfied ourselves that the location appeared eminently suitable for Mr. Eaton's hotel.

When we were ready to end the site visit and return to Havana, we were told that we had to look at the site from the sea. Our protests that this would not be necessary, and in any case it was getting late, were of no avail. Out at sea the boat's engine broke down and there was no radio on board to call for help. The boat drifted towards America and it was getting dark. The crew fired flares to attract the attention of any Cubans and Americans on the lookout. Eventually another boat arrived to help us, but after tying a rope to our boat, it raced off and snapped the tether. My architect friend and I dared not speak but watched the sky for the U.S. Coast Guard. Eventually, the Cuban rescue boat managed to tow us back to safety.

The next day, we had a tour of Hemingway's house and his favourite pub, and visited the Canadian and Russian hotels at Varadero, before we returned to our home countries. Once we were back in our offices, we reported favourably about the site. However, Cyrus Eaton had misread the intentions of the American government: there would not be any reconciliation, and thus the hotel would not be built. To this day, the United States considers Cuba to be a dangerous enemy.

The second odd experience involved President Johnson's War on Poverty, which launched numerous programs in poor areas and in Indian Reservations across the country. RRNA was asked to assess the results, and a few of Nathan's staff went on a tour of several projects. As to be expected, results varied considerably and one experience of my trip stands out. On our drive through the hollows of Kentucky, we passed a wooden hut where I saw an old man sitting on his stoop next to a new refrigerator. I stopped and had a chat with him about the refrigerator. An enterprising salesman had sold him the refrigerator at a good price – yet there was no electricity for miles around. I prayed that another program would supply electricity to the area.

Port Harcourt, Nigeria, 1966

> Two mornings later, with corruption very much on our minds, Sonny and I drove along the traffic-logged expressway leading out of Port Harcourt. Sticking out of the tall roadside grass was a billboard with a government message that said: DON'T BADMOUTH NIGERIA! THINGS ARE CHANGING.
> —Noo Saro-Wiwa, *Looking for Transwonderland: Travels in Nigeria* (2012)

Less than a year before the Biafran War began, when three southeastern states sought independence, RRNA sent me to Nigeria. This was my first assignment in a poor African country. The term "developing country," whatever its meaning then or now, had not yet been generally adopted. The contract was for a highway feasibility study, meaning that we needed to calculate whether the measurable benefits of a new road would be at least equal to or greater than the cost of building it. The proposed divided highway went from Port Harcourt to Aba in the new "oil country" of eastern Nigeria.

The transportation economist in charge of the project had returned from a reconnaissance very disappointed because much of the essential basic information needed did not exist or was unreliable. Therefore I was sent to find such information, either by collecting or creating it. First there were no maps, neither of the town nor of the route to Aba. I visited the Shell corporate office, suspecting the company would have an interest in better roads. I was right. The person I spoke to readily gave me up-to-date maps of the town and surrounding area. Data on land use along the highway corridor had never been collected. Although there had been a population census the previous year, it was the informed opinion that neither the size nor the distribution of the population data could be trusted in Nigeria. The intense rivalry between the numerous ethnic groups in the country led to interference in the collection and publication of population figures.

A complete census was out of the question. I had to devise a sample survey. I walked around Port Harcourt to get a "sense" of the town and discovered that it had three types of residential developments: the old centre of substantial colonial and post-colonial housing; modern, mortgage-assisted suburban housing; and the majority of the town's self-built unorganized housing developments. We would count the population in a few areas to arrive at typical population densities (i.e., persons per acre) and apply them for the whole town.

Fortunately, as a benefit of British colonialism, Port Harcourt had been divided into enumeration areas and census districts in the same way as in England, which was a familiar system for me. Except that the boundary descriptions were, for the most part, not by street names and house numbers. A usual description of an enumeration boundary would read: "Start at Mrs. Munuru's fruit stand on the main Port Harcourt-Aba Road, follow along a path in a north-easterly direction for 52 yards to a mango tree, thence north ... etc." In this particular instance, Mrs. Munuru and her fruit stand were no longer there and enquiries were needed in order to establish were she used to be.

Before coming to Nigeria from Washington, I had arranged for students interested in survey work from the universities of Ibadan and Nsuku (Eastern Nigeria) to meet me in Port Harcourt at my hotel, a very modern Israeli-built and Israeli-owned building, managed by a Swiss. After I explained the work and warned them that they would be out in the heat all day interviewing people, I selected fifteen of them. I tried to get an even mix of boys and girls, and gave preference to those originally from Port Harcourt.

In an office provided for our work by the government, we had one day to review all the instructions: the maps of the town and the selected enumeration areas for the survey, a separate map for each area, and the forms to be used to record the use of each building and, if it was a residential building, the number of occupants by age and sex. I sent them out the next day for a dry-run; reviewing their work, I found a few mistakes, one of which was an amusing one: a building on the major road was recorded as "residential" and occupied by thirteen young females and one middle-aged man. I questioned the unlikely classification of "residential" and the young lady student started blushing, agreeing that it was a commercial enterprise.

I did not accompany the students during the survey, because I wanted to give the impression that this exercise was a local activity. Until one day, when the survey was well underway, a few of the students returned to the office with a problem. The local chief of one of the areas would not let "his" people answer any questions until he had talked to me about the road project in his part of town. Like any astute politician anywhere, he had his price. When I met him he demanded an assurance that his people would be hired for the project. I told him that I had no say in the matter as I would not be involved in the construction work. His response was: "Ah, but you can make a recommendation in your report." I agreed and suggested taking a photo of him so I could remember him. He went into his hut and reappeared in his flowing robe. Before I could snap the camera, he rushed back into the hut to put his sandals on. "His people" co-operated with the survey.

Once we completed our sample census, measured the size of the enumeration areas, calculated population densities, and applied them to the relevant "typical" developments of Port Harcourt, we arrived at a new population total for the town. People who were in the know, such as federal and local officials, considered the total to be "pretty good" or "about right." For the transportation economist back in Washington, we produced an area map showing the census population of the town, and then we continued the land-use survey along the main road through Port Harcourt to complete the assignment.

By this time the political situation had reached a critical stage, I was glad to be on my way. However, I will not leave my account of Port Harcourt without my most unforgettable and humbling encounter.

In the early days when I was walking around the real Port Harcourt where the majority lived I met a woman standing in black, stagnant water holding a baby. The baby's face was covered in festering sores. Seeing a white man who was not in uniform, the woman took me for a priest. She pleaded with me to understand and begged me to touch her baby's face and pray to heal it. Having done the best I knew how to, the poor woman's face lit up in a smile. She had absolute faith in my miracle power to save her child. I saw much poverty in years to come, especially in India, but this encounter has always stayed with me.

As it turned out, the road feasibility study and my part in it became so much dust, except for my experience. The Biafran War started in July 1967. Although down the road many years later, I received evidence of the busy highway at Port Harcourt. One of Rene's relatives, Charles Hope, a consultant to oil companies, sent me a photo showing him standing in the centre strip of the divided highway near Port Harcourt, where he was held up due to an accident.

> Most members of my generation, who were born before Nigeria's independence (1960), remember a time when things were very different. Nigeria was once a land of great hope and progress, a nation with immense resources at its disposal – natural resource, yes, but even more so, human resources. But the Biafran War changed the course of Nigeria.
> — Chinua Achebe, *There Was a Country: A Personal History of Biafra* (2012)

Postscript to Port Harcourt

This postscript goes well beyond the description of the Port Harcourt project. My work in Port Harcourt was my first experience in a so-called developing country. What I learned there was just a beginning, a fragment of what I learned later in other developing countries which, like Nigeria, have not developed. This postscript, therefore, is about understanding the background of a developing country, about the international aid industry, and about development economics.

As in most of Africa, Nigeria was created as a country by colonialism by one of the colonial powers: Britain. Before colonies were established, thousands of tribes with different ethnic and religious backgrounds lived throughout Africa peacefully or otherwise, many of them migrating in search of food and better land. In the late nineteenth century, Britain, France, Portugal, and Germany staked their claims by invasion. Britain colonized several areas in Africa, including land north of the Gulf of Guinea in West Africa where the Niger River flows into the Gulf west of Port Harcourt and named the possession Nigeria.

In time, colonization of this area created the largest African colony, whose population reached perhaps 40 million. Today, Nigeria is the largest African country with 140 million or more people, about half of whom are Muslims. At independence, in 1960, three regions under a federal structure governed the country: a Northern Region of mainly Fulani and Hausa, an Eastern Region (with its government in Enugu) of mainly Ibo, and a Western Region of mainly Yoruba people. I say "mainly" because there are some 250 ethnic groups who speak their own languages in Nigeria. The minorities' discontent led at first to the creation of twelve states to give the larger minorities a say in governing their area. Now, there are thirty-seven states within the Federation.

Though the official language is English, the majority of the population speaks one of three languages: Hausa in the north,

Yoruba in the southwest, and Ibo in the east. All this illustrates why Nigeria has been and still is a difficult country to govern, because it is not "a country" in the conventional sense. Add to that the fact that the country's main foreign income comes from one source – oil – and from one location: within and to the north of Port Harcourt.

In *Dead Aid*, Dambisa Moyo writes, "No one can deny that Africa has had its fair share of tribal fracas. But by the same token it is also true that there are a number of African countries where disparate groups have managed to coexist perfectly peacefully (Botswana, Ghana, Zambia, to name three)" (p. 33). Nigeria is not one of those countries.

What was done cannot be undone easily, if at all. The legacy of colonialism is widespread, painful, and lasting. One particular example is Persia. The damage done is not just ongoing but escalating. The Anglo-American coup of 1953 in Iran, just a few years before Nigeria's independence, which has come to be regretted by America, created an impasse that now threatens us all. The people of Iran elected Muhammad Mossadegh to lead them along a democratic path. During his second term he nationalized the Anglo-Persian Oil Company because he had failed to obtain better royalties (commission) for the extraction of Persian oil. This action proved to lead to the end of his rule of Persia. His government was overthrown in a coup d'état orchestrated by British MI 6 and American CIA under the direction of Kermit "Kim" Roosevelt. We all know what this action led to in Iran and no one knows how to defuse the dangerous situation.

The Port Harcourt-Aba Road was not the only foreign aid project underway in the area when I was there. On weekends, at the hotel bar, I met quite a few aid workers from three sponsoring agencies: the World Bank, the Peace Corps, and U.S. A.I.D. The

Peace Corps youngsters and the U.S. A.I.D. clique usually kept apart, except when having heated arguments.

On one occasion, my project took me to the regional government office in Enugu. I went by government car via the market town of Onitsha. We saw a young man with a backpack walking ahead along the road – obviously a foreigner. The driver, though not permitted to give rides, picked him up. He was with the Peace Corps and on his way to a remote fishing village where he would spend a couple of months teaching up-to-date fishing methods with modern equipment. We went out of our way to drop him closer to the village. Then the driver told me how Nigerians had come to like and respect the Peace Corps – they were doing useful work and they had little money just like them.

A little further along the road we were on a deserted, new divided highway. The driver could only tell me that it had been completed recently by an American construction company. I was puzzled for days about this road in the bush without traffic; until I found an American aid official with an explanation. There had been a feasibility study for a major road along a lengthy corridor which recommended the building of the road in stages, as justified over time. Bids were invited from international companies, indicating that the first stretch was to be built now. An Italian company responded with the lowest bid for phase one. Subsequently, a U.S. company matched or undercut that bid for phase one under the condition that additional phases were built at the same time. It seemed to me that the much talked about Nigerian corruption was encouraged by foreign aid.

Port Harcourt was a bewildering experience as well as a learning process for me. It was good to know that I could operate effectively in a technically primitive environment to produce the required information. At the same time, there was much I did not understand and a lot of aid activity failed to make sense. Admittedly, those were the early days of aid to developing countries. The "why" and "how" of giving were scarcely defined. But the problems and conflicts were beginning to show.

As I left Port Harcourt, I think I was beginning to question why public money, foreign or domestic, should pay for the construction of a road needed, at that time, by only one user: the embryonic oil industry which could well afford to pay for it.

To give an account of the rise, extent, and complex nature of foreign aid is more than I can do here, or am able to do properly. Yet, it has been part of my working life and has become a hotly argued subject, so I will speak my mind.

Both altruism and self-interest supported the aid industry from the beginning and made it grow, support that came from the World Bank at one end and Medicine Sans Frontiers at the other, leading to some good results. Political considerations like the Cold War and national, commercial motives certainly played a role in investment decisions. The success of the Marshall Plan in Europe also influenced the growing support for aid to poor countries, despite the great difference between helping developed countries with investment experience recovering from a war and poor countries without any experience in economic development.

In any case, the rush to help created a dual competition: Western countries competing among themselves in giving money, and developing countries competing for the ever-mounting cash. Whatever the theory or proclaimed goal of foreign aid, the practice of giving aid has produced mixed results but rarely has it produced "development." Altruism still plays an important role, especially in aid from non-governmental organizations. National aid giving never was pure in the sense of being solely in the interest of aid-receiving countries. International aid givers like the World Bank or the Asian Development Bank may operate according to prevailing economic theories but are often influenced by pressures from developing countries.

Some aid-receiving countries were quick learners about the aid agencies' policies and budgeting system; they structured their requests accordingly. For example, they learned that unspent annual funds would be forfeited. The sophisticated countries began to hold out for larger contributions than what were offered long enough to sign a better agreement. But it must also be said that the World Bank, however misguided, is not heartless. The Bank has an honourable record in establishing and enforcing humane rules in development projects involving the relocation of people, as in the building of reservoirs. Involuntary resettlement demands that the people relocated shall not be worse off after resettlement and, if possible, have better lives than before. This criterion caused the Bank not to financially support the construction of the Three Gorges Dam on the Yangtze River.

The real problem of why aid to developing countries has failed has to do with mistaken beliefs, dogmas, doctrines, and theories, call it what you like. It all comes back to the failure to look at failure simply because so many are quite happy with the process.

Here is one more example of aid not coming through as it should from the sphere I am more familiar with: housing assistance, which is a continuation of my exchange with Helen Hughes at the World Bank. In our project in Nassau, Bahamas, Martin negotiated home improvement loans with the government's bank, which happened to be a Canadian bank, at rates below par. When the recommendations for the Grants Town Improvement project were reviewed by the World Bank, the favourable loan terms were strongly criticized because they constituted a "subsidy" that was unacceptable to the Bank. Martin pointed out to the Bank official, who by an odd coincidence was called Mrs. Nassau, that financial institutions everywhere offer favourable rates to their better customers. Mrs. Nassau could only reiterate that the loan terms constituted a subsidy that was not acceptable to the Bank. This time, therefore, the Bank "was no different from the commercial bank down the street."

Fortunately, the Bank's opinion did not matter. The government of the Bahamas – which, in the words of the World Bank, had "graduated" and was no longer qualified to receive the Bank's assistance – went ahead and started the improvement project. In fact, the government put Doug King, the study's project manager, in charge of the improvement program.

But where did development economics originate? Peter Bauer is credited with being the godfather of development economics. He was born in Hungary, educated in Cambridge, and worked and studied in Malaysia and Africa. His creative period was spent at LSE (1960–83) and he earned emeritus status in the ensuing years. His most influential books were *Dissent on Development* (1972) and *Equality: The Third World and Economic Delusion* (1981). The more recent godmother of development economics, helped along by William Easterly (*The White Man's Burden*, 2007), is Dambisa Moyo, who was born in Zambia and has established herself as today's most learned critic of foreign aid. Her book *Dead Aid* (2009) is dedicated to Peter Bauer. Moyo's later book *Winner Take All* (2012) points out that China's resource development projects in Africa appear to be a better way for Africa's own economic development. Both Easterly's and Moyo's scepticism about current development aid was aroused, I imagine, during their time at the World Bank.

I hope and expect that a Bauer-Moyo offspring will continue the good work, but also broaden the analysis of development economics by including the thorny and tough question: Who benefits from economic development? And in which countries, both developing and developed? After all, we need to remember that the beginning of the Iranian tragedy was caused when Mossadegh's appeal to the Anglo-Iranian Oil Company that it toe the line and pay 50 percent of their profits, as all other oil companies did, was refused; AIOC only paid 20 percent (and was calculated based on their private records).

The question about "who benefits" is an appropriate introduction to the next Selected Project.

Recreation as an Industry, 1967

In 1963, President Kennedy established the Appalachian Regional Commission (ARC), a federal–state partnership, to tackle the unemployment problem in this depressed region of the United States. President Johnson's Economic Opportunity Act of 1964, his War on Poverty, broadened the concept into a countrywide initiative and provided increased funds. The ARC's first development activity was well underway – construction of new roads to provide better access to Appalachia's beautiful countryside – and the Commission was searching for other, direct, and lasting ways of creating employment. Tourism was touted as "the fastest growing industry," and the Commission was ready to launch into recreation development.

The Commission's executive director at that time cautioned that tourism may not really help the people living in Appalachia, even if it was successful in boosting the tourist industry, because of the undeveloped nature of the region. He suggested looking at this issue before committing large amounts of capital and hiring RRNA for the research and analysis. In effect, answering the question posed by Robert Nathan himself: "Who would benefit from the growth of the tourist industry in Appalachia?"

The team, under Nathan's direction, pursued two parallel lines of enquiry: (1) a theoretical one – the multiplier – which is a statistical way of calculating a number or multiplier by which a local, regional, or national economy increases its income due to a given investment – a kind of economic multiplication "trickle down" fix; and (2) following the trickling down of the actual dollars spent by tourists at a tourist destination to the local recipients.

We selected a number of tourist locations in the Appalachia region: parks, hotels, resorts, and a racecourse, and we also selected the town of Stratford in Ontario, Canada. The town of Stratford was of special interest because of its history. Originally Stratford had been a busy railway hub and, when the railways moved away, the town declined rapidly. The mayor of the day saved the situation. He suggested capitalizing on the town's name by establishing a Stratford Theatre on this side of the Atlantic that was similar to the one in England.

The data collection in the field for both enquiries had to be coordinated to ensure comparability for the multiplier analysis and to alert all teams of emerging findings. I was put in charge of the coordination in addition to the fieldwork at Harper's Ferry and at an upscale summer resort. The coordination was a bigger job than it would be today – there was no internet and even the fax was not yet available.

While at the high-class hotel in the mountains, I already suspected the outcome of the project. The hotel was only open in spring and summer; the well-paid chef was from New York and occasionally he went back home, which meant he spent little to no money in Appalachia; the hotel's bed sheets and table linens had to be sent to a town outside Appalachia because the village laundry could not handle the volume; and much of the best food had to be imported. The only local benefit was the seasonal employment for the low-paid chamber maids.

The overall results of the study supported the suspicions of the ARC's executive director. The recommendations established the basic conditions necessary to ensure local benefits from tourist investment. I came away from the experience, as did others from the study team, questioning (privately) the usefulness of the "multiplier."

RRNA released its report, *Recreation as an Industry*, in 1967. It received interest and wide circulation when it was published. This was most likely because it was a rare example of a public federal agency, with funds to spend, initiating the research to look first at the likely results before making any investments. Though, of course, governments often know quite well who will benefit: their supporters.

Milwaukee Braves & Green Bay Packers, 1965

This is really about two related jobs, which fall under the topic "Only in America" and which concern baseball and football (that is, American football).

The Boston Braves baseball team moved to Milwaukee in 1952 and became the Milwaukee Braves. In 1965 the owners of the team announced their intention to move again to Atlanta for financial reasons, claiming that they were losing money in Milwaukee. Up to this point, there had been a history of teams moving freely around the country in search of bigger audiences and better TV deals because the baseball industry was unregulated.

Prominent and influential persons and organizations had been anxious for an opportunity to launch an anti-trust suit against the Braves and the National League. It was suspected that the Braves managers were profiteering. A number of Washington law firms with anti-trust litigation experience asked Robert Nathan (RRNA) to be their economic expert and give evidence on two accounts: the loss to the Milwaukee economy if the Braves went to Atlanta and the profits realized by the Braves while in Milwaukee.

Robert asked Jane Arendt and me to assemble and organize the data for his evidence. I must confess that I am not sure that

Mrs. Arendt's first name was Jane; she was a young economist from England with experience in financial analysis and married to a scientist who was also from England. Jane and I had worked together before successfully but the amusing fact in this instance was that we were the only British staff members and had never been to a baseball game – not that it mattered, we were looking for profit and loss data and not analyzing the Braves' performance.

Robert sat down with us to explain what he would need and listed the range of information and the level of detail we should present to him. Above all, the data had to be documentary evidence and not hearsay, which meant that every number used had to be supported by an acceptable document. That's when we found out that Robert also had a law degree and knew all about the rules of evidence.

Whenever Jane and I completed the first draft on any specific topic at issue we returned to Washington from Milwaukee for Robert's review. He never failed to spot the weak points in our material, which we knew about. But he did not complain because he understood the problem, we just discussed the best way to solve it. Information on the likely financial loss resulting from the departure of the Braves was easier to collect than to get at the Braves' profits. Losers are more cooperative in sharing information than profiteers. But we managed – Jane was very intelligent and inventive, as well as charming, in extracting closely guarded information, therefore she searched for the alleged loss of the Braves' income and I took on the easier task of making the case for Milwaukee's economic decline if the Braves were to leave.

Meantime, the boxes of documents grew, each item with its reference number so it could be retrieved instantly if and when information would be challenged in court. About a week before the start of the court hearing the retinues of opposing lawyers, experts, secretaries and stenographers assembled on separate floors of the round towered Pfiser Hotel in downtown Milwaukee to prepare for the court battle in Madison, the capital of Wisconsin.

The usual preparation of Robert, who was once again the chief expert witness, turned out to be less than customary. The leading lawyer who would take Robert through his evidence started off by saying, "After having heard your qualifications, I will ask you the following question to which you will answer..." Robert heard him out for the first prepared exchange and then stopped him and proceeded, without notes, to outline his scenario of the evidence he was going to present to the court. The assembled lawyers listened to him without interruption and with bated breath until he had finished in about half an hour. They unanimously agreed that "that was it."

On the appointed day, the hearing started in Madison, but not at the court house because none of the court rooms were big enough to hold the crowd having expressed their interest in attending the case. Instead, it was held in a very large hall, and even then there was standing room only. After a day or two of legal arguments, Robert was called as the first witness and he was on the stand for two and a half days of presentation and cross examination. Although there was a microphone, he did not use it because his powerful voice filled the large hall.

Jane and I and our boxes were behind the witness stand throughout Robert's presentation, ready to pull out the relevant document when facts were challenged. In any event, we were rarely needed. The judge was very attentive, looking towards Robert and taking notes all the time. The audience was hushed and seemed to follow his arguments. The cross examination was another story. The calm and quiet presentation turned into an aggressive and belligerent drama that Robert handled with ease and composure. He refused objections so conclusively that opposing lawyers became abrasive. One of them asked how much Robert was charging for his services in this case. Robert told him his time and cost so far. "How much more are you going to charge?" asked the lawyer. Robert replied, "That all depends on how long you keep me on the stand." And he was on the stand for another whole day.

In due course, Judge Elmer Roller, former professor at Marquette Law School, ruled that the National League acted in restraint of trade and fined the defendants $55,000. He also enjoined the Braves not to move but demanded they "stay put." Significantly, the judge's decision mentioned that "the Braves had used accounting tricks to turn six-figure profits into paper loss for 1963 and 1964." Jane's painstaking work had paid off.

In the end, however, the Supreme Court of Wisconsin by a 4 to 3 vote reversed the decision, which allowed the Braves to move to Atlanta. That decision, in turn, was appealed to the U.S. Supreme Court, which denied the appeal petition. In total, eight justices voted: five against and three in favour. The three justices who had voted in favour of hearing the case were Justices Douglas, Black, and Brennan. The very recently appointed Justice Fortas did not participate in the Court's deliberations. So it was a close call: if just one of the five justices who voted against the appeal had switched his vote, it would have been a tie and the U.S. Supreme Court would have reviewed the case.

As I mentioned earlier on, ever since college I have had an interest in the U.S. Constitution and the role the U.S. Supreme Court plays in its ongoing interpretation to justify or deny government actions, so I was pleased to have played a part, however minor, in the Braves case. It again emphasized to me the essentially political role of the court in cases of this kind. In addition, by having the chance to work closely with Robert, I got to know him better and learned a lot from him, which increased my respect and admiration for him.

While the Braves' case was in court, it dominated the news in print and on the air, baseball being the major spectator sport in the

United States. The legal, economic, and political issues raised by the case got the attention from everybody – and from none other than Vince Lombardi, who had a personal interest.

Lombardi was the head coach and general manager of the Green Bay Packers, a leading football team at the time, which unusually played in two "home towns": Green Bay, in northern Wisconsin, and in Milwaukee. I don't think that Lombardi lost any sleep over the anti-trust aspect of the Braves' case but took a great interest in Robert's account of all the money being spent by the spectators coming to the games. So he wrote to Robert asking for a similar economic impact study concerning both Green Bay and Milwaukee. Robert had no interest in taking this on, for reasons that became clear to me only later, but he asked Jane and me whether we would like to do the job without his participation. The British team once again got involved in an All-American sport.

I went to meet Lombardi in Green Bay for a preliminary discussion to find out about source material. The attendance records, season ticket holders with locations, and the sales at the games were in good order. Lombardi gave me a tour of the town and stadium with his wife and young son – the jovial family man. But I had some uncomfortable impressions of the man, which were confirmed by his wife in her comments to me when she was able to make them. It turned out to be an early warning.

Jane and I later decamped to Green Bay and Milwaukee to start our data collection. At Green Bay, for local colour, we were taken to the locker room of the Packers in training and introduced to the team. We shook hands with Bart Starr (team member from 1956– 71), who was the all-American football player of the day. When I told the office about this special event, Jane became the envy of all young, and not so young, women at RRNA. I must admit that Bart Starr's physique did not seem to faze her one bit.

Nosing around Green Bay, talking to municipal officials and sports journalists, I heard a lot of criticism about Lombardi's demanding behaviour. He constantly asked for improvements to the publicly owned stadium without making any contributions, as apparently other successful teams elsewhere had experienced. The stadium had just completed installing a lawn heating system, which made sense in Green Bay, but it was a very big expense for such a small town. Now I knew why Robert had no interest in being involved in the job: he knew, like probably most Americans, that Lombardi was a great football coach but a "nasty piece of work," whereas Jane and I were just ignorant foreigners.

I sent our report to Lombardi with a customary covering letter expecting him to be grateful about the substantial benefits that the Packers' games brought to both Green Bay and Milwaukee. Under separate cover I sent him another letter mentioning the numerous complaints I had come across about his stinginess (using a more respectful phrase) and suggesting to him a number of ways in which he could support the young and old of Green Bay to enhance his popularity at very little cost. RRNA never received a reply or even an acknowledgement of having received our report – though the fee was paid promptly.

With that silent end to an amusing project, let me turn to a more meaningful piece of work.

Community Growth and Water Resources Policy, 1971–1972

> "There are three parts to any project, to get it, to do it and to get paid for it, and I like the first and last best."
>
> —John Bousefield

John said this in jest. I know this because he loved his work and was very good at it. He established the longest-operating planning consulting firm in Toronto, and it will outlast him on the strength of his name. But John had a point. There is something exciting about outsmarting the competition.

In 1971 the U.S. National Water Commission was established to examine the country's water supply and use, and to make recommendations to the President and Congress on the future use and control of water resources. Usually, national commissions prepare reports in-house, with or without consultants, and draw conclusions before publishing draft reports for comments at hearings. Uniquely, the National Water Commission started its deliberation by travelling around the country holding public meetings, inviting questions and submissions so they could learn about the public's concerns.

One concern raised repeatedly at these meetings was the concentration and growth of populations in large urban areas, and the following question was frequently raised: "Is it possible for the federal government, by utilizing the financial and construction resources at its disposal, to direct some significant measure of future population and economic activity into smaller communities and less developed regions?" To find answers to this question the Commission issued a general RFP (request for proposal) open to all interested organizations and consultants.

Rivkin/Carson (R/C) responded, knowing that the competition would be formidable if not hopeless for a tiny firm like ours, largely unknown and consisting of only six professionals. Long ago in my career I had acquired a taste for competition. I had also learned that success often depends on bribery. Corruption being endemic everywhere in developing countries as well as in the West, we neither had the means nor the desire to enter that kind of competition. Yet, a national commission is not like a regular government department where corruption is well established. We therefore decided to enter the competition and emphasize our combined experience in urban development in the U.S., Canada, and the UK. We spent a considerable amount of time coming up with a responsive and creative proposal. Although costs may not have been relevant for a national commission, we were certainly more competitive in price, since our overhead was minimal compared to that of a large research firm. At any rate, we got the job, and I was set to direct it.

The task assigned to us was to determine the extent to which water resources development could be used to further a policy of population dispersal, should the nation adopt such a policy. The study was to provide (1) a basis for evaluating proposals aimed at influencing the distribution of future increases in population, and (2) a realistic assessment of the role water resource development could play in encouraging the creation of new cities, increasing the growth rates of small cities, and improving the living conditions in small rural communities. We were not asked to evaluate the desirability of existing or likely patterns of population distribution.

All three R/C partners worked on the study, along with a few others of our staff. In addition, our proposal mentioned that we would receive the assistance of outside experts: Charles Cicchetti, an economist who would be responsible for a multiple regression analysis of water resources investment data related to population changes; and Marion Clawson of Resources for the Future, who would make some of his current work in population analysis available to us and discuss with us the findings of our population analysis.

Our report to the Commission claimed that the conclusions of our study provide the following: a realistic framework for understanding population growth and change in the United States; an appraisal of the present objectives of federal water programs; an identification of the role of water in community development; and directions for water policies which might suitably complement larger national growth policies.

The general conclusion of our study was as follows:

Water policy can have an effect on the manner in which urban settlement is created. Although the impact of water policy on where population and economic activity locates may be minor indeed, such policy can influence how urban development is to take place and at what standards of efficiency, environmental quality, and amenity. The positive impacts of water and allied facilities and services on a settlement pattern can best be achieved through a joint effort with other federal activities, directed to the same places at the same times, and buttressed by appropriate actions on the state and local levels. The essential rule for success is to avoid treating water independently of the development of other resources.

More specifically, our research provided answers to the following questions: Where will a future increase in population tend to go? What special problems impede the growth of small, non-metropolitan communities? How significant are the costs for water, sewer, and related facilities in relation to the total infrastructure and services required for urban development? Briefly, the answer to these questions (which everyone was waiting for) was:

Water supply and sewage treatment are essential to the health, well-being, and functioning of a community. Without them no urban development at modern standards can take place. However, the costs, both capital and operating, for water supply and distribution, sewage collection and treatment, etc., represent a relatively small proportion of community infrastructure and services costs. Road systems and schools, for example, are far more significant.

We addressed more questions: What are the legislative intentions and objectives of existing federal programs that deal with community water-related facilities? Does investment in water resource development and water-allied facilities stimulate growth? Again and briefly, the answer to this key question was:

> The hypothesis that water investment affects the growth of population was tested in four representative states. Expenditures made by federal agencies were arrayed against population trends in each of the counties in the four states, and regression analyses were performed. Neither the metropolitan population nor the least populous counties appear to be influenced in their rates of growth by water resource investments. Indeed, across the board for all counties there was no correlation. Our test confirmed the conclusions found in earlier, more limited studies that water resource projects in and of themselves seem to be ineffective tools for promoting economic development.

In addition, we considered whether new approaches to metropolitan land development had the potential to improve conditions of congestion and sprawl, conditions which contribute to interest in a population distribution policy. Has the federal government been engaged in fostering conscious policies of population distribution and urban growth? Can water resources development be an effective tool in directing a settlement pattern? Is there a role for federal water policy in shaping patterns of population distribution and urban growth?

Our report was released by the Commission and created wide public interest, leading to its publication by Praeger in 1973, a publisher specializing in the studies of U.S. economic, social, and political issues. Entitled *Community Growth and Water Resources*

Policy, our book was subsequently used in universities, including the University of Pennsylvania, for both our findings and our use of research methodology.

Achievement of Environmental Quality in Flood Control, 1970

In 1970, the U.S. Department of the Army, Office of the Chief of Engineers, in Washington, asked R/C (in a sole-source contract) to examine the environmental considerations and the planning process of a particular flood-control project in the City of Mill Valley, north of San Francisco. R/C was to use this case study as a basis for proposing an approach to planning that could ensure high environmental quality in future flood-control projects. Goldie and I worked on this project and wrote the report.

The specific purpose of the research and fieldwork was to develop a method for the Corps that would respect our living environment. Therefore, the study had a practical goal – to provide a workable tool that could handle quality (the environment) in conjunction with quantity (the control of water flow) as required under the National Environmental Policy Act. The Corps had run into criticism because of their "engineering" approach in alleviating floods. Those were the heady days of hopes for the protection of the environment. In addition, the social climate of the times called for the wishes of the people to be heard and their participation in decision-making sought.

The selected case study area, like others in Marin County, California, was a desirable place to live and had maintained its small-town quality. The unusual circumstances in the Corps' preparation of the survey for channel improvement in the late 1960s seem to have led to the project's selection for our study. The required assurance of local co-operation by the County of Marin in 1965 was "conditional" on the project's being "designed, located, and constructed in a manner which is compatible with the natural environment, and which is calculated to ensure preservation of the aesthetic qualities of the area within which the project is located, subject to approval of local government agencies involved."

There was yet another exceptional circumstance. The community proposed, at the recommendation of the city's engineer, an alternative to the Corps' open-concrete channel in the existing stream bed. All this goes to show that the district engineer, being closer to the local situation and to the community's objectives, was prepared to work towards a project design that would meet the hydraulic requirements of the city and at the same time satisfy the community's environmental concerns. In the end, partly for cost reasons, a concrete-lined riverbed devoid of natural features was constructed, resulting in an outburst of anger that was supported by an eminent landscape architect living in the area. It was implied that our work and report would be for the eyes of the Corps only, allowing us to be frank, candid, and even critical of the Corps – in a polite way. Through reports, interviews, and visual inspections, environmental considerations in the planning of the project, and subsequent discussions with Corps of Engineers officials at all levels (the Office of the Chief of Engineers, Division and District), we gained as broad a perspective as possible on the environmental issues involved. We did obtain divergent and conflicting views which, because of their diversity, were extremely valuable in making our appraisal.

In our appraisal, we stated: "When viewed as a process to achieve both flood protection and environmental objectives, fundamental alterations in the present approach are required. These alterations, in turn, demand a fresh outlook about flood control which is different from the traditional views held by engineers, local officials, and even conservationists and interested citizens. In this respect the study is controversial, and its recommendations counter many long-held views."

We concluded that project formulation for flood control measures in an urban region like the San Francisco area required a two-part work program – one aimed at the regional level and one for the stream valleys. We needed the regional context in order to understand how the streams were functioning at the present time as well as how they were going to function in the future. On the other hand, studies at the stream valley scale would require detailed analysis, adoption of objectives, and project design. We therefore proposed that an area-wide study (Mill Valley Area in our case) should consist of the following:

1. Analysis of the environmental character of the river basin
2. Watercourse analysis
3. Hydrological analysis
4. Identification of natural resource elements
5. Development of a waterways plan

In terms of the work elements for a stream valley study, we concluded that the following should be included:

1. Stream valley analysis
2. Visual scene analysis
3. Development of objectives and standards
4. Assessment of environmental reaction to change
5. Project planning

On the difficult relationship between the Corps and the community, we developed, discussed, and made recommendations towards a seven-step planning and decision-making process. With some overlap, projects should be developed through the following interactive stages:

1. Data gathering and analysis
2. Formulation of a statement of problems and possibility for solution
3. Development of program alternatives
4. Adoption of a final program for the design
5. Conception of alternative designs
6. Selection of a final design on the basis of criteria set forth in the program
7. Execution of the design

Having discussed our final report draft with the Corps and having made amendments, we submitted it. If or how the recommendations were put to use I do not know, but I do know that Robert Gidez, the instigator of the project, was satisfied with the results of our work. And I should say a word about this unusual, intelligent, and pleasant man.

Bob was the assistant chief of planning at the Office of the Chief of Engineers. He was not a military man, unlike most senior Corps officials, and had an academic background of studying and teaching. We – the Rivkins and I – had come across Bob while working at Nathan's on a number of projects dealing with water in one way or another. Bob, as an intellectual, was not interested in pure knowledge. For him all research should lead to practical and useful actions. Wherever he saw a problem in the use or misuse of water, he was keen to find solutions. It seems to me, now, that the Corps and related federal agencies turned to him for advice and help whenever an issue or a problem concerning water needed a solution. And he seems to have been free to embark on research projects of his own choosing.

Bob was a man of few words; he was not one for small talk at all. He was obviously respected within the federal establishment since he appeared everywhere: at the Appalachian Regional Commission, the National Water Commission, and at the Corps' concerns about flood control. I have come to believe that Bob was responsible for our selection in the Water Commission study, and I have no doubt that he decided on seriously injecting environmental considerations into flood control projects. And I believe that it was his position at the Corps of Engineers that permitted him to come to us directly, without going through the usual public bidding process.

Athens, Greece, Late 1960s

For me, this unlikely assignment in the late 1960s did nothing for Athens, though it was a pleasant experience, as I had never been to Greece before. The project also added to my understanding of how countries can manipulate international aid and support agencies. The Organization for Economic Co-operation and Development (OECD) – established in 1961 to help governments improve economic and social conditions, mainly in the European Union countries – deemed that the ancient city of Athens, capital of Greece and a major tourist destination, was suffering from multiple growth problems. During the "Regime of the Colonels" (1967–1974), OECD funded a study by foreign experts to work with Greek government officials to identify the "growth problems" of Athens and to make recommendations. I was included in the group of experts at the suggestion of a Greek colleague at RRNA, Nick Georgulas.

At some point earlier on, some background papers about conditions in Athens had been prepared describing traffic congestion, air pollution affecting the ancient monuments, and other problems. An appointed group of politicians and government officials formed the committee supervising the study. In addition, private Greek professionals were invited occasionally to attend the meetings according to their expertise. For example, Konstantinos Apostolou Doxiadis, author of *Ekistics: An Introduction to the Science of Human*

Settlements, and a former chief town planner of the Greater Athens Area, attended one meeting to give his perspective on Athens's growth problems.

Aside from attending the committee meetings, I spent much of my time with city and government officials asking for detailed information about specific programs and budgets and about the absence of actions concerning known needs. I soon perceived the real problem. But first, a word about my personal difficulties in adapting to working conditions in Athens.

The midday being very hot for most of the year, offices worked in two separate shifts, resulting in four rush hours a day instead of two, which added to the air pollution. The first shift started in the early morning, and after an early light lunch at home, everyone went back to bed. In the late afternoon, around 3:30 or 4:00, everyone went back to the office until 8:00 pm, or later. Dinner, at home or more likely at a restaurant, started late – restaurants did not open until 11:00 pm. I had no option but to do in Athens as the Athens office workers did. It took me about a week to get accustomed to the new routine.

My memory for names had always been poor, to the point that I ceased listening to names at introductions. This had always been a handicap for me in my work. Greek names being long and usually ending in "opulous," I decided to use the opportunity to test myself and see whether this forgetfulness was really laziness on my part or truly an inability to remember names. At large meetings I jotted down the names of all the committee members around the table when everyone was introduced, and looked at their faces as I did so. And when addressing them in the discussions, I always used their names. Miracle, it worked! But, admittedly, in my post-Athens life I went back to my lazy ways.

It did not take us very long to find out what the fundamental and principal problem for Athens was, and what to do about it. The real issue was money – the government was always short of funds. Then, as now, half a century later, the Greek citizens avoid paying taxes. This has always been a popular national game, untouched by all governments in Greece. (All countries, worldwide, are only too familiar today about tax evasion, but the discussion about it didn't take place until major powers ran into seriously high deficits.) The urban growth problems of Athens were well known. If they had to be documented for action and costs, the Greek government had only to hire Doxiadis to spell it out for them; though I suspect the government could not or would not pay his high fees. I thus came to seriously suspect that the government mounted this study in the hopes that this sham of an exercise would persuade the OECD to come up with the cash needed.

To save my conscience, my contribution to the project was to be honest. In discussions and memos, I listed and endorsed the city's rediscovered growth problems and what needed to be done about them, and I added an order of priority. Meanwhile, there was plenty of free time throughout the project for me to visit some of the historic sites outside of Athens, such as the harbour town of Peiraias, the amphitheatre at Parnassos, and the lovely island in the Aegean Sea, Skopelos, which I visited one weekend. On yet another weekend, I visited Istanbul, a city of great historic interest, with places such as the Blue Mosque, Topkapi Palace, and the underground bazaar – though in the latter, much to be annoyed about as well, including the greedy and grasping behaviour of people. The biggest pleasure of my stay in Athens, however, came after the completion of the project, when Ann and Jacki came to visit – Ann from France and Jacki from Amsterdam, where she had been spending the obligatory time within her teenage years to revel in a "free" life and grow up. We had a wonderful time together sightseeing and visiting "my" island, Skopelos. Then we took a train to Vienna to see Dorli, Rene's sister, and her husband, Salo.

Some weeks after my return to Washington, I was visited at RRNA by an official dealing with applications for U.S. citizenship, interviewing me about Nick Georgoulas – no obvious connection with Greece, but you never know. He had clearly talked to many people about Nick already. One of his questions to me was, "Do you think Mr. Georgoulas would make a good citizen?" I replied that I imagined he would but that perhaps I was not the proper person to answer that question since I was not a citizen myself – end of interview.

Lest we chastise only the Greeks for non-payment of taxes (though they may have started the practice earlier), the outcry is now universal. According to the economist Edgar Feige, who has followed the "underground" economy for thirty-five years, in 2013 Americans failed to report $2 trillion to the IRS and, as James Surowiecki writes, "If the government managed to collect taxes on all that income, the deficit would be trivial" ("The Underground Economy," *The New Yorker*, April 29, 2013). Even the IRS estimates losses in the hundreds of billions. Apart from the multinationals who can readily manipulate their receipts from earnings outside the country, the off-the-book activities made in cash hide the incomes of both large and small earners. The same is true in England and other European countries. But I believe, though have no evidence, that tax evasions are neither as extreme nor as common in certain Western democracies, such as the Scandinavian countries, Holland, and Germany.

The practice of tax payment evasion is closely related to political ideology. Where the majority of the electorate believes that "governments waste their tax income" on social programs while entrepreneurs know best what to do with their income, that majority will condone non-payment of income taxes. While that view was held for a long time, with deficits skyrocketing today, it is no longer so easily applied.

Kampung Improvement Program and Our Life in Indonesia, 1980s

Thinking now about our time in Indonesia in the late 1980s, I am at a loss in writing a clear summary, or even in characterizing Rene's and my individual and changing responses to the country and its people. We moved for the most part in different circles, worked in different fields, and met people of diverse backgrounds and occupations. I'll begin with KIP (the Kampung Improvement Program), my role in the project, and how I got involved in it.

A "kampung" is a densely developed urban area of unorganized, self-built housing. The houses are put together with second-hand materials and are usually too small for the large families living in them. Above all, a kampung lacks services: no sanitation, no drainage for the heavy rainfall, unpaved paths, limited or no water supply, no electricity, no street lighting, etc. The KIP, rather than tearing down and completely rebuilding kampungs in the manner of Western "urban renewal," introduces services without moving families from their homes and improves conditions gradually according to agreed-upon priorities and the availability of funds. It is a very flexible program, and there in part lies its management problems.

⌁

The World Bank had been funding KIP in Indonesia for several years. In 1984 the government of Indonesia asked the Bank to double its financial support. The Bank agreed in principle but recommended a countrywide review of KIP's past performance since the program had grown rapidly without any examination. The government readily agreed to the review, since the Bank would pay for it.

It was agreed that the KIP review would consist of a two-year program. In the first year, the different administrations put in place on the islands would be inspected, to record what had been attempted and achieved, and to identify and quantify failures such as delays and cost overruns, and failures in staffing and supervision. The first year's work would conclude with detailed recommendations for the program's future administration, considered to be the guts of the project. In the second year, the changes agreed upon between the Bank and the government would be introduced with the assistance of the study team.

The government selected, from a small number of consulting firms pre-approved by the Bank, a U.S. company to perform the evaluation. Surprisingly, the Bank was satisfied with the proposed work program but did not approve the nominated project director who was formerly on the staff of the World Bank. It seemed that the consulting firm thought they were smart in the selection of their project director, but were not smart enough to find out why he had left the Bank.

My first instinct, when I was offered the project director position, was not to accept it for two reasons: first, I did not know the firm, and in fact had never heard of them; and second, and more important, I had not been involved in the preparation of the study and therefore had no idea who I would be working with. However (and there usually is a "however" when one acts against one's principles and better judgement), the project was exceptionally interesting. Also, I had previously worked in Bandung, the capital of West Java province, a large and pleasant city not far from Jakarta, which made me want to see more of the country. But above all, my decision to take the job was influenced by the fact that Rene was very keen on going to Indonesia because of her interest in the marine life in the islands' waters.

We were fortunate to find an idyllic place to live in the southern part of Jakarta: a single-storey house of modern design set in the middle of a large, slightly sloping and beautifully landscaped garden, which included a lychee tree. The house had an internal courtyard, which served as the dining room next to an open kitchen. Ahead of and under the stone front porch was a narrow moat full of goldfish.

Our house, built by a local family who had moved to a larger house nearby, adjoined a kampung. I had learned by this time that it is quite normal in poor countries for well-off people to live next door to poor people living in dilapidated houses. Upwardly mobile families also prefer to stay near family and friends. No derogatory or taboo feeling is present in this practice, which for wealthier people has the added advantage of finding reliable household help.

The owner of our house, Mrs. Manurung, provided us with a houseboy named Kardi, who was nineteen and handsome like most Indonesian men. He looked after the garden, went shopping with Rene, and, I believe, was told by Mrs. M. to watch over Rene while I was at work. Rene became so interested in the life and people in the kampung that she took walks there almost daily, and would talk with those living in the kampung once she learned the language. Kardi always followed, unseen, to make sure she came to no harm.

There was also a maid, Tari, who cleaned the house daily and delivered messages between Mrs. M. and Rene. Through my work, I was also provided with a car and driver, Kersidi, since expats involved in accidents were faced with exorbitant claims for damages and injuries. Rene and Kardi quickly established a friendly relationship. He was the first Indonesian she got to know well and to start speaking with in Bahasa, the country's language. This was a "first" for Kardi, too, and, after all, it was his duty to help, guard, and protect her. He is frequently mentioned in the first diary Rene started to write in Indonesia. Her observations and comments describe a growing fondness for him, a kind of mother-and-son relationship. She talked with him about his early, and much poorer, life and about what his hopes were for the future. This was from the beginning all part of Rene's increasing interest in the local people in general.

One day Kardi brought Rene a present of a bird in a cage. Indonesians love colourful birds in their homes and there is an exclusive bird market in Jakarta which has a greater variety of tropical birds than you can see in any zoo. Rene thanked Kardi for his gift, but after a couple of weeks she told him that an even greater present for her would be to give the lovely bird its freedom. When they opened the cage, the bird gingerly looked out for a while, and then flew away. It must have been around this time that she made mention in her diary, disapprovingly, of Kardi's "forward" behaviour, of putting his hand on her bare shoulder.

Rene and I started taking private lessons in Bahasa, an artificial language based on Malay. After the third lesson, our teacher politely told me that I was holding back Rene's rapid progress, and she suggested that it would be better for both of us to have separate lessons. I soon stopped taking lessons, claiming that I was too busy – a pity because it would have been very helpful in my work had I persisted.

It was not long before Rene discovered the National Marine Biology Institute, which was unfortunately located on the opposite side of Jakarta, over an hour's drive from our house with Kersidi. She met the head of the Institute, Dr. Kamis Musa, who set her up with a desk and a powerful microscope suitable for viewing tiny Bryozoans, and gave her all the assistance she needed.

Rene tried to go to the Institute once a week for the rest of our stay in Jakarta and wrote up the lab results of her work at home. When members of the Institute went to collect samples along the coast and around the reefs, they often brought back jars with Bryozoans for Rene. On weekends, when we went to beaches and offshore islands near Jakarta, Rene would also collect her own samples.

She mentioned to Dr. Musa her concern about collecting without having obtained a permit. His response: "Don't be ridiculous. It will be best if you pretend to be a tourist combing the beach. Nobody bothers about permits." All these activities kept Rene interested and busy, and sometimes frustrated as well, as is normal in research. However, she managed to write papers and to my knowledge at least one of them was translated and published by the Institute.

As soon as I began work on the KIP project, I realized that the staffing, supervision, and public advisory arrangements were inadequate – to put it mildly – although the full extent of the deficiencies emerged only gradually. The KIP evaluation was different from the regular projects supported by the World Bank, such as the building of a dam or road at one location. This was an evaluation of an established urban improvement program, taking place in many cities and on a number of far-flung islands all over Indonesia. As well, different provincial administrations were competing for the same funding, and the participants in the project in general were numerous: a central government-appointed supervisory committee, local consultants hired to work with us, KIP organizations within the "KIP towns," the exceptional two World Bank offices (in Washington and Jakarta), and us – the selected consulting firm for the project.

These "participants," in fact, did not participate, although collectively we had all the information required for the review of KIP. Included among these non-participants was the firm that I was working with. I state this fact at the beginning of this brief, sorrowful, and admittedly angry, post-project reflection of my experience in Indonesia.

Before getting in touch with the kampung improvement community, I walked around some KIP areas in Jakarta to see the work in progress, noticing different degrees of dilapidations. Having also seen an unimproved kampung near our house, I realized that there is no "standard" kampung and, therefore, no handy way of using a standard or average measure of the cost per acre or per number of houses. That fact makes it very difficult to readily identify overcharging or corruption taking place by contractors, local officials, or both.

In hindsight, I realize that I should have found and used a Dutchman working for the government who could have advised me on local customs and practices. At the time there were still a few Dutch professionals living in the area from colonial times who, for mutual benefit, found a niche in the administration. Before I left the project, while I was doing the rounds to say my goodbyes, I discussed the KIP project with one of the Dutchmen, who said, "Don't worry about the lack of response to your work. Indonesia has a history of picking up advice in time."

To do my job I had to discern (because my firm gave me no guidance and probably did not know) which organizations, offices, and teams were relevant to the KIP evaluation and which I would have to manage, work with, consult, and receive information and take advice from. These were as follows:

1. A supervisory committee consisting of senior government department leaders involved in KIP. I was required to submit

reports to this committee at regularly scheduled meetings, which I expected would be discussed and direction and feedback then provided to us about our work. My expectation was wrong, as became clear at the beginning of the first meeting of the supervisory committee. The report had been circulated in good time with a translation, but I was asked to read the report out loud to the committee, after which the meeting ended without a discussion. Although I had posed a number of important questions in the report, which needed to be addressed, no answers were ever forthcoming.

I was annoyed by the uselessness of the committee meeting and asked a senior government official, whom I had gotten to know, why committee members failed to read the report for discussion, considering they received payment for sitting on the committee. He responded: "Yes, they get paid to come to the meetings, but not to read the reports." The reason for this charade is explained by the fact that the base salaries of senior civil servants were very low. To add to their income, they tried to get appointed to as many committees as they could, resulting in not having enough time to see to even their regular duties, never mind reading committee reports.

This did not, however, apply to the chairman of the committee. He, a Chinese Indonesian, did read reports and occasionally made some pertinent comments to his colleagues. (I discuss working with Chinese Indonesians below.)

2. Local consultants, also called "counterparts," who offer cheaper services and are used in foreign aid projects to, supposedly, assist the foreign consultants and upgrade their skills. On the KIP project, their work was unreliable, caused delays, or not done at all.

3. The KIP units in the field, consisting of the local and provincial staff, plus their work teams. While considered a vital source of information, and expected to furnish the

information needed for testing the success of their work, I felt strongly that they had been told by the government in Jakarta to bamboozle me and give me the impression that everything worked well – that all they need was more money. They entertained me and showed me the sites along with some positive results in improved kampungs, but avoided specific answers.

The entertainment was especially lavish when Rene was with me, but we soon learned to avoid the unnecessary and time-wasting routine and go off on our own: Rene would head to where she had planned to go and mix with the locals, while I, along with my colleagues in Jakarta, would perform unsupervised data gathering, which produced some useful results.

4. The U.S. consulting firm I was working for. Their office provided good secretarial and translating support. Beyond that, however, I was given only one full-time professional: a resident U.S. engineer. The firm gave no further help.

5. The World Bank. Normally, the Bank supervises their projects from Washington by periodically sending "missions" to countries in which they fund projects. At the time, the Bank had an office in Nairobi, Africa, as well as one in Jakarta that looked after some projects in Africa and Asia. Larger projects like the KIP evaluation, however, were still the responsibility of Washington. In any event, none of these Bank offices seemed to be responsible for KIP. Although missions from Washington came to Indonesia, they did not come to us, presumably thinking that the Bank's local office would keep an eye on KIP.

Given this incredulous situation, as I encountered it, I realized that I was pretty much on my own. But the lack of all-round co-operation could not be allowed to delay the project. Having reviewed Jakarta's KIP areas and spoken to those in charge at the various locations, I organized visits to KIP towns in Java (Bogor, Bandung, Semarang, Surabaya, Yogyakara, and others) and Sumatra (Pelembang, Padung, Bukittinggi, Medan, and Banda in Aceh Province). Rene came along on the longer trips, and the more she travelled the more she liked the country and its people, with whom she could now speak.

As I learned more of the local circumstances, I was able to make comparisons and begin to ask searching questions about, for example, different costs, procedures, and management, and to develop a framework and structure for my monthly reports. Nevertheless, searching for ways to overcome the lack of help and co-operation became frustrating.

The chairman of the government committee, as I mentioned, was more capable and willing to do an honest job. He was a Chinese Indonesian, a group of people, incidentally, who are often called the "Jews of Indonesia," because they are ambitious and clever, and have encountered discrimination in the country.

The Chinese Indonesians account for only 3 percent of Indonesia's total population, which translates into about 7 million. They have lived in Java and other islands for more than 600 years – long before Dutch colonization, which divided the population into three categories: Europeans, Foreign Easterners (Chinese, Indians, and Arabs), and Indigenous people, who were all guaranteed political rights. This changed, however, after the 1740 Chinese rebellion, when 10,000 Chinese Indonesians were massacred in Batavia (Jakarta). Following the rebellion, the Dutch denied Chinese Indonesians their political rights and allowed them only to engage in trade or business, much in the same way that Jews were confined to trade in Poland and some other European countries.

After Independence, the political rights of the Chinese Indonesians were once again acknowledged. However, following the failed communist coup in 1965, the Soeharto government revived anti-Chinese attitudes by issuing anti-Chinese laws and regulations. It was not until the fall of Soeharto in 1998 that Chinese Indonesians regained their equal rights. During my time in Indonesia in the 1980s, unofficial discrimination in public service was evident. I came to know that promotion beyond a certain level (the chairman's level) was restricted. And so, it seemed, was the chairman's freedom of action in dealing with serious changes in the future administration of KIP.

My own bias towards the Chinese Indonesians went in the opposite direction, and I approached them whenever I was looking for help in my work or private life. I was never disappointed.

I was always happy when Rene came with me on field trips, and not only because of her company. She made me see what I always saw but did not look at, or take much notice of, because my mind was preoccupied: the beauty of the countryside and, in detail, its plant life. Indonesia stretches for about 3,500 miles from Sumatra to Irian Jaya, in a tropical climate. This vast area is divided almost half way by the Wallace Line. These two regions, or "life" zones, contain mainly fauna (less so in flora) of either Asian or Australian organisms. The line was established in 1859 by Alfred Russell Wallace and named after him, the co-discoverer with Darwin of the theory or fact, according to your persuasion, of evolution. The line runs between Bali and Lombok, two small islands east of Java.

All Indonesian islands are hilly rather than mountainous. There are no really high mountains, and when the term is used, one finds otherwise. For example, the Sumatra town of Bukittinggi (meaning "high mountain") is named for a few mountains that are under 3,000 meters high – about the maximum height of all mountains in the country. The beauty of the landscape lies in the way "nature" and "man" have shaped it. For over hundreds of years the hills were terraced to grow rice. The year-round warm temperature allows constant planting of rice paddies, which provides more than one harvest each year. In turn, each stage in the growing of the rice produces a different colour, from water reflecting the blue sky, to different greens and shades of yellow, creating an ever-changing colourama across the countryside.

We enjoyed our travels together on weekends and on the job, discovering the "look" and the "life" of Indonesia. However, the people Rene and I met and worked with every day were dissimilar; they came from different walks of life, and consequently we developed almost opposing relationships with them. As Rene explains, *"My impression of the Indonesian people is so completely opposed to John's. I see them as Kardi, the best kind, compassionate, intelligent; John sees the system's corruption and incompetence."*

Yet we did enjoy the performances of the country's ancient culture together: concerts and dances with traditional percussion and string instruments performed by players in exquisitely coloured costumes, recitations of old legends in specially designed gowns, or shadow plays behind white sheets (with explanatory notes in English).

Today, reading Rene's diary, I can more fully understand what was happening to both of us at the time. I know that sometimes I was bad company, letting off steam, coming home after a frustrating day at the office, while Rene was increasingly stimulated by Indonesia's common people at the lab and around the home.

At some point, I cannot remember exactly when – it must have been a creeping revelation – I knew that none of my efforts would make any difference towards a better Kampung Improvement Program. However accurate my information, or useful the resulting recommendations, nothing was going to change because no one wanted change. This inevitably led to my decision to leave the project at the end of the first year, not wanting to hang around for the second year of idleness and frustrations. But what about Rene? Her mind was set on another year in paradise.

For the immediate future we had planned an excursion to Krakatoa to see the remains of an island which had mostly disappeared in 1883 when a volcano erupted, killing all of the 3,000 inhabitants and thousands more on adjacent Java and Sumatra, scattering lava dust all around the world. Rene's cousin, who lived in London, was also scheduled for a visit, and the two had planned to look at the temples at Borobudur in Java and, further east, the site where the skull of the "Java Man" was found in the late nineteenth century. We also spent some time with our Australian friends, John and Vera, who I had met on my earlier job in Bandung, where they still lived.

Rene's work on Bryozoans at the lab seemed to produce more results. And while her Indonesian horizons were expanding, I was looking forward to an early end to my work in the country. I started to drop hints to Rene to try and soften the blow, mentioning that I may no longer be needed on the project after the end of the first year.

Before I got very far along with my hints, however, Rene decided on a visit to Montreal, to be with Ann after the birth of Claire, who needed an operation. This meant accelerating the process of preparing Rene for the disappointment to come – it might all be decided by the time of her return. As I read many years later in her diary, she had got the message anyway and returned from Montreal prepared, but crushed, to face the sad end of her charmed life in Indonesia.

While she was away, I wrote a letter to the official in charge of KIP at the World Bank in Washington. This was strictly against protocol; the fiction was that a consultant is employed by the government of the country in which he worked, though paid by the Bank. After acknowledging that it was inappropriate of me to write to him, but indicating that a copy of the letter had been sent to the appropriate minister in Jakarta, I thought he should hear from me directly why I recommend the termination of the KIP evaluation at the end of the first year. My letter described the situation of the actors in the program and their non-performance, including the Bank's odd situation with two offices, both of which failed in their normal supervision.

I was aware that the Bank had no standard procedures for ending a project prematurely, though there never seemed to be a problem in finding funds to extend projects. Nevertheless, I wrote that I felt I had to inform the Bank that I was withdrawing from the KIP evaluation.

I did not receive a direct response to my letter, but a copy of the letter sent to the minister in Jakarta stated, "Your consultant recommends termination of the KIP evaluation project at the end of the first year. May I please have your comment?" I do not know what that comment was.

CHAPTER 6

A Found Year

I had given no serious thought to what we would do after the unplanned end of my work in Jakarta. Our house in Toronto was leased for two years, though we could have found a place to rent. Rene could return to the Royal Ontario Museum (ROM) for work, but I was not sure that was what she wanted to do, and I was right. In her diary, on her return from Montreal, she wrote:

> *I know I do not want to pick up life where I left off.*
> *Though I liked the ROM, I have overstayed my time*
> *and usefulness. I now must find myself something for*
> *which I need to strain with effort. Something where*
> *there is a time deadline. This does not happen inside*
> *the walls of a museum. So much towards Toronto.*

I had no job to return to, but that had never worried me before, being a firm believer in the wisdom of Dickens's Mr. Micawber: "Something always turns up." The decisive consideration turned out to be income tax. At the time we left Canada it was the law that if one stayed outside the country for two years or more, no income tax was payable. I calculated that the income tax savings for not returning were attractive enough for us to take a year off. And considering Rene's unhappiness, almost mental unbalance, I thought that a slow voyage home to Toronto might be of some help for her condition.

With the exception of the time marked by our sorrow over Jacki's fatal accident, my decision to cut our Indonesian stay short created the most agonizing period in our life. I was desperate to find a way to help Rene. Even now, I still turn over in my mind what else I could have done for her then to accept a life away from Indonesia. My pathetic excuse to myself was that it would have been just as difficult for Rene to leave the country after two years.

Of course, I could have anticipated this problem before deciding to send my letter to the Bank, and stayed at my job for a second year. But I cannot imagine what that would have done to our relationship; I would have been more than bad company with tragic results.

Deciding on an itinerary for the very long trip home (both in time and distance) proved to be difficult. Rene could not focus on where to go, and she was not ready to leave anyway. This gave me a clue as to the beginning of the found year. Since we could continue to stay in our lovely place in Jakarta, and since there were lots of islands and specific areas we were looking forward to visiting, Rene readily agreed to do just that for a start. I was all too aware of the fact that this could have the counterproductive result of satisfying her wish of seeing more of the country she loved and wanted to stay in, attaching her even more firmly to it. Never mind, it eased her stress and stopped her from thinking about leaving.

I was vaguely thinking about three destinations and mentioned them to Rene: the chain of small islands to the east of Java; the large island of Sulawesi (Celebes); and one or more islands of the Malukus east of Sulawesi. We could take our time and travel the way we liked best: no fixed timetable. We could select places to stay in that took our fancy and move on when we had seen enough or when someone tells us of a place of interest worth visiting. We could travel by bus, boat, and minor airlines, like Merpati, which have small aircrafts that can touch down on grass landing strips.

But before setting out on the easy part, seeing more of Indonesia, I decided to discuss our longer travel plans with a travel agency to find out how we might stretch our open return tickets: Jakarta to Toronto. This was in the days when airlines allowed some flexibility with open return tickets. I went to a Chinese-Indonesian travel agency and the good lady at the agency looked at the tickets and asked me for a detailed list of places where we wished to stop over, with dates on the way back to Toronto – a wish list. I told her that I would be back shortly, hoping to get some input from Rene or at least agreement on the countries to visit on the way home. I received very limited response from Rene to any of my suggestions and was obliged to guess her preferences.

The itinerary which emerged was as follows: after more trips in Indonesia (which did not affect our return tickets) we would fly to Sydney – India – France – Austria – England – Toronto (and make sure to get back at least a week or two after our tax-free absence). Returning to the travel agency with my "wish list," the good lady arranged flights with the stop-overs without extra charge!

The destinations chosen by me were not arbitrary: at each stop-over there would be a "connection" to Rene's life; quite apart from sparking new interests. My thought was to try and lead Rene out of her attachment to Indonesia back to "connections" in her previous life. To anticipate, I believe it helped.

And so we set off on our final flings to Indonesia's missed attractions: Bali and the small islands to the east, Sulawesi, and the Moluccas.

⁓

Landing at Danpasar, the tourist trap on Bali largely taken over by Australians, we quickly moved north to Ubud, an exclusive artist village of absorbing interest: painters, carvers, and sculptors. My memory of our days on Bali is one of a spellbound mix of beauty, of graceful processions of women in beautiful costumes on walks to the temple in the early mornings through the gentle countryside, and of spending nights looking at the moon from the porches of simple huts, with showers open to nature – trees, flowering bushes, and tall grasses. You could not be farther away from the rest of the world. We were able to relax completely for the first time in weeks, or maybe months.

From Bali we took a ferry to the east across to Lombok and more important scientifically, across the Wallace Line, so named after Alfred Russel Wallace, the co-discoverer with Darwin of the theory of evolution. The significance of the Line is that it separates the Australian and Southeast Asian fauna. Not that you can see the difference at this imaginary boundary between the species but to Rene, the biologist, it was important to have been there. In any case, Lombok and the next island to the east, Sumbava, were pleasant especially for their shops selling traditional artifacts.

Relaxed and after a few days back in Jakarta, we set off on the much longer and eventful second trip to Sulawesi (Celebes) of over 500 miles by buses from Ujung Pandang in the south to Manado in the north provides enough material for a very long essay. I will just mention three highlights: Toraja and its people; a long trip by bus to Lake Tempe and on to Manado; and snorkeling in the Celebes Sea at Manado.

The more than one million Toraja people with their own history and culture live in unique wooden houses, built on wooden piles and covered in split bamboo. The window openings of the houses have carved solid windows. When we visited, one of those houses was being demolished and I bought one of the carved windows which I mounted as a decoration at Curry's Rest.

The longest trip from central Sulawesi near Toraja to Lake Tempe took from early morning to well after midnight, for the most part in heavy rain in an overcrowded bus. Rene and I shared the front bench with the driver. The windshield wiper only functioned when Rene pressed two wires between her fingers. The unpaved dirt road turned to mud and near the highest part of the road a number of buses, including ours, got completely entangled in deep mud. Now, here is the thing: the six or more bus drivers reviewed their situation and calmly, slowly organized in heavy rain and mud the separation and dispatch one bus after another until they all reached a more passable stretch of road to Lake Tempe in pitch darkness, where our driver took us to the only place with a room for the night. No light inside, we lay down "on the bed": a door laid out as the bedframe with a thin mattress on top. Being very tired, we went to sleep quickly.

At first daylight Rene found her soap and walked along the sandy beach of the lake away from the little village, stripped, thoroughly washed herself, and had a long swim in the clear lake. We found a place to get breakfast. People were very friendly, talking with Rene and telling her about previous visitors from Europe and America.

Refreshed and strong we boarded a sizable boat to the north end of the perhaps 40-mile long lake at Tentena. All passengers crowded inside the boat. I went on the roof, lay in the sun, looked at the big lake and surrounding land, and went to sleep. From Tentena, we took buses for the 250 mile journey to Manado, today reputed to be one of the best places for scuba diving and snorkeling in the world. A motor boat took us the next morning to a spot close to the town where we could wade in just five feet of water and snorkel to watch the teeming fish life. When I saw a large, three-foot-long fish I called out to Rene asking her what kind of fish it was. She swum over to have a look at it, and almost shouted: get away from it, it is extremely poisonous! – saved by the expert.

For the last place of our last trip in Indonesia we flew from Manado to Ternate Island in the Moluccas, famous for its spices, especially clove. The little town on the island is charming and in the centre of the island sits its presently calm volcano, tall and steep. The oldest and biggest clove tree grows "some way up" this steep mountain. Rene had to see it and a guide was glad to show her. I joined the expedition, but after a short time I gave up, exhausted (having by this time seen lots of clove trees), while Rene carried on, determined to see "the big one," and she took a photo to prove it.

And that was literally the "high point" and The End of Rene's Indonesian saga.

We began our first leg home to Australia and New Zealand by flying into Sydney. The connection: A few of Rene's professional friends, mainly from the ROM, but also from Vancouver, were at that time at the Australian Research Station on Heron Island in the Great Barrier Reef.

We were welcomed by a change of atmosphere and life. Sydney is a wonderful city, both in terms of its scenery and its "matey" people (cordial but not very sociable). The city is located on a bay, which is "almost like a large lake." We saw the sights: the Opera House, museums, and different districts of the city for a few days. Then on to Brisbane, mainly to pick up a Toyota van which readily converted from daytime use to nighttime use. Brisbane, located on the sea, is another bustling place, warm year-round. But time was short as we had to be in Gladstone, another 280 miles further north along the coast, for Rene to take the launch to Heron Island where she would be with her friends for a week.

I drove inland from Gladstone to the Blackdown Table National Park. On the way, I came across an abandoned precious-stone quarry (I believe mainly opals), but upon climbing in found no gems.

The large national park was well laid out and well equipped. In addition, nearby were a couple of small caves with ancient wall paintings, much like the Paleolithic cave paintings at the Lascaux Caves in southwestern France.

In the mornings when I got out of the van I was greeted by wallabies (they are smaller than kangaroos), waiting to share my breakfast.

On one day I had to drive back to Gladstone to take a driving test because my international driving license was about to expire.

In the meantime, Rene recorded her experience on Heron Island: *"I experienced the beauty of Heron Island, the research station, the laboratory, the museum and snorkeled ... I experienced the beauty of the world and freed myself of the need to score with people around me – just happy to rest, to look, to understand. Why was I born under a lucky star?"* She went also in a submarine among the coral reef ... *"It was a fantastic experience."*

Altogether a good rest, mental recovery, and reaquaintance with her friends.

We met on the dock on her return to Gladstone and started "park hopping" back to Sydney – Australia is well provided with national and provincial parks in the Outback.

After some more time in Sydney, we flew to Wellington on New Zealand's North Island. It is the capital of another country with different people: less "matey," more sociable and communicative – and don't ever take a New Zealander for an Australian. Most remarkable of all was New Zealand's South Island's landscape, which possesses all the land formations found in all of Europe – meadows and mountains, glaciers and fjords – but is only about 500 miles long and 130 miles across.

We spent less time on the North Island, though my strongest memory of it is a visit to the Maori Peoples Museum in Wellington.

When we wanted to take the boat from Wellington to the South Island, the sailors were on strike, so we had to fly, thereby having to leave behind our van and renting a car on the South Island, where we spent nights mostly in public stop-overs: simple huts with limited facilities or in small hotels. We drove around the entire island, which gave us lasting memories, especially of the fjords in the south of the island.

India

Our next major stop-over was India, where we stayed for two months.

Multiple connections: In England after the end of the war the interest in India increased considerably, politically and spiritually. Politically because of India's demands for independence; and spiritually because of the discovery of and curiosity towards yoga and meditation, which seemed to be of special interest to college students. The well-to-do youngsters even went to India and spent time at yoga and meditation retreats in the mountains or at residential schools – Ashrams – in Maharashtra. The "movement" was in the air.

Then there was Rene's friendship with the Indian student at the Chelsea Poly ... So I suspected that she was interested to visit India, which was confirmed in her diary, *"... which had been my desire since the 1940s."*

Though knowing that it was a good idea, it did not prevent my anxiety because I knew the country, did not have good experiences there, and disliked the disregard for the poverty of the majority of its people. However, apart from Delhi, I chose places of historic and architectural interest or of known, exceptional beauty: Rajasthan, Kashmir, and Ladakh, though the last two are not really a part of India proper – Kashmir wishing to be independent and Ladakh being totally Tibetan.

In Delhi I took Rene first to the places I knew, like the impressive British Colonial Government buildings designed by Sir Edwin Lutjens, which now serve the Indian Government. We then explored other sites, like the very old and large Red Fort, which used to be the residence of Mughal emperors. Of more interest was the Gandhi memorial building in which Gandhi's life is fully documented, and to which we would pay another visit when passing through Delhi later.

Rene was much bothered by the crushing crowds, freely wandering cows, and the dirt. So I arranged for a car and driver to take us on the long journey to Rajasthan, which took fifteen days.

On the way there, we, of course, had to stop and admire the one sight every foreigner and Indian visitor goes to see: the Taj Mahal, the white marble mausoleum with reflecting pool at Agra – very spectacular. Then to the west to Rajasthan, the "Land of Kings" in the desert, bordered to the west by Pakistan.

Apart from a land of forts and palaces, we also found a bird sanctuary with egrets, herons, whistling teal, kingfishers, storks, cormorants, ibises ... Rene was excited by the palaces and tightly built towns with narrow streets, and she filled her daily diary, as she did throughout our India trip, recording almost everything.

An amusing spectacle for us to watch was a group of upper-class Western travellers: riding on camels and "doing Rajasthan the native way" – almost, because they were accompanied by a small army of servants bringing along tents, beds, tables and chairs, and lots of food and drinks. Which reminds me, and I will digress: our big problem, as we found out progressively, was the Indian food. We did not have a stomach for Indian food over those two months. We began to eat less and less, and started losing weight and strength, and I was frequently ill, making me poor company. We did not yet notice this in Rajasthan but towards the end of the trip in Kashmir and Ladakh, others appeared to notice. For example, when driving towards an all-female monastery in Ladakh, we were stopped by an Indian Army major who checked our passports because the area close to the Chinese border is in dispute between the two countries. He looked at my passport and then at my face and said, "It does not look like you." When I replied, "Well, that's what travelling in India does to you," he chuckled and waved us on. Finally, when later on our homeward journey we came to Vienna, Rene's sister, Dorly, berated me severely for not looking after her sister properly because she was so skinny.

Our hotels in Rajasthan varied from palatial to scruffy, sometimes or mostly due to our driver, who tried to put us up at places where he would get a commission. We were on the go every day. To give some impressions of Rajasthan and of Delhi, to which we returned in order to go to Kashmir, let me select a random group of sketches from Rene's diary.

> *Haipur – I am sitting in our suite in the Karfika House hotel which was once upon a time the moghul's palace. It must have been beautiful but now it is completely neglected, like most places we've seen before in India, carpets full of stains, furniture sticks with chipped paint, floors not washed in years ... garden huge, lovely and walked to shrine of silhouette of the filigree of leaves and twigs, the peacocks as they headed down in the uppermost lavenders against the pale orange sky. There was the calling of an Imam – not a tape, and chanting to the sound of a string instrument ... Ringed doves, blue and buff birds, the cranes and the most beautiful brown birds with two shades of bright turquoise.*
>
> *Udaipur – We reached Udaipur at the shore of a very large lake. A city with a botanical garden where I sank in the mud, a place with beautiful stone sculptures,*

mostly marble. The windows are intricately carved grills with coloured glass. There are pools and gorgeous chambers where at one time swings were suspended from the ceilings. In the palace are paintings, balconies with vistas of the lake and surrounding mountains. We took a short boat ride, walked in two more lovely gardens ... we watched artisans at work painting local scenes. We ate a substantial good meal and are now resting in a clean hotel.

Ranakpur – Jain temple built in 15th century. Returned to palace to take photos. What a desolate journey. The road led from semi-desert to full desert, not sand desert but stone and mud. The people live in straw though probably there are mud walls beneath the straw cover. Others live in rectangular stone houses which blend completely into the landscape from which the building material is taken. There is patchy agriculture in the valleys where the now dry stream beds may fill with water during the monsoon season ... It is an unusual place in many respects. A Muslim temple underground, a Hindu temple above ground. Built in the 14th century, it contains 144 columns not 2 of them alike, intricately carved marble ... Soft haired monkeys acted as guards outside.

Started for Jaisalmer early in the morning. The road straight as a ruler. Few trees, shrubs with prickly thorns. The layers of orange soil deep with ripple marks. Camels run loose, settlements are rare, fewer people along the road run old cement covered water ducts. People live in low mud houses with straw thatch, often tents. We meet more and more army trucks. Some bring the daily water supply to the women waiting by the roadside. After 6 hours we saw the fort on a flat topped hill. Booked into a lovely hotel at entrance road to citadel – so clean that tables of mock marble are wiped without special request. Visit citadel within enclosed confines is the 13th century City. People still live in the houses with the delicate stone carvings ... After dinner a group of musicians appeared in the courtyard. They were engaged by a diamond merchant from Bombay who had brought his wife to this desert town on the Pakistan border for tomorrow's festival. The musicians dressed in colourful garments, played drums, sitars, flutes and various old instruments I had seen in the Jodhpur museum, including a dulcimer ...

Sariska – Visited Sariska Wildlife Reserve, halfway to Delhi ... We met a young English couple, Brian and Allison, and had the longest chat about good old England. At dusk we got the first glimpse of wildlife. Saw many peacocks, gambler deer, spotted deer, wild boar families and blue Nilgai; the latter was kneeling at the waterhole, drinking.

Back in Delhi – We made our travel arrangements for the trip to Kashmir, buying railway tickets and an India guide book, then onto the Gandhi memorial. The place is near the river and the burial site lies in a huge, well-tended ground. The grave is a black slab of marble and an eternal light in a bronze lamp. Worshippers place flowers on the grave. There is a raised walkway from which there is a good bird's-eye view of the tomb. It's in excellent taste in its simplicity, much visited as a national shrine. We crossed over to the Gandhi memorial museum. The documentation of his life and work brought back memories of the days when his history took place as much of it occurred during our adult life. I liked best three sculptures of Gandhi, one bronze, one white marble and one black marble, the latter was created by a S. African and shows only one arm, one leg and half face, but it's the most impressive of the three.

Kashmir and Ladakh

Our expedition from Delhi to Kashmir and Ladakh consisted of: Delhi to Jammu (Kashmir) by overnight rail-sleeper); Jammu to Srinagar (over 100 miles) by bus; and Srinagar to Leh (Ladakh, and adjoining China and Tibet) by plane.

In the early morning before arriving in Jammu we got our first sight of the Himalayan mountain chain above Kashmir's green meadows and river valleys. Rene wrote:

We are installed in a filthy hotel. Jammu is a fascinating city. There is much life, many stores, the streets full of people. I saw another naked man lying in the dust on the sidewalk, like yesterday ... there are many shops ... Food is prepared in the usual ways but in some places they have large tile stoves, like in Russia, one which one can sleep. Furs and woolens are sold everywhere, John bought a nice green length of wool which we use as a blanket at present ... We moved across to the Tourist Bungalow, located in a beautiful house ... I am fascinated by the bubbly activity of this place ... we went to buy the bus tickets for tomorrow's ten hour bus trip to Srinagar ... The trip turned out so interesting that it seemed almost too short ... Soon after we left Jammu the snow-capped peaks appeared ... And the chain got closer and closer until we felt we could reach it. We crossed mountains and passes, the highest pass was Patnitap at 2024 m.

> *The road gave the best opportunity for bird's eye views into the deep gorges of the narrow valleys ... Shops along the roadside open. There are terraces and padis and all the glacial features I had learned about in my geology lessons ... When we finally got to Srinagar, we found a great business centre with wooden houses and "bakshish" hunters ...*

We spent four days in Srinagar, which is quite a large town located on a lake on which houseboats offer accommodation for nights. We looked at a silk weaving factory with machines from France and Germany ... *We went to Palagam on much higher ground and closer to the glaciers for a few days ... As I am sitting in front of a wood fire in our room at Aksa Lodge* (in mid-April) *I see in the garden a patch of snow and from the window I see steep slopes covered in snow ... Though but four days ago, the buds of many trees had not yet opened, now the whole valley is a carpet of gold with mustard blossoms; this with the glacier-covered Himalayan chain as a back drop ... Back in Srinagar and tomorrow we fly to Leh in Ladakh. There is a road from Srinagar to Leh, but it is still covered in snow.*

We find a room in a guest house. Due to the elevation, we had been warned to take a complete rest for at least one day to get acclimatised. We found this to be good advice. Two young foreigners, who were on our plane, went hiking right away and were in bed for the next few days.

We spent five days in Leh and surrounding area, with trips to smaller settlements outside Leh – it was a unique experience, literally "out of this world." We tried to understand how the Tibetans manage to survive in this climate with a very short growing season, and yet they are a happy, gentle people, content to live their traditional life.

We visited a number of monasteries, were permitted to observe their prayers and offered tea with yak butter, which Rene claimed she liked to drink, all in sight of the Himalaya range – and we watched a wedding in the open with music, dancing, prayers and games lasting from early afternoon to beyond our bed time.

Flying with the view of the Himalaya glaciers much of the way to Chandigarh, where we hoped to stay for a few hours and look at Le Corbusier's Capital Complex – legislature, court house, etc. – we were not allowed to leave the plane for some undisclosed reason and flew on to Shimla, the summer capital of British India – now a hub for India's tourism sector. We spent a day pretending to be tourists, had good food and rest. Then to Delhi – the end of India for us – and off to Europe.

The last part of our journey home, in Europe visiting family and friends, was an anticlimax. However pleasant it was to see each other again after two years – I might almost say that we had become strangers. Rene, after Indonesia and her most recent experiences in India could not comfortably relate to relatives and old friends. And I was really becoming impatient to get back home and re-start work.

⟲

CHAPTER 7

Two Heroes

William Holford and Robert Nathan were the two heroes in my life for two reasons:

1. From our first meetings and throughout our extended relationships they showed interest in me and treated me as if I were an equal, despite the fact that they knew little about me and were at the top of their professions and extremely busy men.
2. They taught me most of what I needed to learn in the sphere of my work: urban planning and economic analysis.

William Holford (Prof)

We met for the first time in 1951, as I mentioned in chapter 4, before the Royal Commission on the Qualification of Planners cleared the way for social science graduates to enter the planning course. At the time, I was trying to register into the town planning course at University College, London, where he was the head of the department. Everyone called him "Prof," and he remained "Prof" after we graduated, and even after he became "Sir William," and later "Lord Holford." I resubmitted my application for the two-year evening course with a surprising result: the department's secretary

144

called to tell me that Prof said I might be able to do the course in one year, and that I should come and see him. Prof arranged for me to attend some first-year urban design courses while in the second-year program, which I could complete in one year. This clearly showed how Prof took a personal interest in every student.

Prof was born in South Africa, was educated in Cape Town, and studied architecture from 1925 to 1930 at the University of Liverpool. He began lecturing at the university and eventually became Professor of Civic Design there, succeeding Patrick Abercrombie, the author of the Greater London Plan. In 1948 he again succeeded Abercrombie as Professor of Town Planning at University College, London. Most important to us students, Prof was the principal author of the British Town and Country Planning Act of 1947, the first and foundational planning legislation in Britain, and was a practising professional. He, like his students, would come to the lectures after a day at his architecture and planning office, where he worked on projects in England and abroad.

Prof was the most inspiring and motivational teacher I ever had because he never ceased to learn from his ongoing work. I remember him discussing the traffic problems in Piccadilly Circus, which he had been asked by the government to help with, and saying "every large city deserves a glory hole." (His recommendations for a raised pedestrian piazza above the traffic were not accepted because his scheme did not allow for sufficient traffic increase, and the government was more concerned with vehicular traffic than pedestrian safety.)

Prof enjoyed discussing the many planning issues of the day and usually sat on the table in front of the class without watching the clock, continuing the discussion beyond quitting time. On several occasions, his wife Marjorie Brooks, a mural painter, would wander into the classroom to take him home for dinner.

From time to time, Prof's office would organize meetings with past and present students, for us to meet and keep in touch and for him to follow how we were getting on professionally. Whenever I applied for a better job, I used Prof as a reference and let him know about it, with the exception of one time when I forgot: when I applied for the Toronto job. As we assembled for another meeting Prof came up to me saying, "John, you are applying for positions all over the world." He was not concerned about my failing to tell him about it beforehand, but as it happened, he had just returned from Toronto where he sat on the panel selecting the winning design for the city-hall twin towers. Prof's old friend Hans Blumenfeld, who was deputy at the Metro Planning Board, asked him about me. Prof told me: "They are very interested in you." The very next morning the fateful letter arrived offering me the job I had applied for. His recommendation advanced my career, but at the same time, it meant that I would never see him again and talk about planning issues in London and elsewhere.

Prof died in London in 1975 at the age of sixty-eight, loaded with distinctions and remembered by his many friends.

Robert Nathan (Bob)

I already mentioned how I came to join the large and prestigious economic consulting firm Robert R. Nathan Associates in Washington. Malcolm Rivkin, who recruited me when he came to Boston, gave me a general rundown of the firm; but he left me totally unprepared for the towering personality of Robert Nathan, the founder and president of the firm. Like my Harvard friend, he probably assumed that I must have known about Bob, which is what everyone called him.

a. Robert Nathan, the man:

Three Steps from the Ivory Tower

The establishment of Bob's firm (RRNA – Robert R. Nathan Associates) was a slow and shaky affair, due to his other commitments, mainly his work with Americans for Democratic Action (ADA), as Kenneth Durr describes in his book, *The Best Made Plans: Robert R. Nathan and Twentieth-Century Liberalism*.

> Just ten years earlier Nathan had been prepared to shut the firm down entirely, but by the late 1950s, he was committed – at least in principle – to making this unconventional business a success. In 1960 Nathan produced a marketing brochure that explained what was so different about it. *Three Steps from the Ivory Tower* compared the trajectory of economic consulting with Nathan's own career. The first step was into the government, the second was industrial mobilization for war, and the third step came when economists went to work on a consulting basis. (p. 132)

The Nathan Associates Inc. website (http://www.nathaninc. com/company/history) elaborates on "The Three Steps":

> In founding one of the world's first economic consulting firms, Robert Nathan took what he called the "three steps" from the ivory tower of academic economics.
>
> He took the first step when he surveyed the unemployed during the Great Depression for one of his professors at Wharton. Of that experience, he said "Once I saw how the widening depression ground into the dust ... lives and enterprises as though they were cigarette butts, I could no longer continue to distance myself from damaging problems and policies."
>
> He took the second step as deputy director of the Office of War Mobilization and Reconversion

(OWMR) and chairman of the Planning Committee of the War Production Board. Drawing on that experience in Mobilizing for Abundance (1943), he reasoned that the same economic principles applied to achieve wartime victory could be applied to get the peacetime economy rolling again. Economists, he believed, could be effective in all spheres, from postwar recovery at home to advising developing countries.

He then took the third step in January 1946 when he established Robert R. Nathan Associates, Inc., within walking distance of the White House.

b. Robert R. Nathan, the firm RRNA, now Nathan Associates Inc.:

Under the heading "Leading Economic Development and Regulatory Analysis: 1960s and 1970s," the website includes the following history:

By the 1960s, the firm had emerged as a leader in developing master plans for economic growth, sometimes spending years in a country. In Afghanistan, from 1961 to 1976, the firm helped the Ministry of Planning evaluate economic and social development plans ... In Malaysia from 1976 to 1981, Nathan Associates advised on a scheme to resettle 500,000 people in new and expanded urban areas.

By the mid to late 1970s, the firm consulted in most sectors of the U.S. economy – estimating the local economic impact of the Green Bay Packers, conducting major studies on deep-water ports for the U.S. Army Corp of Engineers, designing use surveys for ASCAP to ensure fair distribution of license fees to songwriters and music publishers, and representing corporate clients before regulatory agencies. The firm also began shaping landmark antitrust cases ...

In 1978, when John Beyer became president of the firm, the firm's work was evenly divided between domestic and international work and about half of the firm's employees were working in 35 countries.

I should mention that Bob had also studied law at Georgetown University, receiving an LL.B. in 1938, in addition to his studies at the Wharton School of the University of Pennsylvania, and that during the war he successfully introduced one of Roosevelt's proposals: the Wage and Price Control, which was designed to prevent inflation. After the war, Bob served for two years (1957–59) as National Chairman of Americans for Democratic Action (ADA), a liberal advocacy group founded by Eleanor Roosevelt.

The RRNA was managed, in my time, by Bob and five or six other partners. Each project came under the direction of a partner, according to experience and availability, although there was collaboration on larger and more complex projects. I came to the attention of Bob, I believe, because my early and successful work for the firm in Nigeria was under Ed Hollander, the partner closest to Bob. Because I was seen, I think, to be capable of searching for and evaluating information under difficult circumstances, Bob started calling on me for assistance.

To work for and with Bob was a pleasure. He had a quick and penetrating mind. He loved to attack your conclusions to see whether they could pass scrutiny. He cross-examined you, like the lawyer he was, on your findings, to be sure you produced the proper results. If you stood up to him, he was happy and respected you for doing so. I had never worked with such a brilliant mind before – nor have I since. Some of the staff members were scared of Bob's aggressive examinations, not realizing that his approach was not personal, but a way to find the truth.

Occasionally, Bob went to Congress for presentations to Senate and House committees on national economic issues affecting current legislation. It became customary for Bob, on his return from the Hill, to give anyone interested a brief account of his views on the congressmen's lack of understanding of the country's problems – in a conference room and usually punctuated by colourful invective that I cannot repeat here.

As a result of our good working relationship, both Bob and Ed Hollander made me project manager of some jobs, and I became a regular RRNA associate – in the role of an economist, since Malcolm's expectations to bring urban planning to the office were not realized.

We, Bob and I, did not lose touch after I left the firm. As mentioned before, he invited me to stand in for an otherwise engaged staff member in the Trinidad project. And from time to time we exchanged updates on personal events – he was even interested in and encouraged me to make Dominica retirement plans.

Bob died in September 2001. To honour him and to ensure that his legacy endured, Nathan Associates Inc. established the Robert R. Nathan Memorial Fellowship in applied economics at Bob's alma mater, the Wharton School of the University of Pennsylvania.

CHAPTER 8

Curry's Rest And Dominica

Our decision to retire to Dominica, a Caribbean island located between Guadeloupe and Martinique, was influenced by several factors: the natural beauty of the island, the Curry's Rest site at 900 feet above the Caribbean Sea with its large variety of tropical fruit growth, the potential of restoring an eighteenth-century sugar-estate house, and the possibility of repairing an old sugar mill. But I think the strongest incentive was my vision of living in the old building, restored to its original design on the outside and adapted to modern living on the inside.

Over the years, we gradually focussed our attention more on Curry's Rest than on Dominica as a whole, which is why the heading of this chapter implies a distinction between our new home and Dominica, the island and country.

Finding Curry's Rest

But first, how did we find and manage to buy Curry's Rest, where we lived for twenty years? When our thoughts turned to retirement, Rene and I agreed that it would have to be somewhere warm. We had visited several Caribbean islands on holidays, and I had done some work in Trinidad and the Bahamas. What we had seen on these trips, we thought, was either nice just for a holiday or too expensive to settle. At the time, a real estate company specializing in the Caribbean published monthly reports by subscription for a small annual fee. Each month, a report would focus on one island – describing its population, landscape, towns, sights, etc. After a year of reading through reports, we picked two islands which seemed "right for us": Dominica and Montserrat.

We booked flights for a three-week trip at the end of 1988, allowing for half the time to be spent on each island. For the first few days in Dominica, we drove around the island, staying overnight at guest houses. We liked the island from the day we arrived, though the roads were narrow and hazardous, and like in England, we drove on the left side.

Returning to the capital, Roseau, we settled in a little downtown hotel to see if we could find "a nice place to buy." Unfortunately, there were no real estate agencies in Dominica. The phone book listed one surveyor who, I thought, might know about houses and land for sale: Mr. Karol Winski, originally from Poland. We went to see him and found ourselves having to listen to his life story for half an hour. He was ninety, had fought for Poland in three wars, had received an MBE from the Queen of England, and more.

When we were finally permitted to tell him why we had come to see him, Winski indeed knew of a Mr. Green who wanted to sell a place called Curry's Rest. He showed us his "survey map" of the property, with undetermined boundaries. The total acreage varied from 400 acres to 270 acres to 100 acres. Our interest in the building led to a description of an "estate building," which was set within fifteen acres of cultivated land, and to details of the mill pond, the sugar mill, the boiling house, and the aqueduct.

We were also shown sketch plans for retirement lots covering much of the property. When I questioned the subdivision plans, mentioning what I had learned about the government's policy of not allowing foreigners to engage in land speculation, he replied, "Oh, don't worry about that."

Curry's Rest's Rescue

The next morning, Mr. W. along with three other men drove us from Mahaut, the village at the bottom of a donkey track leading to Curry's Rest, in a Land Rover, the only vehicle that might negotiate (barely) the track, across three rock-strewn river crossings. It took over half an hour to bounce along the (perhaps a bit more than) half-a-mile track to Curry's Rest, 900 feet above the village.

The main building, built with solid stones, did not look too bad except for the corrugated iron roof. But the inside was a dismal sight. Fortunately, Mr. Green, who intended at one time to live in the house, had two men living at Curry's Rest: Mr. Rudolph Georges, a farmer in his early nineties, looked after the cultivated land around the house; and Claude, a highly skilled old-fashioned carpenter, was there to maintain the building. And, of course, both of them were there to prevent people from helping themselves to building materials and wrecking the building, as had happened to most old buildings on the island.

Mr. Georges and Claude slept in a corner of the main floor of the house and cooked in the open. A water standpipe outside was fed by a spring up in the hills. A pit latrine in the bush provided sanitation. Goats and chickens wandered freely, even on the porch and inside the house. There was also a piggery on the way to the mill. The land around the house, said to be fifteen acres, was a more cheerful sight: bananas, mangoes, coconuts, grapefruit, cocoa, coffee, breadfruit, pimento (not that I knew what that was at the time), and ginger; and beyond that was a dense forest of tall trees suitable for restoration work.

I returned to the house and looked at the main floor, attic, and basement to filter through in my mind the squalor and decay and to imagine the hidden beauty of it all, which with skillful and hard work could make Curry's Rest not just liveable, but as Rene called it years later, a little paradise.

Can We Purchase Curry's Rest?

We decided that we would like to buy the place, considering the laws and our means. For non-Dominicans to buy land in Dominica requires an Alien Landholding License, which, if you want to buy say one acre of land, is not difficult to obtain. In our case, however, the amount of land (though not exactly known yet) was substantial. We made an appointment with Winski for the next day, by which time I had prepared a proposal for the government (borrowing a typewriter in an office).

Our proposal for the government's consideration included the following: the purchase of the property as aliens, and not as an alien company; and the purchase of fifteen acres of land, including the house and the cultivated land, plus three adjoining acres, which included the mill pond, sugar mill, and boiling house, to be held by us. The balance of the land would pass to the government for use as a nature reserve. We also proposed to restore the sugar mill and boiling house to a working condition and to build an interpretive centre explaining the sugar production process in the old days to school children and other visitors.

At this point, before going ahead with purchasing Curry's Rest, I perhaps should have paused and considered what was going to be involved: dealing with government officials and local workmen and finding suitable material in Dominica, all in addition to the work which I knew was going to be hard. I confess that I never gave it a thought because I was sure I could handle it, having worked in the Caribbean and African countries before. To address the transfer of the majority of the land to the "the country and people of Dominica," I used the traditional legal words for donating land: "to sell for

EC (East Caribbean) $1:00." The use of the word "sell" got me into considerable trouble in time to come because the government lawyers were not familiar with my usage of the term.

Mr. Winski, when we gave him our proposal in January 1989, thought we were crazy, perhaps just stupid, or both, but took it to the proper government office anyway. The same afternoon he informed us that the proposal had been favourably received. Then I made a major mistake: I failed to engage a lawyer to look after our interests in our absence and to work with Winski. We were booked to go on to Montserrat and I knew no lawyer – a lame excuse. Yet this failure almost lost us Curry's Rest.

A Look at Montserrat

Montserrat is a very different island from Dominica. It is less than a third in size, though hilly, has no mountains or rainforest, and overall is not as beautiful as Dominica, though it has fine beaches. Foreigners wanting to live there were permitted to settle in a small ghetto in the northwest corner of the island, where wealthy British, Americans, and Canadians had built expensive modern houses on small lots. They swam on the beach, played bridge, had parties, and got together at sundown for cocktails.

We had contacted a couple who advertised their house in the Toronto *Globe and Mail*. It was lovely, with a separate office and a garden that was beautifully landscaped – all ready to move in. Doctors had ordered the husband to return to the U.S. to be closer to good medical services. The place was very attractive, but life there would have been dull.

On one of our walks in the south of the island, we saw some disused windmill stone towers and spoke to an old man who seemed to be the caretaker of the place. We had seen, on another Caribbean island, a windmill tower that had been converted into a multistorey house that looked quite attractive. The old man encouraged us to buy one or more of the towers. When we checked with a real estate office in Plymouth, the capital, they confirmed that as foreigners we would never be permitted to buy anything in that part of the country. Just as well, because six years later, a powerful eruption destroyed most of Montserrat. The expat colony was completely buried under volcanic debris, and so was much of the capital.

After our return to Toronto, I exchanged several messages with Winski, who assured me that he was in touch with the government and with Mr. Green, the owner of the land. In March 1990, I went for four months to West Timor, Indonesia.

Hassles, Delays, Aggravations

Finding Curry's Rest was relatively easy, but to become the owners was anything but simple. Although there was a willing buyer and a seemingly willing seller, it took seventeen months from the day we decided to buy the site for the sale to be settled.

On my return to Toronto from Indonesia in July 1990, I checked with Winski's office about how our purchase was progressing and was told that Mr. Wisnki was in London getting married (at age ninety) to a school girlfriend of his, and that they thought that Curry's Rest had been sold. I went post-haste to Dominica. My first stop was at the Papillote Wilderness Retreat near Trafalgar Falls to talk to Anne Gray (originally from New York), the co-owner of this very successful nature hotel whom I had met before, and ask her about a lawyer. She helpfully gave me the name of "the lawyer I always use." Going straightaway to him, I told him my story of our pending purchase of Curry's Rest, gave him a copy of our proposal to the government from six months earlier, and told him that I had just been informed by Winski's office that the property had been sold. He appeared to be a well-connected lawyer. He called the permanent secretary of the Ministry of Land, Trade and Tourism and learned that the government was considering two applications for an Alien

Landholding License for the Curry's Rest land and that the property had not been sold yet.

We went to see the permanent secretary and on the following day were received by the minister, who confirmed that two applications had been received – one from two U.S. citizens, who I noticed, used details from our proposal, and one from a British couple; but no decision had been made yet by cabinet. Our lawyer explained our prior claim and handed the minister a copy of our dated proposal given to Winski for submission months ago.

The next ten days were a whirlwind of activity for me, the most important being that I had to produce documents for our landholding license application, such as references and health records – something that Winski had not mentioned to us. However, what really puzzled me was why there had not been a government decision on the other landholding license application by the Americans, whose proposal had obviously been prepared by Winski using our "crazy" ideas. Normally, the four months of our absence would have been more than enough time for a decision to be made. As it turned out, the the two Americans were gay, which, Dominica being predominantly Catholic, was frowned upon. For once we benefitted from religious orthodoxy.

Having restarted the process of getting permission to purchase Curry's Rest, I met several people to help me learn on my own, without self-interested intermediaries, how things work, or rather how they don't work, in Dominica.

Lennox Honychurch is a historian of Dominica and the grandson of the Napiers, who came in 1932 from England while on a cruise to Dominica. They liked the island at first sight and built a house at Pointe Baptiste in the north of the island. Elma Napier was a writer, got involved in local affairs, and became the first woman to be elected to a West Indian legislature. Having heard that

Honychurch was interested in Curry's Rest, I asked him why he had not bought it himself. There were several reasons: the government was uncertain about the future use of the land and would take some time to make up its mind; it would not be an easy job to settle down there, whoever got to buy the land; and, as a throwaway reason, he did not have the money.

In his view, the future use of the forest as a nature reserve was not favoured because it was all secondary growth. As I learned much later, when we tried to go ahead with our proposals for the sugar mill and forest, the government asked him for his "negative" opinion. Honychurch's advice was to look for an "easier" property and recommended Bois Cotlette, in the south of the island, which was owned by Michael Didier. I went there and met Didier. Bois Cotlette is an old sugar estate with a small, mainly wooden, and dilapidated house, a stone windmill tower, and a row of tiny, old slave quarters. Additionally, the site has no view, except from the rising ground behind it, on which Mr. D. proposed to build guest cottages. He offered a development partnership in which his contribution would be the site in its existing condition and the partner would supply the money needed for the project. And, oh yes, the then ownership was held by his family, who could not agree on his favoured development.

Our lawyer too, not certain of our chances of getting the nod from the government, showed me a number of available properties; none of them were of special appeal. Looking for more insights about Dominica, I went to see Mr. Archbold, the owner of the Springfield plantation and a well-known American public benefactor, who was very critical about the government's misuse and non-use of large tracts of land that he had donated for forestry research.

My most amiable meeting, however, was with the president of Dominica, Sir Clarence Seignoret, a charming and wise man who had been the last head of the British colonial service in Dominica. As president, Sir Clarence took a special interest in conservation and approved our proposal for Curry's Rest, which he had known about from his youth. However, he mentioned that as president, he could not talk to ministers about matters before cabinet, and that he strongly recommended that I talk to as many decision-makers as possible.

When we were properly established at Curry's Rest, Sir Clarence and his wife visited us with an old friend Charlie Winston, the then owner of Evergreen Hotel, and the two old farmers talked about "the good old days." I learned more that afternoon about farming in the first half of the twentieth century than I ever learned through reading official tourist literature or histories about Dominica.

Sir Clarence lived in an original house on King Georg V Street in Roseau. He enjoyed, until his death in 2002, sitting on his balcony, leaning on the banister, and watching Dominicans and visitors go by; and he always waved to me when I passed his house on my shopping trips to town.

***I naturally went to meet Oliver Green, the owner of Curry's Rest, in his beautiful, large, and well-maintained house not far from Sir Clarence's more modest house. He told me that Winski should have brought me to him and that he had not authorized Winski to offer his house for sale. Mr. Green also knew that Winski had accepted a deposit from the two Americans – a completely pointless transaction without a landholding license. We went over the purchase terms discussed between him and our lawyer, should cabinet decide in our favour.

After two weeks in Roseau, in July 1998, having also met some architects and builders, there was no point in staying any longer to wait for the cabinet decision – I was in limbo. I could not act on anything, like instructing a surveyor to stake out our eighteen acres of land, starting detailed designs for the restoration of the house, looking for another attractive property, or even selling our Toronto house, which would have provided the necessary cash.

My anxiety about succeeding had its lighter moments, however. For one of the required character references, I thought of my good friend Wojchek, who was now a deputy minister in the Ontario government. His recommendation on a government letterhead, I thought, should be impressive. He replied, "No problem, but I am very busy – can you write it for me?" This did not surprise me. His life's success was based on his talking (with a strong Polish accent), not his writing, which was done by faithful assistants. Wojchek did not even finish his dissertation for his town planning qualification in London. I did, in all modesty, write about my character, adding that the minister thought that I was an honest man (not suspecting that the Dominican government would later deal with us in a way that was anything but honest). Wojchek thought my draft "was not flowery enough." I told him to add the flowers.

In retrospect, the year and a half of hope, uncertainty, disappointments, and even discouragement seems now unbearable. One moment in particular stands out – the occasion when our lawyer informed us that the agreed-to price for Curry's Rest (signed by Green) had increased. The occasion proved to me what I had suspected: "our" lawyer acted for both parties, a strictly non-acceptable practice. But what could we do, if we wanted to retire to Curry's Rest?

Throughout this long period, I was still working and spent time in Timor, Indonesia, and China on two CIDA (Canadian International Development Agency) projects – both interesting and worthwhile attempts in foreign assistance.

Eventually, when our Curry's Rest purchase appeared to move to a successful conclusion, we sold our Cabbagetown house, put most of our furniture in storage, and rented a small house on a monthly basis on Pears Avenue facing Ramsden Park, and patiently waited.

Now, the true, native and undisguised problems started.

Restoration of Curry's Rest and Disillusions about Dominica

After being told at the end of March 1990 that the land transfer to us had been settled, I returned by myself to Dominica. Actually, the registration of the transfer did not occur until June.

Essentially, I set in motion, simultaneously, all the necessary activities for restoring the building, for repairing the minimal existing services, and for providing new, modern services. I was in my element, mounting a project.

Vehicular access being the first priority, I negotiated with the Ministry of Public Works for (1) the building of bridges over the stream crossing the existing donkey track, and (2) the paving of the track from the village of Mahaut to Curry's Rest, and (3) I offered to pay half of the total construction cost, and pay my share in advance, plus a bonus if the road was completed by the due date – both unheard of incentives.

WHAT REALLY HAPPENED: (1) I was informed, at the contracted completion date, that the Ministry of Public Works asked for the bonus payment. Having asked someone to check the new road, I was told that the road was not even half completed. (2) Within the first year of using what was now a "public" road, we found the road beginning to crumble for the simple reasons that the concrete mix had insufficient cement and the depth of the new paving was in most places inadequate. Every year, for the rest of our stay at Curry's Rest, our handyman Edward and I had to spend time and material patching the road. (Strangely, a few stretches of the road were properly built and never needed any repairs; how come? Public Works had contracted a dozen or more firms to build separate sections and let them do their work unsupervised. Some contractors did an honest job.) (3) Above all, I found out later that our "contribution" was the only cash available for the road construction – the Government of Dominica did not match our contribution, despite the contract.

Being unfamiliar with the local building and planning laws, I thought I would need an architect. In any case it would help Nicholas, who had agreed to be our builder, to have measured drawings of what I expected to be done to the house. I talked to three architects and selected Lynn Giraud, born and educated in England, who assured me that she had historic restoration experience. She gave the basic job of measuring and drawing the building "'as is" to an assistant, which he did very well. I discussed with Lynn my ideas about internal changes to what were really two old buildings joined together: a smaller and older all-stone single-storey building and, at right angle, a larger stone-and-timber structure with a basement.

Her drawings showed some good solutions and some misinterpretations of my ideas. But the set of drawings were good enough for Nicholas, I thought, and sent a copy to him in Washington. I then asked Lynn to supervise a water and sanitary contractor I was about to engage, and set up a trust account for her to be able to pay the contractor's bills while I was in Toronto.

WHAT REALLY HAPPENED: Lynn had never visited the construction site; she just paid the contractor's bills without making any inspections. But more seriously, when Nicholas with his friend David had started work on the house, he discovered a major flaw in the drawings. To provide staircase access and a new landing in the older building, the roof ridges of the two buildings had to be joined. The drawings showed the ridges at the same level when in reality they were at different levels. Lynn had failed to look at her assistant's correct drawings. This meant that the measurements were useless for Nicholas, and he was very upset because he was used to working from drawings. He had inherited from me an impatience for putting up with other people's mistakes. So, we agreed that I would remeasure the areas in which he was going to work for the following day.

Mr. Ambrose, a much recommended plumber and septic tank contractor who used to work for the public water company and who lived in the village was the obvious choice for the following: (1) To repair our water reservoir located high up behind the house. A huge rock had become lodged in the reservoir during a previous landslide. The only way to remove it was to demolish the front wall of a minor dam, push out the rock, and rebuild the dam; (2) To replace the cast iron pipe, connecting the reservoir to the house, with a two-inch PVC pressure pipe and bury it; and (3) to build a septic tank in the ground near the house.

WHAT REALLY HAPPENED: The reservoir repair and the building of the septic tank were well done. But the pipe replacement was not; the size of the pipe was smaller than specified (I wanted to add to the stored capacity) and it was not a pressure pipe (to protect it from falling stones; in fact, we had several leaks over time), yet the billing allowed for more costly pipes.

There was no telephone at Curry's Rest, and so I went to the local company, Cable & Wireless. They gave me a price based on the number of poles, length of cable, and installation. I agreed, and they installed, giving their usual haphazard service.

WHAT REALLY HAPPENED: Heavy storms or hurricanes occasionally felled some mature trees on which Cable & Wireless had fixed their cable, instead of using poles, and the cable snapped. In due time, Cable & Wireless put up the poles we had paid for at the outset of the process.

Curry's Rest had no electricity; the nearest supply point was in the village. DOMLEC, the electricity company gave me an exceptionally high price for cable and poles for their very unreliable electricity supply. Even today there are frequent, unannounced "load-sheddings" or blackouts that can last many hours.

Electricity supply in Dominica has a checkered history. When Hurricane David struck in 1979, a minimal system built and operated by a British company was destroyed. Because the company was not insured, it walked away from Dominica. The government, to its credit, painfully started afresh to build generating capacity and a distribution network. When we came to Dominica, the service was not only unreliable but came at a high price. Some years later the Dominican government renegotiated with the same British company their return to Dominica. The contract guaranteed profits under all circumstances without being able to control charges – a unique arrangement. Since then, Dominica's electricity charges have been the highest of any Caribbean country.

Solar electricity was relatively new and untested in 1990, but I remembered that the cottage country north of Toronto had some solar installations. If it worked there, surely it would work even better in sunny Dominica. I located a Puerto Rico branch office of an Arizona solar-electric company serving the Caribbean islands. Via fax, an engineer asked for a detailed listing of the number of electric outlets, wattage, and minutes of daily use of each outlet. He then estimated the number of solar panels and batteries required, and then sent a sketch plan of the panel assembly and required layout for a battery room separated from the instrument panel and stand-by generator. When everything was in place, the engineer would come to Dominica to mount the solar panels and wire the system.

We intended to install the solar panels on the roof of the house and the rest of the equipment in the basement. However, when Nicholas saw the size and weight of the solar panel assembly, which arrived after he had started work on the house, he said it would be too heavy to put on the fragile cedar roof shingles. I located a site for the "power house" with underground connection from the back of the future kitchen where the cables would enter the house, and left the construction for later. The power house designed itself: the solar panel supports gave me the dimensions for the concrete roof; the only delicate part of the operation was to ensure the proper orientation of the panels towards the sun for maximum sun exposure.

A mason from the village and I built the power house, mounted the solar panel supports on the concrete slab roof, partitioned the inside for the battery room, fixed wood boards for the control instruments in the other half, having dug in the connection pipe to the house for the cables. When the engineer from Puerto Rico came to do his job, he was pleased about the power house because he was used to working in cramped attics. After he finished, he recorded a promotional video showing the installation and featuring an interview of me.

WHAT REALLY HAPPENED: We had a well-functioning electricity supply, under our own control, at a lower cost than what was available from DOMLEC, and we escaped the ever-increasing price of the public supply. Sometime in 2008, after the system had been in operation for around eighteen years, an interested foreigner, considering solar power for his house, asked me what my electricity costs were. I could not give him a kilowatt-hour rate because my instruments were not set up to do that. As I was interested myself, I could come up with an average monthly cost for the eighteen years by adding (1) the original costs of equipment, installation, and power house with (2) the replacement costs of batteries (after seven or eight years), distilled water to top up the batteries, and upgraded instruments. I divide the total costs by the number of months we had used the system. To make the cost meaningful in terms of consumption, I listed our electric appliances (washing machine, refrigerator, etc.), all other electric gadgets, and the number of electric lights throughout the house. The result was impressive: about half the cost for a comparable house in Dominica, and without blackouts.

After more than twenty years, since we installed the first solar electric system in Dominica, there are perhaps no more than ten others; and for two reasons: the initial costs are too high, and secondly, there is no competent local company to give advice, install, and maintain it.

Why Curry?

Having settled comfortably into our newly restored "ancient house," I thought it was time to have a look at the history of the place, especially its name Curry's Rest; but not just the name. I wanted to find out about the two parts of the house built at different times; about the reason for the aqueduct going beyond the existing waterwheel to below the house and, as I later discovered, about the remains of another waterwheel in the woods well below the house.

I went to the Land Registry and found the records and search system unorthodox, to put it politely, having had some familiarity with searching land registrations as a planner in England, Canada, the States, and elsewhere. I had also been told that some time ago there had been a fire at the registry, said to have been arson, which created gaps in the records. I needed help.

Fortunately, a formerly retired registrar had been rehired (I was going to say because he knew the system, but there was no system) to search for difficult-to-find deeds for the government, and he agreed to help me. At first he gave me an ordinary notebook entitled "Index of Deeds for Saint Paul Parish," where Curry's Rest is located, for the period of June 1766 to August 1882. There were nine entries giving Henry Curry as either "owner" (i.e., seller) or "purchaser" between June 1772 and January 1819, each listing the acreage, except one (in 1793) giving no acreage. The last Henry Curry entry (to John Dodds), which also gives no acreage and which, for the first time, uses "Curry's Rest" in the acres column. Interestingly, an early March entry (March 1970) gives the owner as "Crown" – 15,840 sq. ft. My guess is that this was up in the hills in the forest behind the house near the spring, where Mr. Curry built the water reservoir.

Throughout the forty-seven years of Mr. Curry's land exchanges, he seems to have been a bit of a speculator. Right at the beginning, in June 1772, he purchased 215 acres, and then sold 213 acres just five months later. The last three "Index of Deeds" entries were June 1852 from Savernies Francis to John Bpt. William (15 acres "part of Curry's Rest"; May 1866 from Jos. Fadelle to William Baptiste ("part of Curry's Rest"); and August 1882 from Theresa Didier to John Hawley (325 acres).

I extracted the details of all the transactions in the hope of establishing what others, in addition to Mr. Curry, had done before and after him. Returning the "Index of Deeds" (1766 to 1882) to my newfound friend at the Registry, I inquired about the post-1882 records, but he told me that there were none. He said, "In cases like that, you start the search from the present and work backwards," and he agreed to do that for me.

The very next morning he called to tell me that the last transfer document for Curry's Rest stated that, apart from the 18 acres conveyed to us, for the balance of the 479 acres, the Government of Dominica had paid EC$212,000 (Eastern Caribbean dollars) to Mr. Green, and not that we donated the land, as I had told him.

This false document needed to be corrected. I will not go into the details over the seemingly interminable process to achieve the correction, which took seven years. During those seven years I was constantly in touch, by letter or in person, with the Ministry of Land, the Ministry of Legal Affairs, the Attorney General, and Mr. Winston – first as a state attorney and then, and for most of the time, as the registrar at the Land Registry.

Rene and I swore an affidavit in 2000 asking for the withdrawal of the existing Memorandum of Transfer and substitution of another one. Along the way, the permanent secretary of the Ministry of Legal Affairs replied to a letter of mine:

> "Please be informed that every effort is being made to have this matter settled as expeditiously as possible. Thank you for the cooperation and restraint you have displayed thus far."

It took another few years.

After I finally picked up, at 10:00 in the morning, a copy of the corrected memorandum of Transfer from Mr. Winston, I went straight to Cocorico, a favourite restaurant and bar, to have a double scotch in order to celebrate my stubborn persistence and, unknown to me until then, my patience. The French owner, Fred, thought I had become an alcoholic.

After this experience, I lost my appetite for looking further into the history of Curry's Rest. And there were other disappointments with Dominica – the country, not the island.

Restoration Rebuff

Our Land Holding Licence application proposed the restoration of the sugar mill to a working condition, including an interpretative centre explaining its operations and importance to Dominica and its people at the time it was functioning.

We were always interested in restoring older buildings to live in, especially in Reigate, England; Watertown, Massachusetts; and Cabbagetown, Toronto. That's why we were so excited about Curry's Rest.

The first useful repair, after the house, was the mill pond or water reservoir. It had an inlet from the Mahaut River, which was the eastern border of the property, an overflow back into the river and a channel leading to the waterwheel of the mill. The reservoir had a sloping, leaking bottom with a depth of seven to twelve feet and was roughly 40 square feet. The bottom of the reservoir was covered in natural growth of shrubs, flowers, and grass. Very tall trees surrounded the reservoir – it would make a perfect swimming pool and could still function as a mill pond for the waterwheel.

The pool needed a new concrete bottom and new lining for its sides. Knowing by now that I would not find, even less likely supervise, a work crew, I engaged an engineering firm to do the job.

Edward and I built a cabana of bamboo walls with a roof of leaves, used in a traditional way and which has had to be replaced every two years. The cabana was for guests too bashful to change into their swimsuits in the open. Rene swam in the pool every day – ten laps.

Restoration of the sugar mill was a more serious proposition. As I had mentioned in our Land Holding Licence application: "A public trust will be established to manage the land and historic buildings." Talking to some who had shown interest and produced results in preserving structures from the past, like the Old Market in Roseau, I found many were reluctant to get involved. Only one, Dense Shillingford, was ready to join us. He had shown us earlier the estate he had inherited from his grandfather, who had converted the water-driven mill to diesel power. Dense had restored the mill back to water power. He had also built a rum distillery that produced the only Dominican rum – Macoucherie Rum.

The other potential, but reluctant, members of the non-profit Curry's Rest Board I invited to join responded negatively: "What you are attempting to do is too ambitious for Dominica"; "You don't want to have all those tourists come up here"; "Why don't you just relax and enjoy your retirement" (in other words: as new settlers, don't interfere).

I tried to explain the following: (1) It would be quite easy to control the tourist traffic by restricting tourist-boat busses to one per boat and charge heavily to see the sugar mill, which would also contribute to the upkeep of the place and pay for trained staff of the interpretative centre. (2) The whole project was primarily for Dominicans, especially for the school children. (3) The importance of sugar in Dominica's history should not be overlooked: practically the whole population of Dominicans are the descendants of African slaves brought to the island; the behaviour of the Sugar Barons; the French/British colonial rivalry; the effects of the disappearance of cane cultivation, and so on. (4) As far as we had seen in our travels around the Caribbean island, Dominica was the only one without at least one restored windmill or watermill.

Setting aside, for a time, finding suitable and willing board members, I searched for a lawyer who could set up the non-profit trust that would be needed. The only experienced one I found told me that he established such a corporation as a government lawyer for the legal department, but he was now working on his own (which is to say he worked to make money and he could not very well charge a regular fee to a "non-profit" organization).

Despite these setbacks, we were not ready to give up so soon. Fortuitously, I had come across a publication at Tianjin University in China (where they were trying to show off their small collection of English books), entitled *Peasants and Capital, Dominica in the World Economy* by Michel-Rolph Trouillot (John Hopkins University Press, 1988). This could be the first book for the interpretative centre of the restored sugar complex.

I turned to Phillip Nassief of the coconut product/soap factory outside Mahaut for advice on a lawyer who could help us and an engineer with knowledge about sugar mills (having seen the waterwheel outside Mr. Nassief's factory). He came up trumps on both counts.

He put me in touch with an eminent lawyer in Barbados by the name of Trevor Carmichael, Q.C., leader of the Barbados National Trustees as well as supporter of historic preservation throughout the Caribbean. Over the phone Trevor Carmichael discussed our project with me and said he would gladly do all the legal work pro bono because he strongly believed in the importance of preserving all the surviving historic structures in the Caribbean islands.

Mr. Nassief's second recommendation was Oliver Hinds, an engineer also from Barbados, who had for years helped in the construction and maintenance of his factory and who had considerable experience in rebuilding sugar mills, including the waterwheel near the gate to the soap factory. The next time Mr. Hinds was in Dominica, he twice visited Curry's Rest to inspect the remains of the former sugar mill and, in his opinion, agreed that restoration of the wheel and crushing rollers was feasible. We could review the cost of fixing the boiling house later. We discussed alternatives: replacement parts would have to be made in Barbados but the actual reconstruction could be done either by Barbadians or by Dominicans. I asked Mr. Hinds for cost estimates, which he sent to me. They were not as high as I had feared.

Feeling elated, I next wrote to CIDA in Ottawa asking whether the agency might provide financial support for the project. The response was positive: so long as the Dominican government would confirm that the restoration would enhance and complement the government's national development efforts. CIDA also advised me that initial private donations would help them in making funds available; and I mentioned my intention to approach Tate & Lyle in London, probably the largest sugar producers since 1799, which must have been one of the recipients of slave-produced sugar from the Caribbean islands, to make a donation – which would be acknowledged in our literature.

At that stage everything hinged on registering the not-for-profit trust to turn our ideas into reality. Mr. Carmichael kept me informed about his efforts, conducted by a Dominican lawyer in Roseau, which frustrated him because the relatively simple matter took longer than usual, but he would press on. After six months I called him to say that there seemed to be no purpose in further efforts since the authorities in Dominica were not prepared to take any action, and I thanked him. He, unmoved, said he would continue; and he did so for another whole year.

I knew there must be a reason for the government's silence. Even an incompetent administration will eventually, under pressure, respond one way or another. And I found the reason for this behaviour from the highest, most reputable and honourable source in Dominica. The cause of the government's silence was the prime minister of Dominica, Euginia Charles. She had no interest in restoration or in Dominica's past generally. The preservation of Dominica's history started with her. Above all, she would not approve any action that might imply government spending or loss of government income in the future caused by historic restoration.

The prime minister's narrow attitude to public spending was confirmed to me a year or two later. The Richmond Foundation from London had set up rehabilitation homes for teenagers with drug and other problems in both developed and undeveloped countries. The successful formula consisted of building or renovating a suitable building, followed by Foundation staff selecting and training local staff for a whole year. Thereafter, the government, having guaranteed to provide the necessary funds, would continue. The Foundation was available to provide help when necessary.

The founder of the organization, Elly Jansen, had been to Dominica before without success in establishing a home here. One of the board members of her organization, our good friend Rachel Foster, thought I might be able to help Elly Jansen in a second attempt. I will not go into the sordid details of Euginia Charles's treatment of Elly Jansen beyond stating the facts that (1) Euginia Charles declined to promise public funds for the operation of the program, yet (2) Euginia Charles tried to sell her family home in Pointe Michel, which was unsuitable for a teenager home, to the Richmond Foundation for an outrageous price.

Lennox Honychurch was right in one respect: what we were trying to do was "too ambitious for Dominica," but he never told us why Dominica is so different from other Caribbean countries. I gave some thought to finding the answer in later years. (For my views on this difference, see below: "What's Wrong with Dom?")

Life at Curry's Rest

We were rather slow to become consoled by the fact that the government was neither interested nor willing to support the restoration of the sugar mill or the establishment of a nature preserve. So we withdrew – we pulled in our horns. There was much to do and to learn at Curry's rest, and much to explore on the island, which, after all, brought us here.

Nicholas and I discussed who, out of his work crew, I should keep on as a handyman. I preferred Edward because he was the strongest. Nicholas had some reservations about him and suggested another good worker. At first I used both of them for a time because there was much heavy work to be done around the house, like rebuilding collapsed stone walls. Eventually, I kept just Edward.

To help Rene with her housework, we ended up with Heather, who had approached me in the village one day when on my way back from town. Little did we know that Heather and Edward had been close friends but had drifted apart. Months later Heather phoned me one Friday (pay day) evening to ask whether I had paid Edward for the week. It turned out that Edward was the father of Heather's first child – a daughter. By local law or custom, Edward was required to pay a weekly child support. After Heather's repeated complaints, I got them to sit down with me and suggested that I would deduct the child support from Edward's pay and add it to her pay. But no: Heather wanted Edward to acknowledge his responsibility and pay her directly.

That their daughter was born out of wedlock was normal. The majority of the population was; though Catholicism was the predominant religion. And mothers had their first child as teenagers, which meant they became grandmothers when they were forty years old or younger.

To my surprise, Edward did not really know how to look after plants properly. He was good at mixing concrete, swinging a sledge hammer, and climbing a ladder to pick fruit – just like me as a little boy – but he was not a knowledgeable farmer, everything was allowed to run wild.

Mr. Georges, the experienced farmer, was by then ninety-five and was no longer strong enough to trim trees and rake the ground around the trees, so Edward continued the tradition, not taking any notice of what Mr. Georges told him. I knew from Asia that coffee trees are regularly trimmed to keep them short. We had just one coffee tree that was well over twenty feet high, and it produced coffee beans. I took the cuttings and planted a new row of trees, telling Edward to go to the Syndicate Estate, in the north of the island, to look at the coffee trees there along the road, which are kept no taller than ten feet.

After Rene and I returned from a trip to Grenada, I showed Edward some photos of a cocoa plantation on that island which looked like a cathedral: straight, clean trees like columns growing out of a raked forest floor that was as smooth as a marble floor. Edward ignored all my efforts to turn him into a proficient farmer: "You would not know anything about Dominican plants. You are from Canada."

There was more to learn about unfamiliar plants. A spice merchant from Roseau came up one day looking for "the pimento trees." He knew Mr. Green had planted some – the only ones in Dominica – and exported the red fruit. The pimento fruit grows on evergreen trees of up to thirty feet in Central and South America. It is also called allspice because it tastes like a combination of clove, juniper berries, cinnamon, and pepper. Jamaica is a major grower of these trees and exports the fruit by the tonne.

We found several pimento trees not far from our cocoa trees. The spice merchant wanted to pick the ripe, red fruit right away. I had no idea what the market price was and told him that he could go ahead and pick the fruit; we would discuss payment later. I paid a visit to Mr. Georges in the village to get the lowdown on Mr. Green and the pimento fruit. He had no idea; Mr. Green exported the pimento and that was all he knew. No one else in Dominica, not even DEXIA, the public agricultural trading agency, had the slightest interest in this valuable tree.

Edward and I planted our cuttings into plastic bags and spread the word that anyone interested could come and pick them up. I gave the first one to Jackie Dupigny of the Cartwheel Café to plant in her Giraudel Estate. Before you knew it, pimento trees were growing all over Dominica.

Vanilla used to be grown fairly extensively in Dominica in the first half of the last century. It almost disappeared, mainly because the growing and processing of the vanilla beans require a skillful, lengthy, and labour-intensive operation. My interest was stimulated by a newly published book I had picked up in Toronto: *Vanilla: Travels in Search of the Ice Cream Orchid* by Tim Ecott.

I bought a vanilla plant from a farmer near Mahaut and planted it next to a tree to find out whether vanilla would grow at Curry's Rest. Vanilla is a vine or climbing orchid producing narrow four-to-six inch pods that contain the vanilla beans. My single vine did very well, growing up along the trunk of a tree and producing flowers. The unusual, perhaps unique, characteristic of the vanilla plant is that it needs to be pollinated by hand and within days of the flower opening. That job is invariably done by women because of their delicate touch. Sir Clarence had told me that his sister and her girlfriends used to leave home early to do the hand-pollinating on the way to school.

Once the vanilla pods are ripe, they go through several months of drying, during which they need to be turned repeatedly to ensure proper drying, before they are sold for further processing. So, now you know why vanilla requires a lot of work and why it is so expensive.

Though vanilla grows in several countries, Madagascar became the major producer of quality vanilla in the later twentieth century. It must have been fairly early in the twenty-first century when a blight struck the vanilla plants in Madagascar, which caused the price of vanilla to rise steeply in the following years, and Tim Ecott's book was published in 2005, just about the time I had become interested in vanilla.

At that time, the weekly *Chronicle* newspaper in Roseau published a letter urging Dominicans to mount a sale campaign to promote its vanilla – which Dominica no longer produced in quantities. For once I was roused to write a letter to the editor, pointing out that (1) at a time of shortage, a producer does not have to spend money because the market finds the available supply; (2) Dominica had nothing to offer since it no longer produced vanilla in any quantity; and (3) if Dominica wanted to enter the market the real question was "Who would produce the vanilla beans?"

"Furthermore," I continued, "I am told that in the distant past girls did the hand-pollination on the way to school but they no longer walk to school, they go by bus and they probably would not do it for free anymore. In addition, since most Dominicans have left agriculture, who is going to do the hard work of drying the vanilla beans?"

On the day of the publication of my *Chronicle* letter I was shopping in Roseau and by chance met Lennox who said to me, "You are right about 'who is going to do the work,' but you are wrong about the girls doing the pollination!" I had not mentioned to Lennox Honychurch that it was Sir Clarence Seignoret (the former president of Dominica) who had told me that it was his sister's duty to pollinate the vanilla flowers – an impeccable source.

But then, Lennox Honychurch's reputation as the local historian of Dominica is well-established, to wit: Diana Athill, the writer and famous editor had this to say about Lennox:

> I'd heard several times about Lennox Honychurch,
> the local historian of the island of Dominica (where
> Jean was raised), who was always described by
> people researching as "wonderfully helpful," and I
> had formed a picture of an elderly and earnest black

schoolmaster, so that was what I was looking for when Valeria told me that he, too, would be coming over for the film, on my plane, because luckily he happened to be visiting England. And before I left a shy Caribbean voice spoke on the phone, and I told him what kind of hat I'd be wearing, and he told me he'd be wearing his green white and bluer scarf. So I peered about at Heathrow, and there sure enough was an elderly and earnest black schoolmaster, but he didn't have such a scarf, and was obviously not looking for my hat. So I went back to reading my newspaper – and a Caribbean voice suddenly said "Diana Athill?" – and there stood a most enchanting young man, white, with the most beautiful greenish hazel eyes and an elegant black moustache, looking barely thirty years old (actually he's forty-six) a truly Lovely Surprise. And he turned out to be, indeed, a perfect honey. It's his lonely fate to be the only intellectual white person living in Dominica, his family is one of the very few remains of the plantocracy,[1] and he has made his own career as a historian of the Caribbean (is at present at Oxford doing some special research). (*Instead of a Book: Letters to a Friend*, 2011, p. 130)

After years of learning how to manage problems at Curry's Rest, I was confident that I would be able to deal with any complication that might arise – until I faced a problem created by nature. On a periodic inspection and clean-up behind and around our water reservoir, I noticed that the steady trickle of water flowing down from the natural spring had been reduced to a small dribble. Checking

---

[1] His family arrived in Dominica after the end of the sugar cane production.

the water level in the tank, I found it to be half full (or half empty, depending on your outlook on life).

Looking for an expert, I found a water engineer formerly with DOWASCO, the public water company. He climbed up the steep water course to its source. His diagnosis: the water course near its source had been mainly diverted in another direction due to any number of natural causes but probably by a minor landslide. After scouting along the new course through the forest, his recommendation was to build a small, shallow concrete basin as close as possible to our reservoir and from there to drain the water by pipe back to where it belonged.

This good advice I accepted, and while he promised to do the job, he never finished it. After several months of starts and stops and no further progress, by which time the water engineer and his men had half-finished the small concrete basin, Edward and I completed the basin and installed the long pipeline to the reservoir. During the period of construction, the dribble of water kept us going as long as we economized our water consumption – like California during a water shortage: "Take a shower with a friend."

Friends and Visitors

Acquaintances and friends often asked us, "Is it not lonely at Curry's Rest, up a hill and miles from people?" Our short and honest answer was "No, it never occurred to us." Sure, we had adjusted to the obvious change but we also found that after a crowded life, we were happy to be by ourselves, that we were pretty busy anyway since keeping up Curry's Rest meant a lot of work for both of us, and, to be honest, many people we had to deal with in our working lives we did not miss. And, furthermore, we were not lonely because of new friends we made at Curry's Rest and old friends who came to visit.

Our new friends were a colourful lot, and not just because of their different skin colours, and they included both Dominican-born, long-term residents or, like us, more recent arrivals. Altogether some two dozen people became our friends, and they came from many countries; it was not a crowd you would frequently meet in London or Toronto. We met in town, on the beach or on hikes, at their homes around the island, and at Curry's Rest, which, probably at first, was the greater attraction than Rene and I.

Let me mention briefly a handful of our good friends and events I remember well. I already introduced Sir Clarence and Charlie Winston. One of the earliest friendships started with Ivor Nassief, a third-generation Lebanese-Dominican who at the time was assisting his father Phillip manage the coconut product factory. More important, Ivor had recently been married to charming Nancy. Ivor had studied economics at York University in Toronto and, following the sale of the soap factory, he launched one successful business after another. He was a born entrepreneur and had realized that Dominica's very small market allowed for only limited profit in any one business. We enjoyed Ivor and Nancy's company, and enjoyed watching the arrival and growth of their three children. Over the years, Ivor gave me a lot of good advice on the ways and practices that make the country tick or fail.

From the successful business man to the successful artist: Darius. Darius had spent his life as a male nurse in the psychiatric ward of the Princess Margaret Hospital. Untrained in art, as I believe also untrained in psychiatry, he had started to paint when still working at the hospital. He painted less from reality than from memory – scenes from his early life: cane cutting, village life, dancing under the trees, playing cricket on the village green, whatever caught his fancy from the Dominica of the past. And his work sold, especially to American connoisseurs. When we got to know him, he was long retired and living in his own house in Roseau, where he had been banished by his wife to the basement. (This intriguing plot would make a wonderful story by an accomplished writer. He had a caring girlfriend nearby, where he spent much of his spare time.)

Dominicans had bought his work but, there being no galleries to speak of, there were few places where one could look at his paintings, except at Darius's own place or at Ivor's home and office, where you could find the largest collection of Darius's work in Dominica. Therefore, we visited Darius often when in Roseau to look at his works in progress. He had taken photos of many paintings sold to Americans and, one day, he showed us a shoebox full of those photos. Among them was one that Rene particularly liked of a man and wife harvesting cane in their traditional clothes: he cutting with his cutlass and she was bundling the cane. Darius and Rene talked about the painting at length until Darius said he would paint a similar one for her. Rene suggested a smaller, more simplified reproduction.

On our return a couple of weeks later, I could tell right away that Darius had taken no notice of Rene's request for a "smaller" painting. So Darius went back to his easel and we were then able to admire a smaller rendition of his lovely painting.

From one painter to another: Marie Frederick, a French artist from Deauville. Some years ago she had drifted to Dominica via other Caribbean islands, where she married Clem, a Dominican of many parts – a land owner, planter, and builder – and they settled on his land at Borne in the north of the island. Clem built her "Indigo's Art Gallery and Tree Cottage," a unique wood structure that, in part, literally hung in the air.

We often went to Indigo with our visitors, and Marie frequently dropped by Curry's Rest on her shopping day in Roseau. On one of her shopping days, Marie came early and well prepared with a small canvas on its frame saying that she always wanted to paint at Curry's Rest. She set herself up on the front terrace. In two hours or so, she had produced a lovely painting of trees and flowers, which she gave to us. It now hangs alongside another of her paintings – a scene of Indigo – she had given to Rene. In 2012, I took River, my youngest grandson, to Indigo Tree Cottage, and after that, River began to only sleep in a hammock, even when at home in Washington.

Another "partial" settler, Polly Pattullo, who I regard as our friend, has for many years visited and lived in the Caribbean, including spending several months each year in Dominica. We were fortunate to meet Polly soon after coming to Dominica. She is a writer, editor, and publisher, having started her career at the *Guardian*. Polly's experience in the Caribbean islands, particularly her critical appraisal of the tourist industry published as *Last Resorts: The Cost of Tourism in the Caribbean* (1996), helped us understand Dominica sooner and better. She is also the co-author of *Home Again: Stories of Migration and Return* (2009).

The friendship between us was strengthened years later when Adrien and Althea, our grandson and his wife, became Polly's tenants in her lovely home in London's Clapham Common area. Polly has always offered me the bed in her study when I have visited London.

The diversity of our friendships in Dominica is confirmed by Father Bechamps, a Canadian friar, partly educated at the Sorbonne, who was responsible for spiritual and educational needs of Dominica's prison inmates. He was a delightful man whose hobby was pottery, which he practised in his own workshop. He tried teaching the craft to some of the prisoners. One could often find him in the Old Market in Roseau where he sold his wares.

Father Bechamps visited Curry's Rest on one special occasion when we hosted a Sunday musical afternoon, featuring a peculiar mix of violin, guitar, flute, and voice. This gives me an opportunity to mention just one more couple: Andy Medlicot and his beautiful wife, Ninfa, from Honduras. Andy, an English agricultural advisor who was working for U.S. Aid for International Development, was teaching Dominicans how to grow better fruit. When I started to serve the red Chilean wine Casillero del Diablo (variously translated, but most appropriately Cellar of the Devil), Ninfa saw the label and, as a devout Catholic gasped at the name and nodded towards Father Bechamps. I put my hand over the label and all was well.

There were other friends whose company brought us great pleasure. This sample should suffice to convince anyone who may be wondering why we were not bored at Curry's Rest.

⌁

Many artists live in Dominica, many are natives like Darius and others are immigrants like Marie. Artists like Marie continue to grow in number – attracted to the island by its exceptional combination of the rich plant life, beautiful rivers and waterfalls, stunning topography and endless sunshine. The most accomplished of the homegrown artists is Earl Etienne. His paintings have brought him Caribbean-wide recognition. One remarkable characteristic of his work is his changing style. When you think you can readily recognize any of his paintings, he produces something new. I have spent a lot of time at his studio, which never disturbed him because he mostly works at night. Earl's younger friend Moses, whom he had taught to paint, developed his own style; he is not an imitator of the master. They continue to exhibit together in Martinique and on some of the other islands.

Another transient artist of note is Rojas. He came with his American wife: she looked after the business side of his atelier – and had expensive taste in clothes. Her thing was riding. She understood or had "read" Rojas's artistic eye and rode through the forests searching for scenes for him to paint, which saved him a lot of time while she had fun on her horse.

Rojas had two shows while in Dominica, they both sold out. Moses did the framing of his work. Rojas painted non-stop for about two years in Dominica, then moved on, exhausted – he had done Dominica. I have one of his mesmerizing paintings, which might have been painted somewhere at Curry's Rest. I look at it often, remembering him, his wife, and her horse.

Last but not least is the captivating couple Roger and Sarah Pinfold. We met them first at the annual Queen's birthday party given by the High Commissioner at the State House (formerly the Governor's House) in Roseau. Roger, a lawyer from Suffolk, England, had just arrived to take up his appointment as director of public prosecution for Dominica. Sarah, an imaginative and joyful lady, originally from upstate New York and other places, kept Roger happy and soon came to know almost everyone worth knowing in Dominica.

When Roger had his first meeting with his new boss, the Attorney General, Sarah asked him whether Roger, as the first non-Caribbean (i.e., white) would encounter any difficulties, the A.G. replied: "He will be the first honest one." In fact, Roger was more than that. He taught Dominican policemen their job: how and what to write in their notebooks when arresting suspects, how to present evidence in court, and other matters that would help him in his job as prosecutor. Sarah kept a hospitable home, and we often enjoyed her cooking and meeting new friends there. Nowadays, whenever I visit England, I go to see them in Southwold or Woodbridge, where Sarah is busy restoring old houses.

You do not lose your good friends from younger days wherever they live, in the same city or across the sea, and so it proved at Curry's Rest. Many perhaps came more to see our curiously odd place and Dominica rather than us, but they came and we were glad. Of course they included members of our family who came more often, but even friends made repeated visits. They came from Boston, Florida, London, Montreal, Philadelphia, Toronto, Vienna, and Washington. It was fun, and it was work. Occasionally, we asked Fred and Sidoni from Cocorico to come up and cook an extra-special French meal.

What's Wrong with Dom?

From the beginning of our life in Dominica, we could not understand Dominica's relative backwardness compared to underdeveloped countries we had lived in or other Caribbean islands we knew. Our choice to retire to Dominica was based almost entirely on the island's beauty. Other considerations such as level of development, lack of choice in shopping, and limited entertainment were not important to us. We had to take note of property prices and consider start-up costs. We neither worried about nor had time to investigate the attitudes of the locals towards foreigners or the country's politics because we were used to adapting and "fitting in."

Yet we quickly noticed the absence of the kind of native enterprise or initiative found in other Caribbean islands, except for the businesses owned and operated by foreigners: French or Lebanese who had arrived a long time ago. Even the new growth industry of tourism had barely started up when compared with other islands. Not that we were sorry about the absence of mass tourism; we had come to Dominica precisely because it was less touristy. Only later did we realize that it demonstrated Dominica's inability to capitalize on its major asset – nature. Over twenty years later, after we had departed, the Wai'tukubuli National (Nature) Trail was constructed – a gift to eco-tourism that was paid for by a foreign agency.

While other islands have erased much of the poverty of the post-sugar era and begun to prosper, Dominica was stagnating. It was troubling to appreciate Dominica's outstanding natural beauty while watching it slide economically further behind other relatively less attractive Caribbean islands.

There may have been several and diverse reasons for this difference, but I believe the major ones point to subtle dissimilarities in the "plantation life": during the colonial period, and after the decline of the sugar industry in Dominica and on the other islands. Another reason, a consequence of the first two, was the later exodus of many of its ambitious school graduates who left for jobs and educational opportunities elsewhere; leaving behind the less ambitious.

The first two major Caribbean sugar islands were Barbados and Jamaica, both with large areas of generally level land. The "sugar barons" built huge estate houses on both islands. Other islands like Antigua and Martinique were soon developed. Dominica attracted few colonials because of its hilly and mountainous nature that was less suitable for cane cultivation. Most of those who did establish small plantations did not settle in Dominica. Once they developed small sugar productions, they put local supervisors in charge and left for Barbados and the good life. Once or twice a year they visited their little estates, rode around on a horse to make sure all was well, but did not stay.

The colourful and brutal history of sugar colonialism created a great variety of situations, depending on the island, the colonial settlers or non-settlers, the slaves and their treatment, the condition of the land and buildings, and many other factors. But all, around the end of the eighteen century, colonials and slaves faced the decline of the sugar industry unprepared and in unequal circumstances. Not surprisingly, their responses varied considerably with very different results.

I believe the reasons why Dominica, unlike other Caribbean islands, failed over the long run to build a new life when the only source of income vanished were as follows: few colonists coming to Dominica settled permanently in the first place; those who settled had generally smaller estates and smaller houses; and, most important, few colonists stayed in Dominica after the decline of the sugar industry.

There were some colonial settlers who stayed and went into farming or trade, these were mainly the French like the Dupigny family who helped the country get on its feet. They set up the Dupigny Technical School which was renamed years later, after independence, in order to eliminate the French donor's name.

However, even today, Dominica still lacks an entrepreneurial group comparable to other islands. Three Lebanese families – Astaphan, Nassief, and Raffoul – who came to Dominica in the 1920s and 1930s have to some extent taken the place of the missing original British and French settlers who, on the other islands, had started the flourishing business sectors.

As mentioned, a major misfortune to befall Dominica for many years was the steady departure of the country's bright and ambitious young in search of jobs and education on other Caribbean islands or in London, New York, and Toronto. Meanwhile, the country continued to experience a lack of enterprising people. Ironically, in recent years when the first "returnees" – those Dominicans who spent their working lives in London – came home with their cars and pensions to enjoy retirement, they were not welcome in their home country. They were considered as foreigners or as "English" because they were rich, knowledgeable, and keen to help. This caused new conflicts. This sobering fact has been well documented in *Home Again: Stories of Migration and Return*, co-authored by Polly Pattullo and Celia Sorhaindo (which I just mentioned above).

Other backward countries that have failed to develop have lacked marketable resources. But this is not the case for Dominica: it has an outstanding resource of unspoiled nature (which tends to be spoiled nowadays by natives and visitors alike). In fact, Dominica advertises itself as the "Nature Island of the Caribbean," which is not an idle boast. Yet it has failed to capitalize on it.

In addition to nature, Dominica has old buildings from the eighteenth and nineteenth centuries that, if restored, would be wonderful attractions for tourists. Historic restoration is dependent on original design and original materials. Dominica's record of historic preservation is very spotty. The restorations of the guard house and the powder magazine at Fort Shirley in the Cabrits National Park to the north of Portsmouth were well done some years ago. However, the more recent major restorations of the largest building at Fort Shirley – the officers' quarters – has been financed by the European Union, whose supervising office is in the Barbados. The work being done is closer to a Disney restoration with a red metal roof and mostly modern materials. The only "original" material used, apart from the stone walls, is the use of lime instead of cement for the rebuilding of the outside walls. For the rest, no attempt was made in design or materials to match the original. The new materials of steel, metal alloy, concrete parapet, and so on did not even exist when the officers' quarters were originally built.

The interior of the building was reconstructed without knowing how to use the space, but it would have made a fine boutique hotel. Rooms could have been named after Admiral Rodney and his officers at the Battle of the Saints (April 1782), which was known to the defeated French as La bataille de la Dominique.

Other Caribbean islands of identical origins as Dominica – slaves and colonialists under the control of the sugar barons – slowly recovered after the decline of the sugar industry. Why not Dominica? A good example for comparison from which to get an answer is Nevis, and Nevis is not exceptional.

Nevis is part of the Federation of St. Kitts and Nevis, which is located about 120 miles north of Dominica and to the west of Antigua. Some 10,000 people live in Nevis compared to 70,000 in Dominica, which declined by 10,000 in the last twenty years. Nevis is a completely round island with an extinct volcano (3,230 ft.) in the centre of it; the size of Nevis is not even one-third the size of Dominica.

Nevis is well known because of two famous historic figures: Alexander Hamilton who was born there, and Lord Nelson who lived there and married a Nevisian woman, Frances Nisbet. Nevis started its slave-supported sugar era like other Caribbean islands but came out of it prepared for a new and better life for all Nevisians.

All sugar plantations on Nevis had substantial, well-built estate houses that were occupied by their English masters who stayed through the decline and afterwards built a new life on their land. In a remarkable, if slow process, the masters and servants transformed the sugar economy together into a diversified community of farmers, skilled workers, and tradesmen. They first produced, like immigrants anywhere, the basics for their own life, and then looked around for new opportunities, like trading with nearby islands. The point is that the former masters did not leave the island; they liked the place and were reluctant to leave it.

In the longer run, when tourism began, the Nevisians were eager and ready to respond. Estate houses were turned into guest houses, windmills were fixed to show tourists how cane was crushed. The fine beaches all around the island were cleaned up; lanes became roads – initiative and enterprise were alive. Nevisians took to the new opportunities provided by tourism with enthusiasm, skill, and cooperation.

Five former plantation estate houses with their windmills were the first tourist destinations in Nevis. They led the way for foreign tourist investments, including a Four Seasons resort with a golf course, and a variety of investment opportunities like the purchase of luxury vacation homes which Four Seasons manages for the owners. Other foreign investors and developers found the enterprising atmosphere helpful: today, Nevis has a small but successful off-shore investment business.

Nevisians are proud of their island and its history. An insignificant but telling example involves two brothers who manage a real estate business and whose advertisement reads "In business on the island for five generations." Historic memory is a pervasive presence on Nevis, starting with the excellently restored George Hamilton House in which is located the Museum of Nevis and the Nevis Historical & Conservation Society on the ground floor and a meeting room for the Nevis House of Assembly on the upper floor. Several of Nelson's buildings have been preserved for visitors, as have the slave market, the Jewish Cemetery and a Jewish Walk, a Nevisian Heritage Village (a reconstruction), a New River and Coconut Walk Estate, and other sites.

The Historical and Conservation Society runs a year-round active program and publishes regular newsletters. It is a centre for scholars and laymen alike, and not just for Nevisians; historians from the United States and Latin America come to hold seminars and exchange experiences. In comparison, the museum in Dominica – that houses a fine collection of historic artifacts and provides a good summary of the country's history – is an inactive show for foreign visitors.

The pride in Nevis and its history is well illustrated by American author Vincent K. Hubbard in his book *Swords, Ships & Sugar: History of Nevis to 1900*. One of his apocryphal stories about the arrival of the slaves in Nevis claims that, in the early period, the slave ships from Africa docked first at Nevis where the strongest men and prettiest women were bought until other Caribbean islands complained about getting the "leftovers." True or not, as we noticed, the story illustrates a certain pride by the descendants of the slave masters in the intelligence and adaptability of the descendants of the slaves which allowed them to work together as a team. It demonstrates my belief that a country's success has a lot to do with the quality and unity of its people. It's a fact that in 1675, Nevis was made the headquarters for the slave trade for the Leeward Islands.

When compared with Dominica's failure to make it, I hesitate to push the fact of Nevis's success too far. Yet the comparisons have given me the answers to my question "What's wrong with Dom?" But first, one more comparison: tiny Nevis has a book store, Dominica has none. After the sugar era in the Caribbean Islands, Dominica struggled in the following ways:

- It was without business men or managers because there were few plantation owners to begin with.
- The sugar plantations it did have were relatively small and produced probably less capital than on other islands.

- Its population lacked the initiative to start other economic activities, above all.
- There was a steady and persistent departure of the bright and ambitious to follow educational and work opportunities on other islands and in other cities, especially London, New York, and Toronto – a constant brain drain.

There are, as always, exceptions: some recent new tourist accommodations are taking advantage of the island's natural beauty. Perhaps the best of them is the Jungle Bay Resort and Spa on the southeast coast of Dominica, on a site overlooking the Atlantic Ocean. This "geotourism/ecotourism" resort appeals to those tourists who are less interested in sitting on a sandy beach for a week, of which Dominica has very few. The resort has, apart from the cottages in the rising forest, a swimming pool and dining room, a large and attractive building for yoga classes, and provides therapeutic treatment, organized hikes, nature walks and visits to Dominica's nature sites, like waterfalls throughout the island.

The main interest to me is the fact that the resort was created by Sam Raphael, who in 1984, after years of studies and successful developments in other northern Caribbean islands – a rare occurrence – returned home with his wife, Glenda, from St. Croix to help his country.

CHAPTER 9

Rene

Love, it seems to me, is that condition in which one is most contentedly oneself. If this sounds paradoxical, remember Rilke's admonition: love consists in leaving the loved one space to be themselves while providing the security within which that self may flourish.

— Tony Judt, *The Memory Chalet*

It took the poet Rainer Maria Rilke (1875–1926) to find the right words. I might have just said a bit of give and take for a compatible life. But that would have been too simplistic and not explain anything about love. But then, I never seriously tried to find reasons for our long and happy life together.

Before I came across Rilke's definition of love, I tried to understand why some marriages like ours turn out well and last a long time by comparing us with three happy couples who happened to be our friends and got married at about the same time: Rachel and Walter (Foster), Myrtle and Joey (Hirsh), and Joan and Howard (Sallis). I already mentioned the first two couples. Howard and I met at the London School of Economics, became friends and went to Sweden on our first summer vacation. He and Joan grew up in south Wales, and that was all they had in common. Howard was the son of a well-to-do haberdashery store owner in Ebbw Vale, while

191

Joan was the daughter of a coal miner; their backgrounds therefore were very different. The Foster and Hirsh couples came from Jewish middle-class families; though Walter was born in Vienna.

I will not describe the unhelpful results of my attempted correlations between family background, education, age, character, personalities, and so on. Instead, since I accept the theory of natural selection, I will say that couples knowingly or otherwise act according to emotional selection. Of course, Darwin's natural selection is a random process: a matter of "pot luck"; and so is emotional selection. Success depends on yet another gamble: the instinctive or intuitive adoption of Rilke's meaning of love – altogether a kind of double lottery. Just one addendum: you don't talk about it, at least we never did.

My point is that Rilke's formulation of "leaving the loved one space to be themselves" implies tolerance, respect for the other, patience, and at times, self-control, which, fortunately, we both had.

Imagine my astonishment when I read Rene's thoughts on the subject in her private diary, written in July 1987, some forty-two years after our wedding:

> *For perfection there is a need to a life in harmony which depends on the needs of the person one shares with, and over the years I have learned that this is created by giving your life companion perfect freedom. If the person loves you he will sometimes do things he does not really care for because he knows you want to do this thing very much. But I never must expect to get this treatment repeatedly. Though we may live side by side the two of us need to lead really our own lives much of the time.*

With Rilke's and Rene's wisdom I am now positive of having found the secret of our long and successful life together. Rene also wrote at the same time:

I learned to understand that John can be happy only
when he has mental work to do, can find whatever he
is looking for without effort and has me around at a
distance and above all, not always.

Both of us had some affairs, or as Rene rightly put it in her
"longest love letter" to me, "flirtations," except on two occasions:
one each, when the flirtations did or seemed to go beyond romance.
In Rene's case the rival, sadly, took himself out of competition. In
my case, when the affair had not even been consummated, although
the friendship was serious, Rene's firmness ended the budding affair.

I have throughout referred to Rene's intelligence and good
qualities: she was better educated and had wider interests than me.
She understood me better than I did myself: *"At times you can be very*
difficult. When things don't function right, then you feel insecure." She
would help me over difficulties rather than complain. Who could
wish for a better partner?

Rene knew her own goal: to become a biologist. She started her
studies as soon as the war was over, before I had returned from Cairo,
and got her B.Sc. before delivering Ann. For the next nine years she
was busy bringing up our three children, pretty much without my
help because of the long commute between Reigate and London. I
was around only on weekends.

When we got to Toronto in 1959, Rene was eager to get back
to work and decided to become a teacher so that her hours would
coincide with the children's timetable. She took a teacher's training
course and became a primary school teacher in the Catholic school
system – they needed teachers and she could claim to have gone
regularly to confession as a child.

On our next stop in Watertown, Massachusetts, Rene carried
on teaching. By a stroke of luck she was actually needed there. The

eastern section of Watertown began to be settled, after the First World War by Armenians who had migrated to the city following the Armenian Genocide in Turkey. They readily found work at the Hood Rubber factory and, as the community continued to grow, the children needed a Catholic education. The school was a pleasant institution and I believe even Nicholas was pleased because he seemed to like his young and pretty Armenian teacher.

Then, after the unexpected move to Washington, Rene got her chance. At last she returned to biology studies at American University and, at the age of forty-four, very easily passed her master's degree after two years, including a "flirtation" with a fellow student thrown in for good measure. During the rest of her active life, she worked and researched at the Smithsonian Institute, the Royal Ontario Museum, and the Indonesian Biology Institute.

The only, and considerable, test to our relationship occurred in Indonesia and had two related sources: our very different attitudes towards Indonesians and my decision to quit the KIP project at the end of the first year.

Our opinions and views about the people were very different because we moved in different circles. Rene worked with, met, and enjoyed the company of professionals at the Biology Institute, and made friends with educated people like Mrs. Manurung, the owner of the house we lived in, and the kampung dwellers living next to us. My contacts were bureaucrats and their hangers-on. Rene described these differences in her journal:

> *How could I always manage perfectly travelling and finding my way on my own in strange countries. I know I am not as organized as John but since I am slow, given time I always get my way without hurting people, make friends and admit that even lesser people*

can and do know things better than I could. Not like
J. who is inclined to mistrust, gets great satisfaction
of pointing out errors and never admits that other
persons can tackle some tasks better than he does. I do
believe his is a pathological condition, not just a case
of immaturity.

Rene did not realize that most of my work in Asia and Africa, including the KIP assignment, consisted of reviews, evaluations, and making recommendations for changes to locally managed projects financed by international agencies. I actually got paid for being critical, finding inefficiencies and corruption – hence my critical outlook and my daily frustrations in Jakarta and in KIP cities in the rest of the country.

I could have put up with the lack of local support if the World Bank had given me some help. In the absence of any support, I had to make a strong statement and leave.

In addition to Rene's sorrow about leaving the people she knew in Indonesia, she was conscious of leaving behind the beautiful countryside of the islands and her lovely garden.

The spell of the garden.
How could I ever forget the evenings in the garden
at Jl. Praja Dalam? The silence of the tropical nights
was broken by the stridulations of the cicadas, the swish
of the tail of the gold fish in the moat, the gobbling of
the gekows eating insects. The scent of tropical blossoms
was intoxicating. And after you went to bed, I was
held captive by the magic spell of the tropical night.
Later, when we were travelling in the islands, I
often imagined the presence of spirits.

Rene was unable or unwilling to discuss our year-long journey home to Toronto (after visiting many more Indonesian islands). She

could not think about anything but the loss of her paradise. I was left
to guess about the places she might like to visit. About India, when
we were there: *"I should not have come to this country – which was
not my intention in any case but had been my desire since the 1940s."*
I guessed right, but Rene seemed to feel the same way about India
as I did. I had not been eager to return once again to this humanely
depressing country. However, the last part of the India journey, in
Kashmir and Ladak, was wonderful for both of us – because these
two areas are not really India.

The rest of the long journey to France, Austria, and England did
not restore her spirit or zest for life. Not until our travels in China
and a brief visit to Kupang (West Timor, Indonesia) was Rene her
old self again. Finally, of course, at Curry's Rest she had her new
and last "paradise."

Rene was welcomed back by the ROM, once we were set up
again in our Cabbage Town house. But she never really settled in
again at the museum. She would have preferred to continue research
rather than exhibit shells and other sea creatures; despite the fact that
she had come to be known as the "Shell Lady," the term *The Globe
and Mail* used when it published an article about her under that title.

Before re-opening my own office in Toronto in 1989, my friend
and former colleague Martin ter Woort invited me to join him on
a large project in China. The Chinese government had asked the
World Bank for financial assistance in building the Tree Gorges
Dam on the Yangtze River. The Bank required a proper "Western"
feasibility study, which CIDA decided to pay for. The study team
consisted of several groups (engineering, hydrology, etc.), and Martin
was the head of the "resettlement" group concerned with China's
preparations (or lack thereof) for relocating the thousands of farmers

and their families required to move to higher ground once the rising waters behind the dam would force them from their land. Martin, having received permission to enlarge his "resettlement" team, asked me to join his team.

The start of the work in China was actually delayed due to the Tiananmen Square debacle, which should be called the FIRST OCCUPY event.

I mention these facts here to explain why, in the course of the study, I could bring Rene to China for an exciting trip. Meantime, Martin's clever and determined leadership in exposing the complete lack of resettlement assistance by the Chinese government was instrumental in the World Bank's eventual unwillingness to provide funds for the Three Gorges Dam project.

Foreigners wishing to travel in China at the time, soon after the Tiananmen rebellion, had to join an approved group and were accompanied by Chinese "guides." To travel alone and follow our own itinerary, I created a "group of two" and used the occasion of a major review meeting on the Three Gorges Dam study in Beijing, to which ladies had been invited. Somehow, because I belonged to the study team, Rene and I were allowed to travel unaccompanied; we just were seen off and met at airports, railway stations, or boat docks and taken to a hotel.

After a visit to the Great Wall near Beijing, we went to Xian to see the remarkable terracotta warriors and horses dating back to 210 BC. Xian was a textile town and we were also invited to one of the factories, where we ended up buying an attractive baby's quilt.

From Xian we travelled to our greatest surprise – Guilin on the Li River in South China, said to be the most spectacular landscape in the country. We would never know the full extent of the beauty, but it certainly amazed us to see the topography of limestone peaks in the shape of sugar loaves and to visit the bamboo and willow forests.

We spent a morning in a tiny fishing boat being paddled on the Li River by a fisherman who used a cormorant to fish: a traditional fishing practice. This consists of tying the bird's throat to prevent it from swallowing and dipping it into the water to scoop up the fish. At the end of the morning the cormorant got its reward: a few fish to eat. We took some more boat rides, without the fisherman, to get closer to the mountains for some hikes. Guilin and surroundings were certainly a highlight of our extensive trip in China.

Our next stop was Chongqing, located at the confluence of the Yangtze and Jialing Rivers, which was inaccessible by large boats before the construction of the Three Gorges Dam. Yet even then Chongqing was considered one of the largest towns in China because it incorporated a vast area of several counties. I had been to Chongqing twice before and chose a hotel I knew in the centre of the town, although our "receptionist" at the airport tried to put us up out in the country in a new and much more posh tourist hotel.

We spent several days in the busy city. I was careful not to exhaust Rene, remembering India. But she had long ago recovered from her year-long post-Indonesia depression.

Not being a travel writer, I will merely give an outline of the rest of the trip. But I must add that the urban areas we visited about twenty-five years ago had completely changed, and had grown beyond imagination. For example, the last time I was in China in 1991 and visited Shenzen, just north of Hong Kong, one of the designated Special Economic Zones, it was a fishing village of maybe 200 people. The first excavations for factory buildings were being dug in former rice fields. Today, the Greater Shenzen area has a population of over 10 million.

To catch a regular (as opposed to a tourist) Yangtze boat, we went by bus to Fuling in the upper Outang Gorge and boarded a crowded boat. We managed to get two sleeping bunks for the journey downriver (which I guess to have been about 550 miles). The overnight journey made frequent stops all the way to Wuhan.

Wuhan was the former capital of the Kuomintang government and the long-time headquarters of the Three Gorges Dam planning office, which included a scale model of the proposed dam for test purposes. The idea for the dam actually goes back to Sun Yat-sen (1866–1925) who wrote an article in 1919 entitled "The Industrial Plan," in which he saw a dam on the Yangtze as part of an economic development for China.

There is much to see in Wuhan and I enjoyed showing Rene the city.

The last two places of or trip were Suzhou on the Grand Canal (from Beijing) and at one time called "The Venice of China" because of several canals faced by houses and crossed by humped bridges. Suzhou had many gardens and was an artist town. We had to buy at least one lovely painting.

The appropriate finale of our trip in China was Shanghai, the largest city in China and the world; though its size is the least important part of its fame. Arriving on September 30 we checked into our reserved room at the old Peace Hotel at a corner of the Bund (embankment) along the Huangpu River. The now-famous Pudong financial high-rise district that would be built on the banks across the river did not even exist yet.

Around midnight we were woken by a strange and loud babbling noise from the street. Looking down from our window, we saw the street packed with people: it was the early morning of the first of October, the National Day of the People's Republic – we had no idea. For the next twenty four hours we became part of the vast, milling, eating, and celebrating crowd with music, speeches and performances along the Bund.

I was very surprised that we got the reservation in the Peace Hotel at this special time because the hotel was rather special. Somewhat like the Chelsea Hotel in New York, it was used by artists and other performing people who might stay for extended periods. This is where Noel Coward wrote his play *Private Lives at the Peace Hotel*. The hotel was also known for its Old Jazz Band in the bar, where we had a drink one evening. Altogether, our final stop turned into a memorable experience.

~

Let Rene have the, almost, last word in her chapter:

Epilogue

> *We have reached the Sunset of our lives. Never in my wildest dreams could I have imagined that you would plant the Garden of Eden.*

> *Nor that after the meagre beginnings we would be living in the most beautiful house I have ever seen. The structure is simple and in good taste. The story of our life together, is evident from the objects within. A mascot is sitting on the post at the bottom of the stairs. He brings us good luck.*

> *When we sit and watch the setting sun, I feel the desire as in the tent, though mellowed by age.*

> *I feel the magic of the tropical night as together we look at the sparkling stars. And somehow a bond holds us so tight.*

September 8, 1995

Rene wrote this on our 50th anniversary when we had been at Curry's Rest for about five years. We were to have another fifteen years there together.

~

After reviewing the recollections of my life, I noticed how little I wrote about our children: Ann, Nicholas, and Jacki, and nothing at all about the grandchildren: Alex, Adrien, Claire, Nicolas, and River. Not even when writing about Rene, the mother of our three children, do I reflect on her major part in bringing up our children. This is odd, considering that Ann started me off on writing my memoir some years ago, when on a visit to Curry's Rest she asked me to write about my childhood, having listened to a few things I had told her about my unusual start to life. And, having read the few pages I wrote about playing with gypsies in the forest, Ann said "Now, carry on," which I did not do for quite a few years.

I suppose there are two reasons for my neglect in writing about our children: (1) when they were young Rene looked after them while I was at work, and I often came home late; and (2) most important, all three of them were independent after finishing high school, studying or working away from home. And Rene and I kept moving around, so there was no fixed "home."

However, I suspect the main reason why there is so little about "the family" is due to the nature of my memoir. I had no clear vision of the focus or audience for my memoir when I started. I had much I could write about, and seemed to have selected an unstated goal: to present how, with a difficult start in life, I managed to overcome a seemingly hopeless future and succeeded in living a satisfying and rewarding life. Hence, our children, who were a pleasure to spoil when young and to admire their easy successes at an early age, did not fit into my chosen theme.

The grandchildren always lived somewhere else and we saw little of them. However, now all five of them are very bright and on the way to successful professional lives. It gives me the greatest pleasure to watch their undoubted progress in their chosen fields. However, I will mention my first great-grandchild, Shotaro, who was born in Japan, lived his first two years in London, Philadelphia, Toronto, and Edinburgh, and is now beginning to sort out his Japanese spoken by his mother, Aska; his French, spoken by his father, Alex, who was born in France; and his English, spoken by his playmates. Who knows which additional language he will pick up without having to "study it." Shotaro is symptomatic of our times.

_ɯ_

I have never believed in an afterlife; a pity, if I did I could dream about meeting Rene again.

Rene in Leicester, England, 1945

Rene with our three children, Toronto, 1959

Rene at Curry's Rest, 2009

CHAPTER 10

Epilogue

> Memories lie slumbering within us for months and
> years, quietly proliferating, until they are woken
> by some trifle and in some strange way blind us
> to life. How often this has caused me to feel that
> my memories, and the labours expended in writing
> them down are all part of the same humiliating and,
> at bottom, contemptible business!
> — W.G. Sebald, *The Rings of Saturn* (1998)

Being by myself, without Rene after my whole adult life, opened a
new chapter in my life. I say "by myself" and not "alone" because
Ann took on the task of watching over me from afar (Ottawa) – it
is perhaps the "Rene" in her.

I had time to read and think about my life's experiences, especially
while writing about my life – so, what did I learn, or better, who
have I become as a result of the experiences? I have to be selective;
therefore, I will confine myself to three topics of greatest interest to
me now: understanding society, the Palestine–Israel conflict, and
my recent rediscovery of the German people.

The reason I discuss, explain, and quote a lot in the Epilogue
is that the issues occupied my mind throughout much of my life
(except in Germany), and I want to know whether my thoughts and

theories were justified. Revisiting Germany was largely an accident but I was glad of it.

Part I: Understanding Society, Or, Where Is Mankind Going?

> It is interesting that today blood flows only where blind nationalism enters the fray, or zoological racism, or religious fundamentalism – in other words, the three black clouds that can darken the sky of the twenty-first century.
> — Ryszard Kapuściński, *Imperium* (1995)

My low opinion of mankind's behaviour is already tempered by Heine, who said, "Man is the aristocrat among animals."

When, where, and with whom I spent my formative years – say, from coming to Berlin (1926) at age five to leaving Germany (1938) at seventeen – had obviously much to do with my developing understanding of society, my *Weltanschauung* (world view). While I never starved in that time, except briefly in Prague at sixteen, I would not recommend to anyone my harsh beginnings and belated formal education; but I think that my experiences provided a more useful grounding for understanding the world today than that of a child born into poverty or extreme affluence.

No sooner had I passed my happy and carefree childhood in Wolfenbüttel when I met a troubling world in Berlin. Not that it troubled me personally at first, but it must have set me wondering. I mentioned that my father started life in Poland as an ultra-orthodox Jew and gradually, after university studies in Berlin which included a Ph.D. in theology, become a liberal or progressive Jew. Essentially, liberal Jews emphasize ethical conduct above ritual observance. In any event, my religious attitude had drifted beyond religion to what I described as agnostic, i.e., someone who neither believes nor disbelieves in the existence of a god, as compared to an atheist who attacks religious beliefs. At some point, I suppose because something had to replace the void of non-belief, I became a humanist without knowing the word or its meaning.

I had read about an organization which asked for money to feed and clothe poor people. I needed practical advice from my father: how to acknowledge receipt of money from a donor? He told me and commended me for my initiative – I knew I was on the right track.

∽

> We think that human beings, at least in ethical theory, all have equal rights, and that justice involves equality.
> —Bertrand Russell, *History of Western Philosophy*
> (1946)

Russell's quote implies that humanists generally prefer individual thought and evidence over established doctrine of faith. Humanist thought has roots in ethical and moral philosophy and history going back at least to the fifteenth century of Erasmus (1466–1535) and Thomas More (1478–1535), and Russell claims that Nicholas V (1447–55) was the first humanist pope (*History of Western Philosophy*, p. 459). Curiously enough, the first Humanist Manifesto was adopted in 1933, the year Hitler came to power.

The manifesto was signed by philosophers, historians, scientists, authors, ministers of the church, and a rabbi, and included among its fifteen precepts are:

- Humanism asserts that the nature of the universe depicted by modern science makes unacceptable any supernatural or cosmic guarantees of human values.
- The goal of humanism is a free and universal society in which people voluntarily and intelligently cooperate for the

common good. Humanists demand a shared life in a shared world.

- (And, as a sign of the times during which the manifesto was written, it also included:) The humanists are firmly convinced that the existing acquisitive and profit-motivated society has shown itself to be inadequate and that radical change in methods, controls, and motives must be instituted.

I, of course, had no knowledge about this at the time and had to gain more advanced education and practical worldly experience. The laudable sentiment of "Love Thy Neighbour" sounded fine in theory, but its practice was hard to locate outside of individual religious groups and did not necessarily apply to others outside the group. It seemed merely a feel-good sentiment of no consequence.

The persecution of the Jews was clearly not a unique phenomenon, nor of recent times, though as practised by Hitler it had reached its most extreme form. Both before Hitler and certainly since then, conflicts have been a constant spectacle worldwide both between and within clans, devout believers and ethnic groups: Hindus vs. Muslims, Arab Muslims vs. Non-Arab Muslims, Shias vs. Sunnis, Hutus vs. Tutsis, Croats vs. Serbs, Sudanese vs. Darfurians, the list goes on.

Ethnic cleansing became the term for the end product of a negative progression from dislike to prejudice to discrimination to restrictions to prohibitions to punishment to incarceration to violence to purges to executions to genocide.

There has been progress in the adoption of humanist principles publicly and privately: the United Nations Declaration of Human Rights (1948), the Canadian Charter of Rights and Freedoms (1982), and the establishment of Amnesty International (1961), Médicins sans Frontières (1971), and Human Rights Watch (1978). And now: Pope Francis is in the Vatican. Bertrand Russell undoubtedly would call Francis a Humanist Pope.

"How I would like a Church which is poor and for the poor," Pope Francis said in his first week as a pope; he chose his name for Francis of Assisi (a twelfth-century saint), a man of poverty, a man of peace, a man who loved and protected creation. I am indebted to James Carroll's profile "Who Am I to Judge? A Radical Pope's First Year" in *The New Yorker* of December 23 & 30, 2013.

Pope Francis started as a Jesuit, became Bishop of Buenos Aires in 1992, Archbishop of Buenos Aires and Cardinal Bergoglio in 2001. During this time, liberation theology, which began in Latin America in the 1950s and 1960s, grew. Liberation theology is a political movement in Roman Catholic theology and is regarded to have been founded by Gustavo Gutiérrez (b. 1928), a Peruvian Dominican priest (*A Theory of Liberation*, 1971), which interprets the teaching of Jesus Christ in relation to liberation from unjust economic, political, or social conditions. In his 1987 book, *Liberation Theology*, Phillip Berryman described the movement as "an interpretation of Christian faith through the poor's suffering, their struggle and hope, and a critique of society and the Catholic faith and Christianity through the eyes of the poor."

Since Cardinal Bergoglio became Pope Francis, much has been written about his position on the liberation theology movement, some of which I have read. As Archbishop and Cardinal, he has been criticized for decisions made against the movement, though he could hardly counter the Vatican's directions. For now, and perhaps for the future too, I think James Carroll's opinion is the right one: "Whatever Bergoglio made of liberation theology during his time as a Jesuit authority, he came to embody its spirit after he was named a bishop, in 1992."

A final point on this issue: In September, 2013, Pope Francis met Gustavo Gutiérrez, the liberation theology pioneer. After the meeting, the Vatican newspaper *L'Osservatore Romano* published an essay stating that, "with the election of the first pope from Latin America, liberation theology could no longer remain in the shadows to which it had been relegated for some years, at least in Europe."

Maybe I attach too much importance to Pope Francis as a hopeful influence for the better in humanist practices internationally. Perhaps, I am just grasping at straws because what can the pope, any pope, really accomplish outside his church? As Stalin is supposed to have said when cautioned to be less aggressive in his comments against the pope: How many tanks does he have?

Few men, or women, have been able to predict the future accurately, least of all historians because of their tendency to rely on their own theories of history. But the Vatican still has some influence in the world, especially when its judgements and opinions are expressed *vox populi* – in colloquial terms, which Pope Francis does so well because of his sincerity and moral character.

Which takes me to my next topic.

Part II: Palestine–Israel Conflict

My interest in the Middle East goes back about seventy years. In 1945–46, when I was a British soldier, I was stationed in Cairo and visited Palestine twice: first for a short holiday on the beach at Netanya with Rene's uncle Fritz, his daughter Janne, and her youngest child Dodi, then perhaps one year old. Later, shortly before my return to England, I was stationed for over a month at a British Forces Education Centre on Mount Carmel in Haifa, where I witnessed, and got involved in, the turmoil in the pre-Israel era between Palestinians, Zionists, and the British.

As mentioned previously, a soldier friend of mine and I wondered how the armed rivalry would, or could be resolved; it seemed insoluble, unless a mutually acceptable accommodation was agreed on. Historically, Palestine was controlled by major powers, and numerous peoples had lived there over a very long time. "Palestine" was carved out of the Ottoman Empire when the British Mandate for Palestine was established in the League of Nations in 1922. A few Jews had immigrated to Palestine in the nineteenth century before the Zionist Organization was created in 1908 to encourage and organize the "Aliyah" (the return to Palestine of the Jews). Between 1882 and 1914, about 75,000 came, mainly from Russia; from 1919 to 1929, about 120,000 came, mainly from Poland and other eastern European countries like Hungary. With the rise of the Nazis immigration increased steeply, 250,000 in the years from 1929 to 1939.

The flow of Jewish immigration reflected (1) the pull of Zionist encouragement, (2) the push due to Jewish persecution, and (3) the fluctuating immigration policies in Palestine and other countries at the time. Especially noted are the U.S., due to its annual quota changes, and Britain, thanks to specific controls such as its White Paper of 1939, which restricted immigration to Palestine.

Of course, not all of the half million Jewish immigrants between 1880 and 1939 stayed in Palestine. The Jewish exodus was greatly influenced by immigration laws elsewhere. Additionally, some Jews used Palestine as a staging point before moving elsewhere, and other non-Zionists did not care for the pioneer life. For example, my brother Max first went to Palestine in 1937, returned to Berlin a year later, and finally went to Argentina, where he stayed for the rest of his life. Argentina, the country which became a haven for Nazi leaders after the Second World War, including Eichman, who was later kidnapped by Israel and taken to Jerusalem for his trial – it's a small world.

Regarding the migration lottery, Jews coming to Palestine until about 1939 were nearly all Ashkenazi Jews, i.e., from Eastern Europe, Germany, and Austria, who, when the war started, could no longer get out and disappeared. The next wave of Jewish immigrants, the Sephardi Jews from Morocco and North Africa, also referred to as Oriental Jews, came much later when the Zionists in Palestine–Israel needed more Jews to oppose the Arabs' belligerence. This caused what may be called an intra-semitic conflict of major political consequences, a conflict that continues in the leadership of Israel to this day.

Finally, the only quasi-legal right for the Zionists to claim Palestine is a letter from the British Foreign Secretary, Lord Balfour, to Baron Rothschild of the Zionist Federation, dated November 2, 1917, which states:

> *Dear Lord Rothschild,*
>
> *I have pleasure in conveying to you, on behalf of His Majesty's Government, the following declaration of sympathy with Jewish Zionist aspirations which has been submitted to, and approved by, the Cabinet.*
>
> *His Majesty's Government views with favour the establishment in Palestine of a national home for the Jewish people, and will use their best endeavors to facilitate the achievement of this object, it being clearly understood that nothing shall be done which prejudice the civil and religious rights of existing non-Jewish communities in Palestine, or the rights and political status enjoyed by Jews in any other country.*
>
> *I should be grateful if you would bring this declaration to the knowledge of the Zionist Federation.*
>
> *Yours sincerely,*
>
> *Arthur James Balfour*

This letter, referred to as the "Balfour Declaration," is really the legal beginning of Israel, although it begs one question: What "rights" is Balfour talking about? I am not sure the then-existing "non-Jewish communities" were aware of any rights they had, or that anyone could have spelled them out for them.

I followed events in Israel from afar after the country's independence in May 1948. When Dodi had grown up, he included me in a group of friends to whom he sent e-mails whenever Israel came under criticism for its actions against the Palestinians, and therefore needed defence or vindication for its behaviour.

Overall, Israeli's prime ministers from Ben Gurion onwards, with one exception, ploughed ahead, ignoring the Palestinians and established settlements in the West Bank. However, Palestinians living in "Israel" proper have the vote and representation in the Knesset (Parliament).

The "exceptional" prime minister was Rabin, who negotiated the Oslo Accords (1993–95) between Israel and the PLO (the Palestinian Liberation Organization) towards limited self-government over parts of the West Bank and Gaza. For this achievement of the Oslo Accords (or perhaps better called "a reluctant peace"), Rabin was assassinated on November 4, 1995.

Throughout its history, Israel had the steady support of the U.S. government in terms of money, armaments, and diplomacy, for two reasons: the influence of the "Jewish Lobby" in Congress and, more important, America's need to maintain a reliable and militarily strong ally for the protection of U.S. oil interests in the Middle East. Until more recently, say, starting in 2013, there had been no change in this situation. But when U.S. home energy supplies – oil, natural gas, and renewables (wind and solar) began to increase towards self-sufficiency, I began to fear that the U.S. government would begin to feel free to turn its back on Israel – what then? Well – today (2014), we almost have arrived at that critical point when the Secretary of State of the United States was overheard using the dreaded word "Apartheid" during his negotiations in Israel.

My frustration to understand how Israel got into its seemingly hopeless situation, from which there seems to be no escape, was answered by three recent books, all written by Israeli-born authors:

- *My Promised Land: The Triumph and Tragedy of Israel* by Ari Shavit (Spiegel & Grau, 2013)
- *The Idea of Israel: A History of Power and Knowledge* by Ilan Pappe (Verso, 2014)

- *Israel's Holocaust and the Politics of Nationhood* by Idith Zertal (New Edition, Cambridge University Press, 2011)

⌒⁀⌒

My Promised Land by Ari Shavit

Shavit is a leading Israeli journalist, a columnist for *Haaretz*, who was born in Israel and has been a long-term critic of the occupation of the West Bank. His book is a candid and honest account of Israel's history; it starts with his great-grandfather's first visit in Palestine in 1871, and is a detailed account based on taped interviews and interview notes with ministers, politicians, soldiers, decision-makers, participants of major events, news analysts, colleagues, and friends. It is an astonishingly fair-minded record of Israel from well before day one.

The aggressive Zionist approach to establishing their home in Palestine is symbolized by Shavit in his chapter "The Tragedy of Lydda," which describes the expulsion of Palestinians from their town of Lydda in the West Bank in 1948: "Even as war rages on in most parts of Palestine, both Arabs and Jews regard the Lydda Valley as a zone of restricted warfare" (p.107). He goes on to say:

> But on July 4, 1948, Operation Larlar, designed to conquer Lydda, is presented to Israel's first prime minister, David Ben Gurion. Although two hundred civilians were killed, negotiations between the two warring sides established the evacuation of Lydda ... By noon a mass evacuation is under way. By evening tens of thousands of Palestinian Arabs leave Lydda ... Zionism obliterates the city of Lydda. (p.108)

Lydda is our black box. In it lies the dark secret of Zionism. The truth is that Zionism could not bear Lydda. From the very beginning there was a substantial contradiction between Zionism and Lydda. IF ZIONISM WAS TO BE, LYDDA COULD NOT BE. IF LYDDA WAS TO BE, ZIONISM COULD NOT BE. (p. 108) (my emphasis – this shows that there was no attempt made to search for a better, peaceful solution; it is the legacy of the history of tribal, religious, colonial, and political power struggles throughout the ages and all over the world. This attitude is, in the case of Israel, supported by justifications, à la the Holocaust.)

For when one opens the black box, one understands that whereas the small mosque massacre could have been a misunderstanding brought about by a tragic chain of accidental events, the conquest of Lydda and the expulsion were no accident. They were an inevitable phase of the Zionist revolution that laid the foundation for the Zionist state. Lydda is an integral and essential part of the story. And when I try to be honest about it, I see that the choice is stark: either reject Zionism because of Lydda, or accept Zionism along with Lydda. (p. 131)

So there you have it; no need for me to quote any more from Shavit. However, I would like to quote an opinion by Shlomi Segall, Associate Professor, Department of Political Science, Hebrew University, Jerusalem, who wrote in a response to Shavit's book:

In the aftermath of the Six-Day War, which ended in the occupation of the West bank and Gaza, a number of Israeli soldiers published memoirs of the war, expressing ambivalence about what they had participated in. In particular, they agonized over the misery they had brought upon thousands of Palestinian civilians. In Israel, this genre was quickly mocked as "shooting and weeping." Shavit elevates the genre to new heights of cynicism. Writing with sympathy for the Palestinian victims of the 1984 ethnic cleansing of Lydda, Shavit ends to shamelessly justify the act. If we were a Serbian national expressing equivalent views about atrocities committed during the Yugoslav wars, he would be considered an apologist for ethnic cleansing. Perhaps because Israeli Jews enjoy a sort of immunity as "eternal victims," Shavit was able to indulge in the exercise of "ethnically cleansing and weeping." It adds insult to injury suffered by the people of Lydda. (*The New Yorker*, November 4, 2013)

As they say in court: I rest my case.

The Idea of Israel by Ilan Pappe

Ilan Pappe is one of Israel's "New Historians," who, since the early 1980s, have been rewriting Israel's history from its creation in 1948. Unlike Shavit, who is a journalist, the historian Pappe and his colleagues are historiographers. Historiography is the study of the methodology of historians generally, the study of a body of historical work as a discipline, and the development of a specific history (for example, Zionism and its underpinning of Israel's political actions since its creation).

Pappe was born in Haifa in 1954 to German Jewish parents. He is a graduate of the Hebrew University in Jerusalem and obtained his Ph.D. from Oxford. He has published a number of books on the history of the Arab–Israel conflict, the most widely read and most controversial of which is *The Ethnic Cleansing of Palestine* (2006). Pappe taught at the University of Haifa, but left Israel in 2007 (after threats were made on his life) to teach at the University of Exeter, England. Pappe is a supporter of the one-state solution for a binational state for Palestinians and Israelis.

I apologise for my lengthy quotes from Pappe's book, but justify them because his analysis explains and answers, for the first time, my puzzlement about Israel's obstinate refusal to confront its hopeless situation in the Middle East. (And, perhaps you, the reader, will be led to read his book.)

Pappe's detailed and well-documented analysis leads him to the following conclusions:

> Every book on Israel attempts to dissect a complex and ambiguous reality. Yet however one chooses to describe, analyse and present Israel, the result will always be both subjective and limited. Nevertheless, the subjectivity and relativity of any representation do not invalidate moral and ethical discussion about that presentation. In fact, from the vantage point of the early twenty-first century, the moral and ethical dimensions of such a debate are no less important than questions of substance, facts and evidence ...
>
> In this book, I will argue that these opposing versions are not about Israel as such, but rather about the idea of Israel. Obviously, Israel itself is not merely an idea. It is first and foremost a state – a living organism that has existed for more than sixty years. Denying its existence is impossible and unrealistic. However, evaluating it ethically,

morally, and politically is not only possible but also, at present, urgent as never before.

Indeed, Israel is one of a few states considered by many to be at best morally suspect or at worse illegitimate. What is challenged, with varying degrees of conviction and determination, is not the state itself but rather the idea of the state. Some may say they challenge the *ideology* of the state; meanwhile some Israeli Jews may tell you they fight for the survival of the *ideal* of the state. This optimal term through which to examine the two sides of the argument, however, is "idea." (2014, p. 3)

Pappe mentions Simha Flapan, a journalist, born in Poland, who immigrated to Palestine in 1930. In his retirement, Flapan went to Harvard and met Wahid Khalidi, a Palestinian historian who convinced Flapan that the official Israeli version of Israel was a fabrication. Flapan wrote in his book, *The Birth of Israel: Myths and Realities* (published posthumously in 1987), "like most Israelis, I had always been under the influence of certain myths that had become accepted as historical truth" (p. 110).

What are those myths according to Pappe? He lists six of them (pp. 110–112), which I will summarize. There is another myth concerning the Holocaust that I will mention later.

The FIRST MYTH was that Israel accepted the UN resolution of 1947 and, therefore, agreed to the creation of a Palestinian state. The acceptance, according to Flapan, proved that Ben Gurion ignored the territorial dimension of the partition and referred to the resolution only as granting legitimacy for the idea of the Jewish state, whose borders the Zionists would determine.

The SECOND MYTH was that the Palestinians followed the Grand Mufty of Jerusalem in his resistance to any UN plan. Flapan shows that Ben Gurion's chief advisor on Arab affairs reported that the vast majority of Palestinians accepted partition.

The THIRD MYTH was that the Arab world was determined to destroy the Jewish state in 1948. Flapan explains that first, the Arab world was fragmented and did not have a unified policy, and second, Iraq and Transjordan were seeking an understanding with the new Jewish state. And, in fact, Ben Gurion concluded a secret treaty with Jordan, under which the two sides agreed to divide Palestine between them.

The FOURTH MYTH was that the Palestinians left their homes because they were told to do so by their leaders. There is "no evidence" for such an allegation.

The FIFTH MYTH is that Israel was a "David" that miraculously defeated an Arab "Goliath." Flapan was convinced that at any given stage in the confrontation of 1948 the superiority of the Jewish forces was never in dispute.

The SIXTH MYTH was that Israel extended its hand for peace after the war and was rejected by the Arab states and the Palestinians. Flapan points out that the Lausanne protocol, created in an international peace conference on Palestine convened by the UN, was signed on May 12, 1949, by Egypt, Jordan, Lebanon, Syria, and Israel. This protocol set three principal guidelines for peace in Palestine: recognition of the earlier partition plan and therefore the existence of Israel, the internationalism of Jerusalem, and the repatriation of Palestinian refugees.

From its beginning, the State of Israel endeavoured to present its history in the context of the Jews' constant, widespread, and drawn-out struggle of resistance and defence against discrimination. Every spark of active Jewish resistance or opposition has been explained in Zionist terms from Ben Gurion onwards. A good example can be found in Pappe's chapter 7, in the section entitled "The Ancestors of the Warsaw Uprising Is the State of Israel":

Mainstream Israeli historiography, the underpinning of the elite, characterised the revolts in the various ghettos and camps as a chapter in the long Zionist history of struggle against those who wished to destroy the Jewish people. This was one narrative. The very idea that there might be another narrative was a bold suggestion, made by post-Zionist scholars in the 1990s. To them, these uprisings had been Zionised in Israeli collective memory and mainstream academia. They saw this process of Zionisation as a typical instance of how national movements tend to define people's past identity in accordance with the needs of the present national movement. (2014, pp. 164–165)

The Warsaw Ghetto Uprising, starting in January 1943, was organized by two groups of Jews in the ghetto: the Jewish Socialist (anti-Zionist) Bund and the Zionist movement. Both groups received aid from the Polish underground. One of the leaders of the revolt was Marek Edleman from the Bund. As Pappe describes it:

After the war, Edelman studied medicine in Poland and ... in 1976 he joined the famous Solidarity movement led by Lech Walesa and became one of Poland's revered intellectuals. In his writing he often addressed issues of human and civil rights around the world and often criticised Zionism and Israel for their discriminatory policies towards the Palestinians. In the late 1980s he became a member of the Polish parliament. In 1993 the Israeli prime minister, Yitzhak Rabin, led an Israeli delegation for the jubilee commemoration of the Warsaw Ghetto Uprising. Polish president Lech Walesa asked Edelman to be among the chief speakers; heavy pressure from the Israeli delegation removed him from the list at the very last moment.

In 1945 he wrote a book on the uprising called *The Ghetto Fights*, which appeared in Hebrew only in 2001. He disliked the way he and his friends were portrayed visually and textually in Israeli scholarship – "none of them had ever looked like this…," they didn't have rifles, cartridge pouches or maps; besides, they were dark and dirty, hardly the ideal type of handsome, Aryan-like young Jews seen in the Israeli museums of the Holocaust and in the pictures decorating official texts.

Edelman explained that for him the uprising was a human choice about how to die (as Primo Levi, too, claimed). But death was not a simple issue for the political elite in Israel, which was always busy shaping the collective memory of a society of immigrants, while at the same time colonising a population and an area that resisted, at times violently. The leaders felt in the past, as they do today, a need to rank death in a hierarchy – to idealise one type and condemn another. Death in rebellion against the Holocaust was commendable, death in the Holocaust without resistance was questionable. Death for the sake of the nation was to be the sublime act of Humanity.

Edelman was ignored in official Israeli texts and representations of the Holocaust. He is known now thanks to Idith Zertal, who, in the relative openness of the public debate during the 1990s, introduced his story to the world. (2014, pp. 165–166)

By bringing Idith Zertal to our attention, we reach the deplorable story of how Israel used, and continues to use, the Holocaust as a founding event in its history and subsequently uses this interpretation of the state's existence to deflect every criticism of its actions.

⟨﹏⟩

Israel's Holocaust and the Politics of Nationhood by Idith Zertal

Zertal is one of the New Historians of Israel. She graduated from Tel Aviv University's School of History and taught at the Hebrew University of Jerusalem. She was the editor of *Zmanim: A Historical Quarterly*, and is currently teaching at the Institute of Jewish Studies at the University of Basel, Switzerland. Her writings include *From Catastrophe to Power: Holocaust Survivors and the Emergence of Israel*. Her current book, previously published in Hebrew under another title, *Israel's Holocaust and the Politics of Nationhood*, has received wide attention and has been published in eight languages. The book has even been praised by Israel's establishment: "This is a brilliant and unsettling book that charts new, deeply submerged territories of the collective consciousness of Israeli society. The book is a major contribution to our understanding of the history of Israeli life and mentality," said Shlomo Ben Ami, Emeritus Professor of Modern History, Tel Aviv University, and former foreign minister of Israel.

I intentionally provide this lengthy background of Zertal to allay any suspicions that I may have selected her book because it answers many of my doubts about Israel. My copy of the book is a new edition, Cambridge University Press, 2011, with a foreword by Tony Judt, and I quote from his long foreword:

> Whereas most of the pathbreaking new scholars in Israeli historiography confined themselves to the classic themes of Zionist history – merely inverting or subverting the interpretation – Idith Zertal has

carved out for herself a unique role. She, virtually alone, has opened up the impossibly painful subject of Israel's use and abuse of the Holocaust.

The relationship of the Holocaust to Israel is in one sense perfectly straightforward. If Hitler had not tried to exterminate the Jews of Europe – and come close to succeeding – there would not have been a Jewish state in the Middle East... But the Shoah changed everything, the Zionists could argue after 1945 that Jewish survival was a moral obligation history had placed on the rest of the world – and that only in a Jewish state could the surviving Jews count on security and a future. But once Israel existed, the moral benefits of being grounded in a great historical crime became unclear ... On the one hand, Jews were the world's ultimate victim, and Israel had a moral case against everyone else which it never hesitated to press. On the other, the victims were not very attractive in Zionist eyes and were often dismissed with something close to contempt: as Zital documents, official Israel even went to the trouble of trying Jewish "collaborators" for wartime cooperation with the Nazis – as though to illustrate just how low Jews could sink in the absence of the sort of pride and backbone that only a state can provide.

...just as the older generation of founding fathers like Ben Gurion were beginning to worry that the arguments of Zionism were no longer as self-evident as they had once seemed (in the eyes of the world, at least). It seemed to them that the Holocaust might now be put to more active service: as an illustration as well as a justification of the cause for a Jewish state. Out of it grew the Eichmann Trial.

The trial, and the agonized debates to which it gave rise, is associated above all with Hannah Arendt's classic account of it, "Eichmann in Jerusalem: A Report on the Banality of Evil." For many years, her work was not translated into Hebrew, and as Idith Zertal documents, she became something of a persona non grata in the world of Jewish and Israeli scholarship.

It is thus multiply tragic that Israel above all is now responsible for the devaluation of the Holocaust and the trivialization of Auschwitz. By forcing the analogy between the challenges facing Israel and the threats to which Diaspora Jews were once exposed, by tendentiously linking Jewish loss and defeat in biblical and post-biblical times to the establishment of the extermination camps, and by forcibly reminding every Israeli schoolchild of the crimes of non-Jews in the past (and implicitly in the future), Israel has linked the fate of the memory of the Holocaust to itself. And in so doing, since Israeli behaviours in recent years has incurred a range of international responses reaching from anger to contempt, it risks inviting the charge that the Holocaust is merely an exploitable (and overexploited) historical myth.

I use the term "myth" advisably, much as Professor Zertal deploys it. There is nothing mythological about what happened in Europe in the 1940s. But the relationship between the situation in which Jews found themselves then and the circumstances that Israel has created for itself today is fictional. It was developed for local political advantage. In this sense, the destruction of the Jews of Europe is a serviceable myth that has been exploited to national ends by a state which did not even exist at the time in question.

This is bad news for Israel – en route to becoming what Idith Zertal wisely describes as an altar and temple of Auschwitz memory – but is also a grim portent for the rest of us. The Holocaust does not belong to Israel any more than it belongs to Jews. It is, as wise Jewish observers have written, primarily a problem and a challenge for non-Jews. (pp. xiv–xvii)

Israel's manufactured history has not persuaded Palestinians, or their Arab friends in neighbouring countries, of Israel's right to destroy them.

We cannot change the past, but we can learn from it. Discussing and debating now the merits and acceptability of One State versus Two States, alternative boundaries, treaty rights, human rights, and historic rights, perhaps at this time, we might start a different approach. Even Shavit's favoured option, withdrawal from the West Bank, is much too late now, if it were politically acceptable. Israel is facing the wrath of the Arabs not only in Palestine but of the whole Middle East, and it is losing the support of the West.

Even among the Israelis of today there has been a change of mood. They love their country and are proud of its achievements, but many are anxious about the country's future; and they are not fatalists. There has always been a steady emigration; especially by graduate students, who travel to universities in England, Canada, and the U.S., and settle in those countries after gaining their Ph.Ds.

Today, the uncertainty of Israel's future is causing many Israelis to consider leaving their country in order to protect the lives of their families. At the *Harper's Magazine* forum, "Israel and Palestine: Where To Go from Here" (held in Jerusalem on June 15, 2014), speaker Eva Illouz, professor of sociology at the Hebrew University and president of the Bezalel Academy of Arts and Design, pointed out that "A comprehensive survey published in *Haaretz* revealed that nearly 40 percent of Israelis think about emigration" (*Harper's Magazine*, September 2014). It is clear that the majority of Israelis are not fatalists.

⌒

In the interest of Israel's self-preservation I suggest my dream solution: that Israel demonstrate its contrition and a new-found neighbourliness by announcing its decision to establish a Palestine Development Center in the West Bank, ideally with the financial and technical support of public and private organizations from around the world.

I have in mind the creation of institutions of learning and production facilities for Palestinians. The teaching facilities would also be available to students from neighbouring countries. I suggest:

1. An Institute of Technology like Israel's Technion
2. A technical school for engineers and craftsmen
3. Construction of appropriate manufacturing plants for the production of goods to serve the needs of the region

Instead of continuing the fruitless negotiations about the future political settlement, let the political settlement negotiations arise once trust has been established between Arabs and Jews in Palestine.

Part III: Rediscovering Germany

When I left Berlin in 1938, I turned my back on Germany. Not to put the country out of my mind, but I was too busy and not a little worried starting a new life in an unknown country, learning a new language, finding a job at seventeen, and looking towards my future.

Within a year, the Second World War had started and Germany was the enemy. Soon, no one from my family would be alive in

Germany. The stories emerging out of Europe later in the war about concentration camps did not enliven my interest about the country of my birth.

It was over fifty years before I returned to Berlin. On a fine day in 1989, Rene and I were in the pretty town of Litomerice, Czechoslovakia, were she was born and lived until she left for England, when we heard that the Berlin Wall had come down. On an impulse and unprepared, we decided to drive to Berlin and perhaps meet an old friend from "Leicester days" who had chosen to live in East Germany and work as a lawyer for the Communist government.

The East German border guards were very excited; they had never seen British passports before. Our unexpected and brief return to Berlin gave me the chance to show Rene where I grew up. The only direct link to my family occurred on a visit to the destroyed synagogue – turned into a memorial/community centre – located in the same street where we lived. I was shown a book listing all the Jews who lived in Berlin before the deportations started, with dates and where their journeys ended – including my sister and her husband. The commemorative document had an eloquent introduction written by then president of Germany Richard von Weizsacker, who had also been the mayor of Berlin from 1981 to 1984. This document was perhaps the first evidence for me of Germany's official acknowledgement of its past crimes.

After Berlin, we drove on to Wolfenbüttel, my first time going back to my birthplace. Our house, located on the *Am Alten Weg* (On the Old Path), was gone, but the forest across the Weg was still there. Wolfenbüttel itself was unchanged from what I remembered. Finally, we visited Belsen, one of the concentration camps nearby. There was little to see apart from mass graves and a visitor centre explaining, with photographs, the history of the camp.

On this short visit to Germany, I had no real contact with Germans to gain any impressions about them. During the years away from Germany, I had not forgotten about the rise of Hitler, the war, and the disappearance of the Jews from Germany and most of Europe. Starting belatedly on my proper education at the London School of Economics in 1946, where I went expressly to find out what went wrong in Germany, and in my subsequent reading of the literature on the subject, I formed my firm but reasoned opinion that the tragic event of the war and the disappearance of the European Jews could have been avoided and were not inevitable. (Anyone interested in the story of the German Jews should read the unique and indispensable book by Amos Elon, *The Pity of It All: A Portrait of the German-Jewish Epoch 1743–1933*.)

Both tragedies were the result of historic "if only cool heads had prevailed" to prevent the disasters. The two main causes of Hitler's rise to power were the 1919 Treaty of Versailles, and President Hindenburg's senility, when appointing Hitler as chancellor of Germany. Both errors were not just perceived in hindsight as faults but were recognized and discussed at the critical times.

The conditions imposed on Germany after the First World War were very harsh, and were criticized at the Peace Conference, especially by John Maynard Keynes who was the principal delegate from the British Treasury. He predicted in his book *The Economic Consequences of the Peace* (1919) that Germany would not recover under the conditions imposed by the treaty. Keynes's economic reasoning, used to determine the very different approach after the Second World War, created the very successful Marshall Plan, which restored the European economy, especially Germany's.

Hindenburg, though revered by all Germans, was well past his prime to understand what was happening in the Reichstag and on the political stage generally. In the second 1932 election, the Nazis actually were returned with a reduced number of delegates and Hitler's appointment as chancellor in 1933 did not reflect his public support. Hindenburg responded to events under pressure from a few confidants who thought and said that "they could control Hitler." Unfortunately, Hitler was quite a shrewd politician with a strong instinct to succeed. He was badly underrated – until it was too late.

⌒⋙⌒

None of my readings about Germany and not even the brief visits to Berlin and Wolfenbüttel had brought me into contact with Germans. Only by chance, after two generations, did I actually make contact. The first occasion was in 2011 when I went to the grave of my parents in Berlin to visit and inspect whether my arrangements for the perpetual care of the grave were carried out.

Fortunately, most Berliners speak English. My spoken German is pretty rusty, though I can still understand it fairly well. As soon as Berliners learned that I was born in Germany they showed a surprising interest in me. The cab driver on the way to the cemetery could not stop asking questions when he found out why I was going to the Weissensee Jewish Cemetery. In addition, there seemed to be much interest in Jewish-related activities: there was an exhibition of Max Lieberman's paintings and other meetings about Jewish-related subjects were advertised.

Pleased by the unexpected demonstration of attention to Jewish subjects and affairs, I put it all down to the fact that Berlin had become a major tourist city and therefore catered to a wide range of tourists' interests. Berlin, I thought, was not representative of Germany as a whole.

By a most extraordinary coincidence the following summer I was proved wrong. Staying at a bed & breakfast near Newfield in southwest Maine, New England, I met a German couple and their son from Erkerode, a village a few miles from Wolfenbüttel. At breakfast, as usual for me, I did not participate in the small talk. Until, someone at my table asked a lady "Where exactly in Germany do you come from?" When she replied, "Braunschweig," I perked up, hesitated, and told her that I was born in Wolfenbüttel. Having finished breakfast I got up and said I was pleased to have met her, left, and set on a bench outside waiting for my daughter and son-in-law to come down to breakfast.

Very soon, Marianne Kröhle, the lady in question, came to join me on the bench and, like the Berliners, asked about my youth in Germany. When her husband, Roland, and son, Max, joined us, Marianne slipped back inside and returned with her home address and said, "Come and visit us the next time you come to Germany."

I had planned to visit Europe the next summer to meet relatives, so I wrote to Marianne at Christmas time that I might come to Erkerode as well. When I made the journey, I was excellently received and entertained, and met her parents and daughter. Theresa and Roland drove me to Wolfenbüttel and all over the countryside. Above all, I was given another astonishing surprise, a book entitled *Jüdishe Familien in Wolfenbüttel: Spuren und Schicksale* (Jewish Families in Wolfenbüttel: Traces and Fates) by Jürgen Kumlehn, published in 2009. A remarkable feat of research which describes, in its first part, the history of the Jews in Wolfenbüttel from 1697 until the rise of antisemitism in the town and the region that led to their disappearance. The second, longer part, describes the fate of some 75 Jewish individuals or families in Wolfenbüttel, including my family.

Unfortunately, the author, who lives in Wolfenbüttel, was on holiday at the time. I contacted him on the internet after my return home and since then he has helped me greatly to understand Germany's post-war response to the Nazi crimes.

I have not remarked before on my frequent chance meetings with persons who were important in my life and influenced my work. This is, of course, normal, but I seem to have had an unusual number and always at a time when I needed them: from the lawyer in Berlin who smuggled me past the Gestapo control out of Germany to save my life, to my heroes and colleagues, to my wife, and others.

And so it was again when I took a renewed interest in Germany and met the Kröhle family who gave me Jürgen Kumlehn's book.

To be honest, I was reluctant to start on this vexed question of Germany's response to its Nazi past; and little did I know how hard it would be to understand it. However, having talked to people in Berlin who were curious about my origin, having met the Kröhles, and having read Kumlehn's book, I knew I had to reflect and comment on what is a crucial part of the history of our time and of my life.

Yet I know so little about the events and circumstances in Germany during the last seventy years. I had read books by Günter Grass, and I read President Weizsacker's well- known speech to the Bundestag in 1985. I also knew of the Adenauer – Ben Gurion agreements of the 1950s about billions of restitution payments to Israel, including, curiously, the delivery of two submarines to Israel's navy, as well as additional restitution payments to individual Jewish survivors. Actually, some friends in England urged me to make a claim – I never did. How would money compensate for my sister's life?

Beyond these selected events, I knew next to nothing; especially not about examinations or reactions to the ethnic exterminations. More importantly, there seemed to be scarce written material, piecemeal or comprehensive, on how the Germans dealt with National Socialism's crimes as they became more generally known. In fact, several aspects about Nazi war crimes have taken a very long time to be examined critically.

A good example is found in the recently published book by Uki Goñi, *The Real Odessa: How Peron Brought the Nazi War Criminals to Argentina* (2003).[2] To quote from the book's back cover:

> This ground-breaking work of investigation by a courageous Argentine journalist unraveling the complex network that allowed hundreds of Nazi war criminals, including Adolf Eichmann, Josef Mengele, Erich Priebke and Klaus Barbie, to flee to Argentina at the end of the war. Among other shocking revelations, it shows that the escape operation had tentacles in Scandinavia, Switzerland, and Italy, and relied on the enthusiastic support of the Vatican and President Juan Peron himself.

Apart from the astonishing information gathered by Uki Goñi, it is significant that this book was not produced by a German, or by a victorious ally, or a European Nazi collaborator, but by an Argentinian who dislikes Peron and his regime.

I struggled to arrive at some overview about Germany's awakening or disillusion from its nightmare and horror but without success. On the other hand, I found no dispute about the principal facts: the Wannsee Conference of January 1942 which deciding on the Final Solution, and the meticulous records about where, how, and when the many were put to death.

Then there is the time factor. It is now two generations since the end of the war. How to find and select the important decisions made. There was the subsequent division of the country into East and West Germany, followed later by reunification – both with their certain and unknown influences. For example: Kumlehn told me that reading the book and subsequently seeing the film *Nackt*

---

[2] This Odessa has nothing to do with the city of Odessa on the Black Sea, it stands for Organisation der Ehemaligen SS-Angehorigen, or, Organisation of Former SS Members.

unter Wolfen (Naket among Wolves) based on the book by the East German author Bruno Apiz, which is about the Buchenwald concentration camp, triggered for him not only the interest in the Third Reich but also his wish to understand, have clarifications about, and be able to "remember" everything.

Jürgen Kumlehn is not a trained historian, therefore he and others like him are looked down upon by the "proper" historians, and sometimes as *Nestbeschmützer* (defilers). He calls himself "ein Erinnerer" – a man with a conscience who wants to record the ills of the past. I would call him a humanist, although he does not use that term. But he uses the right words: unlike historians, he wants to see past events from a "human and personal" perspective. Of most importance to me is his conclusion that it will take generations to overcome the Nazi ideology because, he believes, that it has penetrated "the peoples souls" and there is now a need to restore a sense of sanity.

The real historians and philosophers, the heavies like Ernst Nolte, Jürgen Habermas, Michael Sturmer, and Andreas Hillgruber did not weigh in until the 1980s, debating "why it happened" and came up, for example, with a conclusion "that National Socialism was a reaction to communism and therefore was a defence," and, I suppose by implication was a good thing.

I began to look at Germany's situation in stages: during the war and after the war. For the longest period of the war, the Wehrmacht was well on the road to victory to become almost master of all Europe – until losing the Battle of Stalingrad (February 1943). Even later, during the Battle of the Bulge (December 1944–January 1945), the Wehrmacht raised hopes. All of this, I believe, created not so much a divided nation at the end of the war, but Nazis and disappointed losers. Because, during the war, the Nazis gained some respect from, perhaps, most Germans for their successful warfare. Under those circumstances, what could one expect from them in the way of "remembering"? Those acutely aware of the infamous deeds may have anticipated the punishment of the criminals; the rest would just keep quiet.

In order to try and regain some respect for Germany and establish friendly relations, Adenauer started to pay the compensations – hush money or blood money – to Israel. I assume he could do that without a vote in the Bundestag, as long as he could find the money. So at this stage there were no expressions of confession, remorse, or redemption. Somewhat differently, years later, President Weizsacker gave his well-known speech, a kind of "conscience of the nation address" to both the German people and the international community. This time, contrition and repentance were fully expressed, and it was effective abroad. Did it work at home? I cannot begin to answer that.

This leads me to the important subject of re-education, which I have not explored and which is at the heart of Kumlehn's concern: the eradication of Nazi ideology. Whatever was lacking in making post-war Germans properly aware of their Nazi period has by now been overcome. Significantly, Kumlehn feels quite satisfied that in the last fifteen years the acceptance of the "rememberers" has considerably improved. Today's Germans, especially the younger ones, may have little concern or interest in their Nazi history – and why should they? Germany is now and has been for some time an economically successful and democratic country, an indispensable member of the European Union, and Jewish life has returned. In 1933, about 500,000 Jews lived in Germany. They either escaped or disappeared. Today, there are over 100 Jewish communities with about 150,000 members. I am comforted and heartened by what I learned, particularly when I compare Germany with neighbouring Austria.

Austria, unlike Germany, engaged in denial and deception about the country's role before and during the war. Austria used the catchy, though false, slogan "We were the first victims of Hitler."

Well, here is the truth, as written by Eric R. Kandel in his book, *In Search of Memory: The Emergence of a New Science of Mind* (2006):

> Austria's record is quite clear on two issues: 1. Its role in the Nazi effort to destroy the Jews during World War I, and 2. To try to come to grips with Austria's implicit denial of its role during the Nazi period.
>
> For a decade before Austria joined with Germany, a significant fraction of the Austrian population belonged to the Nazi party. Following annexation, Austria made up about 8 percent of the population of the greater German Reich, yet they accounted for more than 30 percent of the officials working to eliminate the Jews. Austrians commanded four Polish death camps and held other leadership positions in the Reich: in addition to Hitler, Ernst Kaltenbrunner, who was head of the Gestapo, and Adolf Eichmann, who was in charge of the extermination program, were Austrians. It is estimated that of the 6 million Jews who perished during the Holocaust, approximately half were killed by Austrian functionaries led by Eichmann.
>
> Yet despite their active participation in the Holocaust, the Austrians claimed to be victims of Hitler's aggression – Otto von Habsburg, the pretender to the Austrian throne, managed to convince the Allies that Austria was the first free nation to fall victim to Hitler's war. Both the United States and the Soviet Union were willing to accept this argument in 1943, before the war ended, because von Habsburg thought it would stimulate Austria's public resistance to the Nazis as the war ground to a halt... Because it was not held accountable for its actions between 1938 and

1945, Austria never underwent the soul-searching and cleansing that Germany did after the war. (pp. 405-406)

Eric Kandel is an American neuropsychiatrist and won the Nobel Prize in Physiology or Medicine in 2000. Kandel was born in Vienna in 1929 and left for the United States in 1938; he has been at Columbia University since 1947.

In addition to these no-longer disputed facts of Austrian participation in the murder of Europe's Jews, one more case of denial and curious public blindness needs to be mentioned. It is less well publicized, and the victims included few Jews, yet the scale and brutality of the ethnic cleansing by the German army ought to have led to some condemnation of the Austrian officer serving in the German army, instead of appointing him to high office.

I take no pleasure in quoting yet another fine author, telling the important though gruesome story of the prominent man involved. I suggest the more sensitive and squeamish reader skip this passage, taken from W.G. Sebald's *The Rings of Saturn* (1998):

> ... For some time I had been feeling a sense of eternal peace when, leafing through the "Independent on Sunday," I came across an article that was related to the Balkan pictures I had seen in the Reading Room that morning. The article, which was about the so-called cleansing operations carried out fifty years ago in Bosnia, by the Croats together with the Austrians and the Germans, begun by describing a photo taken as a souvenir by men of the Croatian Ustasha, in which fellow militiamen in the best of spirits, some of them striking heroic poses,

are sawing off the head of a Serb named Branco Jungic. A second snap shows the severed head with a cigarette between lips still parted in a last cry of pain. This happened at Jasenovac camp on the Sava. Seven hundred thousand men, women and children were killed there alone in ways that made even the hair of the Reich's experts stand on end, as some of them are said to have admitted when they were among themselves. The preferred instruments of execution were saws and sabres, axes and hammers, and leather cuff-bands with fixed blades that were fastened on the lower arm and made especially in Solingen for the purpose of cutting throats, as well as a kind of rudimentary cross-bar gallows on which the Serbs, Jews and Bosnians, once rounded up, were hanged in rows like crows or magpies. Not far from Jasenovac, in a radius of no more than ten miles, there were also the camps of Prijedor, Stara Gradiska and Banja Luka, where the Croatian militia, its hand strengthened by the Wehrmacht and its spirit by the Catholic church, performed one day's work after another in similar manner. The history of this massacre, which went on for years, is recorded in fifty thousand documents abandoned by the Germans and Croats in 1945, which are kept to this day, according to the author of the 1992 article, in the Bosanske Krajine Archive in Banja Luka, which is, or used to be, housed in what was once an Austro-Hungarian barracks, serving in 1942 as the headquarters of the Heeresgruppe E intelligence division. Without a doubt those who were stationed there knew what was going on in the Ustasha camps, just as they knew of the enormities perpetrated during the Kozara campaign against

Tito's partisans, for instance, in the course of which between sixty and ninety thousand people were killed in so-called acts of war, that is to say were executed, or died as a result of deportation. The female population of Kozara was transported to Germany and worked to death in the slave-labour system that extended over the entire territory of the Reich. Of the children who were left behind, twenty-three thousand in number, the militia murdered half on the spot, while the rest were herded together at various assembly points to be sent on to Croatia; of these, not a few died of typhoid fever, exhaustion and fear, even before the cattle wagons reached the Croatian capital. Many of those who were still alive were so hungry that they had eaten the cardboard identity tags they wore about their necks and thus in their extreme desperation has eradicated their own names. Later they were brought up as Catholics in Croatian families, and sent to confession and their first holy communion. Like everyone else they learned the socialist ABC at school, chose an occupation, and became rail workers, sales-girls, tool-fitters or book-keepers. But no one knows what shadowy memories haunt them to this day. In this connection one might also add that one Heerengruppe E intelligence officers at that time was a young Viennese lawyer whose chief task was to draw up memoranda relating to the necessary resettlements, described as imperative for humanitarian reasons. For this commendable paperwork he was awarded by Croatian head of state Ante Pavelic the silver medal of the crown of King Zvonomir, with oak leaves. In the post-war years this officer, who at the very start of his career was so promising and so very competent in the technicalities of administration, occupied various high offices, among them that of Secretary General of the United Nations. And reportedly it was in this last capacity that he spoke onto tape, for the benefit of any extra-terrestrials that may happen to share our universe, words of greeting that are now, together with other memorabilia of mankind, approaching the outer limits of our solar system aboard the space probe Voyager II. (pp. 96–99)

The nameless person of Sebald's account is Kurt Waldheim (1918–2007) of the wartime German Army Intelligence in Bosnia, previously enrolled in the SA, Hitler's Brown Shirts. How could this man have been selected Secretary General of the United Nations (1972–81) in preference to other qualified candidates? That he became president of Austria (1986–92) is readily understandable, without me having to state the obvious. His U.N. office seemed preposterous, unless you accept the opinion of cynics who say that as a member of the international "elite" he was above the law.

I cannot resist ending Austria's position as a favourite target for writers without mentioning Edmund de Waal, ceramic artist and writer who chronicled his grandmother's Viennese family – the Ephrussis. In his book *The Hare With Amber Eyes*, de Waal, poking fun at Emperor Franz Joseph, adds one more tag to Franz Joseph's long list of titles:

> Emperor of Austria, King of Hungary and Bohemia, King of Lombardi-Venetia, of Dalmatia, Croatia, Slovonia, Galicia, Lodomeria and Illyria, Grand Duke of Tuscany, King of Jerusalem and Duke of Auschwitz.

APPENDIX

Rene's interest in marine biology went beyond technical or professional studies of sea animals. She thought her subject was of interest to everyone and she had the skill for writing about the fascinating creatures, large and small, for the general public. While she worked at the ROM (Royal Ontario Museum) she wrote for the *ROTUNDA*, the museum's quarterly magazine. The article reprinted below had the advantage of being expertly illustrated by Zile, her friend and colleague at the museum.

I remember another of her pieces in the magazine about sponges for which I was, curiously enough, the stimulus. I was ignorant about sponges; did not even know that they are animals living on the bottom of the sea all over the world and that there are thousands of species. While I was working in the Bahamas, in Nassau, I saw an open site next to a beach covered in grey, sand-coloured, shapeless objects, some over two feet across lying in the sun. A few of them seemed to have been washed and looked like very large sponges. When Rene came on a vacation to visit me I took her to the sponge site. She discovered the "sponge house" nearby. In no time she talked to Mr. Pantelis Tsakkos, a Greek sponge diver in charge of the business. Mr. T. told her that the only source of Bahamian sponges, which had been harvested since the mid-nineteenth century, was on the mud flats along the east coast of Andros Island, the largest island in the Bahamas, not far from New Providence Island on which Nassau is situated. He further explained the relatively simple operation of retrieving the sponges at Andros, not far below on the mud flats – unlike in Greece or most other places where you dive for and cut the sponges off the sea bottom. So the work consisted only of cleaning, grading (by type for different uses), sorting, and compressing for packing the sponges.

It so happened that Rene was planning to go to Andros anyway because the island's east coast is next to a very deep sea channel of interest to marine biologists. At the time, the deep waters were also used by the U.S. navy to train their submarine sailors.

FOOD FOR THOUGHT: CRUSTACEANS AND MOLLUSCS

Renate Carson, with drawings by Zile Zicmanis

O NE OF TORONTO'S GREAT CHARMS lies in the many colourful markets to be found in different parts of the city. At the Kensington Market, for example, the names of the fish shops—Portuguese Fish Market, International Fish Market, New Seaway Fish Market, Canadian Fish Market, Esthela's—are as varied as the vendors, the shoppers, and the merchandise. Most of the stands, however, have one thing in common: among the items they offer for sale are crustaceans and molluscs from all over the world. One can find crabs from Alaska, the Maritimes, Cuba, Mozambique, and Honduras; clams, mussels, and oysters from the east coast of the United States and Canada; octopuses from Taiwan and other lands; and squid from Portugal.

One day my assistants and I bought crabs, clams, oysters, and mussels from the Canadian east coast; shrimps from Alaska and Norway; squid from Portugal; periwinkles and a large octopus from unknown localities; and a lobster. That evening, with the boiled animals spread out in front of us on a platter, we had to admire the medley of gay colours, odd shapes, and varied sizes. The greenish-brown lobster had turned *as red as a lobster;* the blue crabs were now an orange-red; the shrimps and prawns lay in a sprawling tangle of intertwined limbs; the clams and mussels had opened partially in the steam; and the diminutive periwinkle was dwarfed by the octopus. Why, I wondered, do we eat only the flesh from the claw of the lobster, from the tail of the shrimp and the lobster, and from the cephalothorax (fused head and thorax) of the crab?

Crabs, shrimps, and lobsters are crustaceans whose segmented soft body parts are enclosed in an external skeleton or exoskeleton. Frontally the segments lie hidden in the fused cephalothorax. On the abdomen the segments are visible since each one is covered by a separate skeletal plate. This makes the abdomen flexible and enables the animal to move more easily. Along the sides of the body there are jointed limbs, which drop off if the animal is trapped or injured; later new limbs will regenerate. (The reason the lobster turns red when it is boiled

241

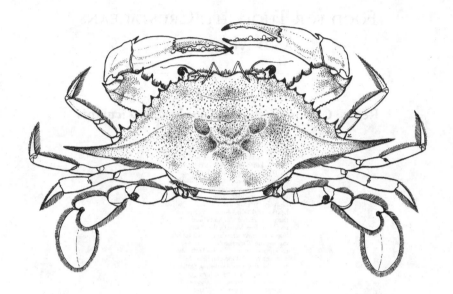

is that the hidden carotene pigment in the skeleton becomes visible when the chemical bond that tied the pigment to a protein is destroyed.) The skeleton of the crab and the lobster is strong; it keeps the animal well protected and provides it with mechanical support. However, the skeleton presents certain drawbacks as well: it is heavy and rigid and impedes the animal's movement, and it necessitates moulting followed by the growth of a larger exoskeleton to accommodate the growing soft parts. When the animal is moulting, it is vulnerable to attack. Moreover, the exoskeleton often forms a barrier to mating. In the Dungeness crab, the male moults at a different time from the female. Before she moults, he intimates his intentions by stroking her abdomen. After she has shed her exoskeleton, he retreats temporarily and waits until her new skeleton has hardened slightly. Only then can mating proceed.

Crabs and lobsters are caught in baited traps. Since they spend most of their lives walking on the bottom of the sea, anything that has eyes and swims above them is quite likely to spot them. But crabs and lobsters have their own protection. The calcified skeleton contains chromatophores, which are centres of concentrated pigment. As the animals move over the mud bottom, their colour changes to blend with the variations in colour tone of the bottom. They have claws too, which serve a dual purpose. They are used for hunting and gathering food and as weapons to ward off other creatures. Some crabs use their claws to communicate—to indicate the boundaries of their territory, or to show that they are ready to fight or to mate. Most restaurants provide crackers to help remove the tough cover from the lobster claws. If you have ever had trouble opening a lobster claw, be grateful that you are not its prey. The flesh that you are seeking is the powerful muscle that closes the pincer at the tip. The larger claw is used extensively for crushing shells and small crustaceans and the smaller one has a serrated cutting edge.

It seems that with all crustaceans we eat the flesh from the parts of the body that during life were subject to the most rigorous exercise. We eat the lobster tail because when the lobster swims, its abdomen pushes the weight of the cephalothorax, and until her eggs are hatched, the female carries them on the swimming limbs attached to the side of her abdomen. Crabs for the most part run sideways on their walking legs. Both walking and swimming limbs are operated by the muscles in the cephalothorax, which supply the edible crab meat.

Shrimps and prawns, which also have claws, are caught in nets since they spend their adult lives swimming at midwater level. They swim with paddle-shaped limbs, attached laterally to the segments beneath the abdominal plates; abdominal movement helps to propel them in various directions. The Alaska shrimp car-

24

ries her eggs under the pleural cover on the side of her abdomen. After the eggs are fertilized, they remain attached to the swimming limbs until they hatch. The shrimp's abdominal muscles are strong and juicy, and they are the only part of the shrimp we eat.

Though the molluscs we find in a fish market are commonly called shellfish, they are not fish at all since they lack an internal backbone and fins with skeletal support. The main constituent of the shell is calcium carbonate, and the thickness or texture of the shell tells us something about the bottom where the animal lived. Clams, mussels, and oysters are bivalves; their shell is made up of two valves, which are kept closed by powerful adductor muscles. It is these muscles that provide the best parts of the molluscs for eating, and as anyone who has tried shucking clams for chowder knows, they are very strong. It is extremely hard to get a knife inside the shell to sever the muscles and separate the valves.

Oysters are often associated with the precious pearl found in the pearl oyster, but edible oysters, like the American oyster, are noted for their delicious taste. They are eaten whole (except for the shell, of course). Since oysters are prone to disease, those we purchase in fish markets have been carefully screened by commercial growers and inspected before they are released for sale.

Oysters live in shallow water, and they open their valves by means of a ligament and close them by means of the adductor muscle, located some distance from the hingeline inside the shell. Before the young oyster settles, usually on pilings, rocks, or the shallow sea bottom, it pours cement from a gland in the foot onto the substrate, and then fixes itself horizontally. There the oyster stays for the rest of its life, or until an oysterman comes along and picks it off with a pair of oyster tongs. Nowadays oysters are often collected with long iron rakes, and commercial oystermen use dredges.

The oyster shell is very thick, and its valves are asymmetrical: the attached valve is convex and the free valve is flat. The shell builds up from flaky layers and each layer represents a different period of growth. The smallest layer is the oldest, the largest layer the most recent. Oysters have a tendency to change sex during their lives, starting out as males and turning into females. This change can occur once or several times during a lifespan, but most oysters end up as females, and they can live to be 20 years old.

Clams live buried in mud and therefore their valves remain tightly closed—held together by the contracted adductor muscles. They dig themselves into the mud with the foot. In order for the animal to maintain life, food and oxygen-laden water must enter the shell. In some clams, a tube protrudes from the hard shell in such a way that the opening is above the surface of the mud, so that water can enter the tube and pass into the body. The clams we bought at the Kensington Market had thick greyish shells with distinct growth lines, not unlike the rings visible in the cross-section of a tree

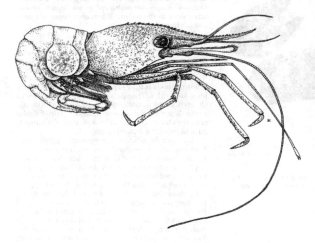

Opposite page: In the process of boiling, the blue crab turns red, owing to the destruction of a chemical bond.

Left: The Alaska female shrimp stores her eggs under the flap on the side of the abdomen.

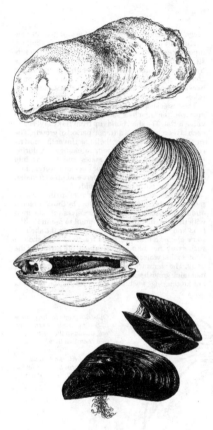

trunk. However, these growth lines are not indicators of age as are the rings of a tree. They simply record the story of arrested and resumed growth, owing to changes in temperature, water turbulence, and food supply. Each growth line formed as the shell began to grow again.

Mussels grow on the substrate, where they appear tall and slender. Compared to oyster shells, mussel valves are quite fragile, and they are patterned with fine growth lines, because in the shallow waters and brackish estuaries in which the mussels live there are constant variations which interrupt growth of the shell. Mussels from Canada's east coast are purple, those from the west coast brown, presumably because of a difference in the mineral content of the bottom.

To remain firmly fixed on the bottom, the mussel ties itself down by means of a waterproof thread exuded from the byssus gland in the foot. This thread is the only soft part of the animal that is not eaten, and it is so strong that chemists have tried to synthesize a similar material for use as a fixative for dental fillings. Once settled on the substrate, the mussel has no further use for its crawling foot. It winds the byssus thread round the foot's stalk, which it then uses as a spool for secure anchorage in changing tides.

The octopus and the squid are fleshy molluscs without an external shell. On their heads they bear a crown of sucker-studded arms on which they crawl—thus the name cephalopods (head feet). Beneath the arms on the sides of the head are two huge eyes with eyelids. An octopus can express its feelings by wrinkling the area around the eyes. This activates the chromatophores, which are scattered all over the body, and the animal changes colour—becoming red, green, brown, almost any colour of the palette. When an octopus is frightened, it literally turns white.

Cephalopods catch fish on the suckers of their arms and then bite the victims to death with the beak. Both the octopus and the squid are very fast swimmers (the squid is the faster of the two) and their bodies are muscular and elastic. For rapid propulsion, water is forced through a narrow nozzle into the body cavity. When the body is fully expanded, the nozzle closes by means of a valve. Then the muscles contract, and water shoots from the nozzle, propelling the animal in the opposite direction. Squids also possess a pair of fleshy fins, which can be used as brakes when the animals wish to swim at a leisurely pace.

Most cephalopods have the remnant of a shell inside their bodies. The vestigial shell inside the squid is in the shape of a pen, and close to it there is an ink sac. Cephalopods compensate for the lack of an external shell by shedding ink into the water to create an ink screen behind which they can escape their predators.

By observing the habits of squids, fishermen found that they could catch them by trailing a dummy squid from the end of a line. The animals follow the dummy, and when they are close enough the fishermen capture their prey simply by scooping them out of the water. The octopus can be caught by a ruse. Fishermen dangle unbaited pots from a line. The animal mistakes the pot

Above: Bivalves, such as the oyster (top), the clam (centre), and the mussel (bottom) keep their valves closed by means of contracted muscles. These muscles are what people like to eat.

Opposite page: The periwinkle and the octopus are edible molluscs. Nowadays they are also used in experimental procedures in laboratories.

26

for a cave in which to hide and crawls into it. Commercially, cephalopods are caught in nets or are speared.

The many and varied seafood dishes listed on restaurant menus attest to the popularity of seafood. Not only does seafood taste good, but it is low in fats and high in protein and provides the energy we require to withstand the strain of modern life. Shrimps are 27.6 per cent protein, and oysters are 6.2 per cent; the protein contents of the other crustaceans lie somewhere between those two figures.

Each year hundreds of these animals find their way into laboratories, where they are studied for a variety of purposes. Ethologists study the octopus to find out more about its capacity to learn. The periwinkle, now of less importance as a food than it was in Dickens's day, has found its place in experiments carried out by geneticists. Physiologists study the nerves and muscles of crustaceans, and geologists use bivalves to determine units of geological time.

Thus with dwindling food resources on earth, man turns his efforts to farming the sea, which yields him a harvest of crustaceans, molluscs, and cephalopods—for food and for experiments that may lead him to a better understanding of himself.

Renate Carson joined the ROM in 1976 and is a Curatorial Assistant in the Department of Invertebrate Zoology. She was born in Czechoslovakia and educated in England and the United States, where she obtained an M.Sc. in biology from the American University. After a short teaching career she joined the staff of the Smithsonian Oceanographic Sorting Center in Washington, D.C. Before her move to Canada in September 1975, Ms. Carson spent a summer at the Marine Biological Laboratory in Woods Hole, Massachusetts.

R. Carson photo by Arnaud Maggs. Used with permission of the Estate of Arnaud Maggs.

BIBLIOGRAPHY

Achebe, Chinua. *There Was a Country: A Personal History of Biafra.* New York: Penguin Books, 2012.

Athill, Diana. *Instead of a Book: Letters to a Friend.* London: Granta Books, 2011.

Bauer, Peter. *Dissent on Development: Studies and Debates in Development Economics.* Cambridge, MA: Harvard University Press, 1972.

Bauer, Peter. *Equality: The Third World and Economic Delusion.* Cambridge, MA: Harvard University Press, 1981.

Benes, Eduard. *Democracy Today and Tomorrow.* New York: The Macmillan Company, 1939.

Berryman, Phillip. *Liberation Theology.* Philadelphia: Temple University Press, 1987.

Blumenfeld, Hans. *The Modern Metropolis: Its Origin, Growth, Characteristics and Planning.* Boston, MA: MIT Press, 1971.

Brogan, Denis W. *The American Political System.* London: Hamish Hamilton, 1933.

Brogan, Denis W. *Politics and Law in the United States.* Cambridge: Cambridge University Press, 1946.

Burnham, James. *The Managerial Revolution: What Is Happening in the World.* New York: Praeger, 1972.

Carroll, James. "Who Am I to Judge? A Radical Pope's First Year." *The New Yorker,* December 23 & 30, 2013.

Carson, John M., Goldie W. Rivkin, and Malcolm D. Rivkin. *Community Growth and Water Resources Policy.* New York: Praeger, 1973.

Cheuse, Alan. *A Trance after Breakfast: And Other Passages.* Naperville, IL: Sourcebooks, 2009.

DeWaal, Edmund. *The Hare with Amber Eyes.* New York: Farrar, Straus and Giroux, 2010.

Durr, Kenneth D. *The Best Made Plans: Robert R. Nathan and the 20th Century Liberalism.* Wakefield, MA: Montrose Press, 2013.

Doxiadis, Konstantinos Apostolou. *Ekistics: An Introduction to the Science of Human Settlements.* London: Oxford University Press, 1968.

Easterly, William. *The White Man's Burden: Why the West's Efforts to Aid the Rest Have Done So Much Ill and So Little Good.* London: Oxford University Press, 2007.

Ecott, Tim. *Vanilla: Travels in Search of the Ice Cream Orchid.* New York: Grove Press, 2005.

Elon, Amos. *The Pity of It All: A Portrait of the German-Jewish Epoch 1743–1933.* London: Picador, 2002.

Flapan, Simha. *The Birth of Israel: Myths and Realities.* New York: Pantheon, 1987.

Goñi, Uki. *The Real Odessa: How Peron Brought the Nazi War Criminals to Argentina.* London: Granta Books, 2003.

Hubbard, Vincent K. *Swords, Ships & Sugar: History of Nevis to 1900.* Corvallis, OR: Premiere Editions International, 1992.

Judt, Tony. *The Memory Chalet.* London: William Heinemann, 2010.

Kandel, Eric R. *In Search of Memory: The Emergence of a New Science of Mind.* New York: Norton, 2006.

Kapuściński, Ryszard. *Imperium.* New York: Vintage Canada, 1995.

Keynes, John. *The Economic Consequences of the Peace.* New York: Harcourt, Brace and Howe, 1919.

Kumlehn, Jürgen. *Judishe Familien in Wolfenbuttel: Spuren und Schicksale* (Jewish Families in Wolfenbüttel: Traces and Fates). Braunschweig: Appelhans Verlag, 2009.

Larson, Erik. *In the Garden of Beasts: Love, Terror, and an American Family in Hitler's Berlin.* New York: Crown, 2012.

Mannheim, Karl. *Ideology and Utopia*. London: Routledge & Kegan Paul, 1936.

Mannheim, Karl. *Man and Society in an Age of Reconstruction*. New York: Routledge, 1940.

Moyo, Dambisa. *Dead Aid: Why Aid Is Not Working and How There Is a Better Way for Africa*. New York: Farrar, Straus and Giroux, 2009.

Moyo, Dambisa. *Winner Take All: China's Race for Resources and What It Means for the World*. New York: Basic Books, 2012.

Orwell, George. *Homage to Catalonia*. 1952. Reprint, New York: Mariner Books/Houghton Mifflin, 1980.

Pappe, Ilan. *The Ethnic Cleansing of Palestine*. Oxford: Oneworld Publications, 2006.

Pappe, Ilan. *The Idea of Israel: A History of Power and Knowledge*. London: Verso, 2014.

Pattullo, Polly. *Last Resorts: The Cost of Tourism in the Caribbean*. Kingston, Jamaica: Ian Randle Publishers, 1996.

Popper, Karl. *The Poverty of Historicism*. New York: Routledge, 2002.

Russell, Bertrand. *A History of Western Philosophy*. New York: Simon and Schuster/Touchstone, 1967.

Sacks, Oliver. "Speak, Memory." *The New York Review of Books*, February 21, 2013.

Saro-Wiwa, Noo. *Looking for Transwonderland: Travels in Nigeria*. Brooklyn, NY: Soft Skull Press, 2012.

Sebald, W.G. *The Rings of Saturn*. New York: New Direction Books, 1998.

Shavit, Ari. *My Promised Land: The Triumph and Tragedy of Israel*. New York: Spiegel and Grau, 2013.

Sorhaindo, Celia, and Polly Pattullo. *Home Again: Stories of Migration and Return*. London, UK, Papillote Press, and Trafalger, Dominica: Dominica UK Association, 2009.

Surowiecki, James. "The Underground Economy." *The New Yorker*, April 29, 2013.

Trouillot, Michel-Rolph. *Peasants and Capital: Dominica in the World Economy*. Baltimore, MD: Johns Hopkins University Press, 1988.

Zertal, Idith. *Israel's Holocaust and the Politics of Nationhood*. New Edition. Cambridge: Cambridge University Press, 2011.

Printed in the United States
By Bookmasters